SPORT IN THE AMERICAN WEST
Jorge Iber, *series editor*

WEST TEXAS
MIDDLEWEIGHT

The Story of LaVern Roach

Frank Sikes

Texas Tech University Press

This book is typeset in Haarlemmer MT Standard. The paper used in this book meets the minimum requirements of ANSI/NISO Z39.48-1992 (R1997). ∞

Designed by Kasey McBeath
Cover photograph reprinted by permission of AP Images.

Library of Congress Cataloging-in-Publication Data
Names: Sikes, Frank, author.
Title: West Texas middleweight : the story of Lavern Roach / Frank Sikes.
Description: Lubbock, Texas : Texas Tech University Press, [2016] | Series: Sport in the American West | Includes bibliographical references and index. | Description based on print version record and CIP data provided by publisher; resource not viewed.
Identifiers: LCCN 2016021435 (print) | LCCN 2016005396 (ebook) | ISBN 9780896729766 (Ebook) | ISBN 9780896729759 (hardcover : alk. paper)
Subjects: LCSH: Roach, Lavern, 1925-1950 | Boxers (Sports)—Texas—Biography. | Boxers (Sports)—United States—Biography.
Classification: LCC GV1132.R59 (print) | LCC GV1132.R59 S55 2016 (ebook) | DDC 796.83092 [B] —dc23
LC record available at https://lccn.loc.gov/2016021435

Printed in Canada
16 17 18 19 20 21 22 23 24 / 9 8 7 6 5 4 3 2 1

Texas Tech University Press
Box 41037 | Lubbock, Texas 79409-1037 USA
800.832.4042 | ttup@ttu.edu | www.ttupress.org

This book is dedicated to

Evelyn
Who never forgot

C. R. "Choc" Hutcheson
True friend and confidant

and to the memory of
Angelo Dundee
Who recognized boxing greatness

Every man's life ends the same way. It is only the details of how he lived and how he died that distinguish one man from another.

Ernest Hemingway

CONTENTS

ILLUSTRATIONS

I HAD the Pleasure & Honor To meet —
LAVERN ROACH ~~and to~~ as a Person & Human
Being — great on Both Counts — He would
Have Been a Fistic star at "any Time" —
CHAMPIONSHIP MATERIAL walked Like a
CHAMP IN AND OUT OF The RING —

Angelo Dundee

P.S. I Became TRAINER +
MANAGER OF Champions Ali° Foreman
Willie Pastrano Carmine Basilio Ralph
Dupas, Michael Nunn etc ete

Letter from Angelo Dundee.

PREFACE

> Boxing changed because of LaVern Roach.
> —*Angelo Dundee*

August 16, 2011, Clearwater, Florida

These were the first words spoken to me by Angelo Dundee as we sat down for lunch at Anthony's Coal Fired Pizza, one of his favorite eating places in Clearwater, Florida. What a remarkable statement coming from one of boxing's most knowledgeable and respected authorities. Those six succinct words from Angelo Dundee provided me with the best reason to write the LaVern Roach story.

LaVern's rise to prominence occurred during an era when boxing shared the spotlight with baseball as the nation's top two professional sports. He became one of the fistic sport's most popular figures during the mid- to late 1940s. For a short period of time, his name and photos appeared in New York City's newspapers and sports magazines more than those of his middleweight peers—champions Tony Zale, Rocky Graziano, Marcel Cerdan, and Jake LaMotta—and even surpassed headliners Joe Louis and Sugar Ray Robinson.

LaVern's sensational amateur boxing career, while serving in the Marine Corps during World War II, culminated with a national Golden Gloves championship. He then turned pro about the same time Angelo Dundee was getting his start in the sport under the apprenticeship of older brother Chris. Chris Dundee and John Abood, LaVern's manager while boxing for the Corps, comanaged the upstart boxer from Texas. One of Angelo's first duties was writing press releases and sending them, along with publicity photos, to the fighter's hometown newspaper. His role later increased to that of a corner man and promoter, working with the young fighters, getting to know them inside and outside of the ring.

Angelo was with the young pugilist throughout most of LaVern's professional boxing career.

I was already familiar with LaVern's accomplishments inside the ring, which included the Best Fighter to Come out of World War II award, presented to him by Gene Tunney, former heavyweight champion and recipient of the same award for his duty in World War I. Other awards included *Look* magazine's Amateur Boxer of the Year for 1945 and the *Ring* magazine's Rookie of the Year for 1947 and Fighter of the Month (January 1948). He was also recognized as a top-ten contender for the middleweight championship of the world.

LaVern's influence outside of the ring was just as significant as his exploits inside the squared circle. A few years ago in his acceptance speech at his own induction into the International Boxing Hall of Fame, Sylvester Stallone stated,

> I've never pretended to be a boxer. I don't possess those skills. What I do think is I have an understanding of what goes on outside the ring. Outside the ring is sometimes maybe an even bigger struggle than what goes on inside the ring, and I was able to capture that. Then I believe that you can identify more with the fighter. They are the greatest athletes in the world. They are the guys that go in there and take the blows and show that if you really put it out there on the line, you are a champion. You may not be the champion of the world, but you'll be the champion of your life.

These words, describing the life of Stallone's fictional character Rocky Balboa, certainly fit the life of LaVern Roach. Six and a half decades have passed since LaVern's last fight, but he is still remembered in his hometown of Plainview, Texas. The annual LaVern Roach Memorial Award is the highest honor that a Plainview High School senior boy can receive. It is awarded, not for athletic talent, but for outstanding sportsmanship, citizenship, and clean living.

Apart from sharing his memories of LaVern, Angelo talked about the early effects of television and the influence that the underworld had on the sport. He shared stories about the boxing personalities of other fighters, trainers, and managers of that day. Last, he spoke of his relationships with Ali, Foreman, Leonard, and others.

As the interview was winding down I slid my notepad and pen in front of Angelo and asked if he would write the letter included on page xv of my book, as he had agreed to in an earlier phone conversation. He collected his thoughts and then wrote them down on the notepad, handing the paper and pen back to me. As I started to read, he retrieved the paper and pen and added a postscript. I was amused by the postscript, wondering if he was concerned that time might forget him and his accomplishments or whether this was way of trying to add authenticity to the story.

As the words, "Boxing changed because of LaVern Roach," still echoed in my mind, I thought, *How many sports personalities can lay claim that their sport changed because of them?* Dundee, whom Muhammad Ali called, "The greatest trainer of all time," and perhaps boxing's greatest ambassador ever, provided me the essence of this book. His parting words to me were, "Good luck with the book. Boxing is in need of a good story."

Angelo Dundee died less than six months later on February 1, 2012, prior to the publication of this book, never having read it or knowing that he was one of three persons to whom this book is dedicated. I hope this book meets Angelo's approval and is the good story that boxing needs.

Boxing not only changed because of LaVern Roach, but may have survived because of him.

ACKNOWLEDGMENTS

This story of LaVern Roach could not have been written without the encouragement of so many friends and contributors who shared my enthusiasm in helping continue his legacy, sixty-five years after his death. Their combined support and efforts have provided material, new and old, that defines the boxer, the Marine, and the man—a champion to a past generation and an inspiration to current and future generations.

The story of LaVern Roach would never have gotten off the ground without the approval of Evelyn Roach Trice. She has been my rock and my pillar since day one, providing the encouragement needed to carry me through the ups and downs of writing that first book. Her memories, collection of memorabilia, and introduction to other key figures in the life of LaVern Roach have been priceless.

The key figure whom Evelyn introduced me to was Choc Hutcheson. Choc, the quintessential archivist, provided me "his letters from LaVern," boxing notes, and memories of LaVern as both friend and sportswriter. Without the letters that Choc has safeguarded all of these years, the book would have been grossly incomplete. Some of the information in these letters, from a friend to a friend, contained material that was a revelation even to Evelyn.

The third person I want to recognize is a name known to all boxing fans: Angelo Dundee. Circumstance brought me to Angelo. Recognizing the magnitude that his relationship with LaVern offered, I was successful in linking up with him. What Angelo brought to the table, in addition to his recollections of LaVern and overall commentary on boxing, was validity to LaVern's role in boxing history.

It was a pleasure to work with Sandy Lindeman, a high school classmate, who helped in the research and interviewing process. Special thanks to proofreaders Dr. Joan Sears and Linda Tarvin. Gratitude to Dr. Travis Bridwell, Gerald Pipkin,

Bruce Hook, Ronnie Roach Birdsong, Rick Roach, Suzanne Knox Rogers, Annalee Schubert, and my wife, Nancy, for their input and encouragement. Thank you to my daughter, Samantha, and her husband, Dale Ritter, for the use of their lake house which provided a perfect getaway for writing in solitude and to my son, Brian, his wife, Dr. Amy, and my granddaughters, Madison and Bella, for their understanding and allowing me to be, at times, an absentee grandfather so I could spend time writing the story of LaVern Roach.

Special gratefulness goes to the National Personnel Records Center in St. Louis, Missouri, for the safekeeping of US Marine military records and allowing access to LaVern's service records.

Eternal gratitude goes to Texas Tech University Press for believing in me and the story, starting with Judith Keeling, editor at the commencement of this project, and Joanna Conrad, current assistant director and editor-in-chief. Special thanks to Sport in the American West series editor Dr. Jorge Iber, and to Reader #1 and Reader #2, who all agreed that this was "a story that needed to be told."

WEST TEXAS
MIDDLEWEIGHT

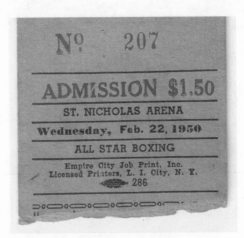

Roach/Small admission ticket purchased by
author from Anita Kivell. Photo by author.
Author's private collection.

CHAPTER 1

St. Nicholas Arena
New York City, February 22, 1950

Each boxing match is a story—a unique and highly condensed drama without words.
—Joyce Carol Oates

"LaVern, are you alright?" referee Frank Fullam asked as he stood in the corner where LaVern, sitting on his stool, was being attended by his manager John Abood and his cornermen.

"Sure!" LaVern said.

"Do you know where you are?" Fullam asked.

"Sure!" LaVern said again. "I'm in St. Nick's."[1]

It was Wednesday evening, February 22, 1950—fight night in New York City. In the late 1940s and early 1950s, every night except Sunday was fight night. Friday evenings were reserved for Madison Square Garden, the mecca of boxing, while Wednesday night fighting took place at St. Nick's. The other nights of the week were divided between the Broadway Arena, Bronx Coliseum, White Plains Arena, Sunnyside, Ridgewood Grove, and the many other venues spread across the five boroughs.

Harsh winter weather in the month of February is to be expected in New York City, but the severity of this snow and ice storm along with record freezing temperatures made it worse than usual. The Washington Weather Bureau issued a special weather bulletin urging drivers all the way from New England to Missouri to drive with caution.[2]

New York State and the upper northeastern seaboard received the brunt of one of the worst winter storms to hit in over a decade. In New York City, the five-degree-above-zero temperature was a new low for this day of the year. Subway and street traffic came to a near halt, and plane

Fight night at St. Nicholas Arena, New York City.
Reprinted by permission of boxrec.com.

flights were cancelled. The grounds, sidewalks, and streets outside of St. Nicholas Arena as well as the rest of city were frozen, covered with a mixture of ice, sleet, and snow, making driving and walking hazardous.

As a result of the adverse weather conditions and the fact that this evening's boxing match was being nationally televised on CBS, only 1,832 fans braved the bone-chilling weather to make their way to St. Nick's. Many of these enthusiasts missed seeing Bobby Copeland defeat Jimmy Taylor in the eight-round preliminary bout. Neither the fans in St. Nick's, nor the nationwide television audience, knew what was in store for them.

Television, in its infancy, was in the process of changing the landscape of all major sporting events in the nation. For boxing, this change was not necessarily for the better. "Boxing planted the seeds of its own destruction by televising boxing matches. Now fans were staying home to watch free televised boxing shows."[3] At the beginning of the 1940s it was estimated that there were approximately five thousand television sets in the

United States. Most were of the five-inch black-and-white variety. By the start of 1950 that number had increased to about 5 million, aiding in the decline of attendance at boxing events.

The first televised boxing match took place in 1931, carried by CBS. Being able to view the event from your living room was still a novelty to many fight fans in 1950. World War II was a major factor in slowing down the development of televised sports. By the end of the war, NBC and the Gillette Safety Razor Company teamed up to produce *The Gillette Cavalcade of Sports* with Steve Ellis handling ringside broadcasting. In 1946 NBC dropped the Monday and Tuesday broadcasts and focused on its Friday night matches at the Garden. In 1948 CBS picked up the Wednesday night void by airing the *Tournament of Champions.*

On such a wintry night, those without the luxury of owning a set often were invited or invited themselves to a friend's or neighbor's to view the event. Hundreds of thousands, perhaps even a million or more viewers were expected to watch the 8:30 p.m. broadcast that evening. A last resort was listening to the fight on the radio, where an equal number across the nation tuned in.

St. Nick's, as it was known by the locals, was located in Manhattan, on the northeast corner of Columbus Avenue and Sixty-Sixth Street. The old, dingy building, built in 1896, was originally opened as the St. Nicholas Rink to serve the needs of ice skating, figure skating, and ice hockey.

In 1906, its name was changed to St. Nicholas Arena. The first boxing matches held there were under the pretense of a "membership club," since prizefighting was illegal in the state of New York. The membership club scheme was just a way to circumvent the law to allow boxing in the city. Boxers were given club memberships, allowing them to legally fight in their own club. In 1911, when pugilism became lawful again in the state, St. Nick's became one of the first legalized venues. St. Nick's continued to accommodate ice hockey, figure skating, and boxing until 1920, when the popularity of the squared circle made the ice rink expendable. The ice rink was removed, and the arena was reconfigured to seat as many as four thousand boxing fans.

Since then, it had been the home to as many as ten thousand or more fights. Some estimates push that figure to thirty thousand or more. Accurate record keeping was often tossed aside and numbers padded to embellish the needs of the occasion. St. Nick's has been billed as the "Cradle of Champions" since many greats—including past champs Jack Johnson and Jess Willard as well as future champs Floyd Patterson and Cassius Clay—either got their start or fought some of their early matches there.

Since the promoters of Madison Square Garden controlled most of the title bouts held in New York City, wanting the Garden to be the only venue worthy of these championship events, few title fights were held elsewhere. The only title match ever held at St. Nick's occurred on October 17, 1938, when Joey Archibald defeated Mike Belloise for the world featherweight title. Fighting in St. Nick's was the next best thing to being in the Garden.

The main ten-round event of the evening was a middleweight bout between Georgie Small of Brooklyn and LaVern Roach of Plainview, Texas. Small wore white trunks, was five-foot-eight, and weighed in at 159½ pounds. LaVern, in black trunks, tipped the scales at 159 pounds and stood five-foot-nine.

Prior to televised bouts, boxers in New York State were required to wear either black or purple trunks, which were easier to clean and get the blood off of than light-colored ones. The advent of television changed the color scheme. Black trunks and white trunks make it easier for the announcer to distinguish and describe the fighters, similar in size and often in looks, to the television audiences. As a result, black trunks and white trunks became customary. Along with this new custom came heated arguments among the television networks and management as to who was going to pay for all of the new silks, an argument that was going on at the time of this fight.

Both fighters were crowd favorites. Georgie Small, a local Jewish boxer, grew up in nearby Brooklyn and had a large following at the fight. Equally as popular with the ringside fans was LaVern Roach, a transplanted Texan, now residing in New Jersey with his wife and two kids. He had won the hearts of many New Yorkers with his image as a bright, good-looking, clean-cut, and clean-living all-American young man. He, too, was very popular in the Jewish community as well as having a large military following, especially among Marines. The two fighters knew each other. Georgie had served as a sparring partner to LaVern a couple of years earlier, helping prepare him for a fight with Tony Janiro. Both liked and respected each other. Expecting the fight to be close, bookmakers had LaVern a slight six-to-five favorite over Small.

The evening's referee, the "third man in the ring," was Frank Fullam, a good boxer in his own day, winning the 1931 National AAU Middleweight Championship. After the obligatory introductions, the two contestants met at the center of the ring, received instructions, performed the perfunctory touching-gloves handshake, and waited for the opening bell.

Two days earlier in a letter to Choc Hutcheson, close friend and sportswriter for the *Lubbock Avalanche Journal*, LaVern wrote,

> Small is a pretty good boy and plenty smart, but doesn't fight too often. It will be a good win for me if I can look good. I am in top shape and should win, but keep your fingers crossed. My nose is a little sore and we thought we'd call it off, but I think I'll be O.K. Hope so anyway.[4]

As expected from his corner, LaVern outboxed Small for the first seven rounds, with an arsenal of rapid long-range missiles to the head and sharp uppercuts to the chin when infighting. The ringside fans, who paid a gate total of $5,343, seemed to be impressed as LaVern displayed his boxing skills at the expense of his opponent. He was so far ahead in points that all he had to do was remain standing at the final bell to win the bout.

Each round lasted three minutes with a one-minute break in between. At the end of the seventh round each fighter went to his respective corner to be toweled down and checked over for cuts, and to receive instructions for the upcoming round.

Different instructions were given to each pugilist prior to the start of the eighth round. LaVern was told by his corner to continue taking the fight to Small, being careful not to let his guard down. At the same time Small and his corner knew that they were way behind in points. Only a knockout could salvage the fight. His corner urged him to become more aggressive and look for an opening to land a knockout punch. If he didn't, the fight was lost. Small showed signs of tiring, which was bad, since the late rounds of a fight usually favored LaVern. Well-known for his superior training and conditioning, LaVern usually held a distinct advantage over his opponents by this point of the fight. Small was frustrated as he approached these final rounds: "He is fresher than I am."[5]

As the bell rang for round eight to begin, nine minutes of boxing separated LaVern from a chance to fight Rocky Graziano or Jake LaMotta for the world middleweight crown, something he had been dreaming of since he was a young boy growing up in Plainview. A featured summer bout in Yankee Stadium with Sugar Ray Robinson was also in the works. The future looked bright.

It was LaVern's twenty-fifth birthday, and a win would be the best birthday present he could receive. A loss might end his dream of becoming a world champ and send him back home to Plainview, Texas, a road that he had traveled once before and wasn't eager to repeat. Not now. Not until his goal was accomplished.

CHAPTER 2

Plainview, Texas, February 22, 1925

I believe one establishes a set of principles through faith,
how we were raised and where we were raised.
—George W. Bush, on growing up in West Texas

It's a boy! Rosa Inez Roach gave birth to Raymond LaVern Roach, adding one more to the growing population of the nation. Earlier that day headlines in the *New York Times* read, "The Population of the United States Today Was Estimated to Be 150,604,000."[1]

Stanley James Roach was the proud father of their firstborn. Stanley was born in Tifton, Georgia, on July 28, 1901. Shortly after Stanley was born, the family left Georgia and moved first to East Texas and then to Memphis, Texas, where other family members had previously settled. Memphis is located in the panhandle southeast of Amarillo and not too far from the Oklahoma border. The Roaches, like many other families, moved west in search of fertile land to farm and to start a new life. Rosa Inez Ferguson was born in Waco, Texas, on March 31, 1906. According to the 1910 census data, farming was the Fergusons' primary occupation. The family left the wooded area of East Texas and moved to the Plainview area for the same reason as the Roach family.

Stanley and Rosa met, and after a brief courtship they married in Memphis, Texas, and soon moved near Plainview. They settled in Cousins, a small farming community located seven miles north of Plainview. Stanley worked as a sharecropper, a system allowing those unable to purchase land the opportunity to live on and farm land while receiving certain benefits, such as a portion of the crop and sometimes even living expenses. Sharecropping—or tenant farming, as it was also called—was

Map of the Lone Star State of Texas, with Plainview boxed in. Reprinted by permission of mapresources.com.

common in this area, especially for those without the means to purchase land, or with limited education, and no skilled trade. Stanley qualified for each.

He was of the generation that grew up during World War I, too young to serve in it. Raised in rural communities and needed for work on the farm, these boys often received a limited education, knowing only how to work with their hands. In the 1930 federal census, Stanley listed his occupation as "laborer and odd jobs."[2] Stanley and others like him became jacks of all trades and masters of none.

Country living was tough, usually without electricity and indoor plumbing. Many of the houses had dirt floors. Most families didn't have the luxury of owning an automobile, making transportation difficult and not an ideal situation in which to raise a family. Soon after Raymond LaVern was born, the family moved from the Cousins community into Plainview, a town with a thriving population of about seventy-five hundred. In town the Roach family at least enjoyed the luxury of electricity. In later years LaVern always referred to Plainview as his hometown.

Plainview is as difficult to define geographically as to its location within the Lone Star State as Texas is hard to define as to its physical location within the United States. The question for Texas is whether it is a southern, southwestern, or western state. A case could be made for each. Plainview's geographical identity within the state is just as perplexing. Plainview has been concurrently known as being part of the Texas Panhandle, the Staked Plains, the Llano Estacado, the South Plains, the High Plains, and West Texas. Ask six different locals the location of Plainview and expect to get six different answers.

Situated on the southern tip of the Texas panhandle, Plainview is located 76 miles south of Amarillo and 47 miles north of Lubbock. The state line of New Mexico is 80 miles to the west, and the Oklahoma state line is about 110 miles to the east. It is situated halfway between the Dallas/Fort Worth area and Albuquerque, New Mexico.

Nothing about the physical landscape of this region appealed to the eyes of its first visitors or inhabitants. The first European to cross this part of Texas, Spanish conquistador Francisco Vasquez de Coronado, led a royal expedition in search of the Cibola and the Seven Cities of Gold. On October 20, 1541, in a letter to the king of Spain, he wrote,

> I reached some plains so vast, that I did not find their limit anywhere I went, although I travelled over them for more than 300 leagues . . . with no more land marks than if we had been swallowed up by the sea. . . . There was not a stone, nor bit of rising ground, nor a tree, nor a shrub, nor anything to go by.[3]

Coronado's impression of the area was echoed as late as 1852 by US Army captain Randolph B. Marcy, who led an expedition encompassing the same region:

> It is much elevated . . . very smooth and level . . . without a tree, shrub, or any other herbage to intercept the vision. . . . The almost total ab-

sence of water causes all animals to shun it: even the Indians do not venture to cross it except at two or three places.[4]

The Llano Estacado (Spanish for staked plains), for centuries thought to be unfit for man or beast, changed dramatically within the next three decades, thanks to a New Yorker with a vision.

The distance from Plainview to New York State is about eighteen hundred miles, but in spite of the distance, Plainview's beginning had a direct connection to the state of New York. Plainview, located near the center of Hale County, is the county seat. The first permanent settler to come to Hale County was the Reverend Horatio Graves, of Ausable Forks, New York. Having earlier made the trip to the area with a surveying crew in 1877, he returned in 1878 and purchased land in the center of the county. On July 4, 1882, he moved his wife and three daughters to a land that was flat and treeless, with nothing but a "plain view" in all directions. Unlike nearby rival towns Brownfield and Littlefield, named after early local business leaders from their respective communities, Plainview simply received its name from the topography of the land. Descendants of the Reverend Graves stated,

> Grandfather Graves did not leave Ausable Forks, New York, where he was pastor of a Methodist Church, because he had poor health or because any member of his family had ill health. Grandfather went to Texas because he felt that the availability of cheap land, where the winters were not as cold as the winters in New York State, made Texas an ideal location for establishing a Methodist colony.[5]

Later in life, as the reverend's health declined, his family moved to California to be close to other members of the clan, but not without feelings of regret for having to leave so many dear friends.

From its beginning, farming was the main livelihood for Plainview, but unpredictable weather often accompanied with little rain brought crop failure as often as it brought success. This changed in the early 1900s when it was discovered that the water table beneath the surface of the land had a depth of less than 150 feet, making irrigation farming feasible. With the arrival of east-west and north-south rail service to move the local crops, which included corn, sorghum, millet, alfalfa, vegetables, wheat, and fruit, the boom was on.

Local land developers, offering what appeared to be an unlimited supply of cheap land with plenty of water, began promoting the sale of the land around Plainview. Prospective buyers were brought in by passenger railcars from all over, but primarily from the states of Georgia, Alabama, Mississippi, Kentucky, Oklahoma, and Missouri, as well as from East Texas, where farming was the chief source of making a living. Most came for the same reason—cheap, available land and an opportunity for a new start in life. The Roach and Ferguson families were among these early settlers.

By 1925 Plainview had two colleges, a thousand-seat opera house, a seventy-room hotel with an elevator, a couple of banks, a hospital, and a modern courthouse. One of the larger towns, along with Amarillo and Lubbock, Plainview experienced a period of prosperity and domestic economic growth. With the Great War officially over, Plainview and the rest of the country entered the 1920s with a great deal of optimism. As prosperity and economic growth increased, it seem like the roaring twenties would last forever.

On the national scene, Calvin Coolidge was in the second year of his presidency of the United States, having assumed the position in 1923 upon the death of Warren G. Harding. New York City passed London in population, becoming the largest city in the world. The states now numbered forty-eight as Oklahoma, New Mexico, and Arizona were admitted to the union during the early part of the century.

The primary modes of entertainment included silent movies, music, and sporting events. The top box-office attraction of the day was Charlie Chaplin. One of the top movies of 1925 was *The Phantom of the Opera*, a silent film featuring Lon Chaney. Al Jolson and Eddie Cantor were two of the leading singers.

Baseball, boxing, and horse racing were the top sports of the 1920s. The Washington Senators were the reigning world champs in baseball, and Babe Ruth was the sport's biggest star. Black Gold, Coventry, and Man o' War were the top race horses.

Though baseball was the most popular team pastime, boxing was the most popular individual sport. Boxing consisted of eight weight classes, the most popular being the heavyweight, light heavyweight, middleweight, and welterweight. The biggest name in boxing was Jack Dempsey, the heavyweight champion. Divisions, weight limits, and title holders in 1925 were:

Division	Maximum Weight Limit	1925 Champion
Flyweight	112 lbs.	Pancho Villa
Bantamweight	118 lbs.	Eddie (Cannonball) Martin
Featherweight	126 lbs.	Louis (Kid) Kaplan
Lightweight	135 lbs.	Benny Leonard
Welterweight	147 lbs.	Mickey Walker
Middleweight	160 lbs.	Harry Greb
Light Heavyweight	175 lbs.	Mike McTique
Heavyweight	Unlimited	Jack Dempsey

Social changes accompanied the peace and prosperity of postwar America. Women gained the right to vote in 1920. Another social concern dealt with the legality of alcohol. The Prohibition issue was debated but would not be settled until a decade later. The tranquility of the United States was not being experienced worldwide. Europe and the Far East were dealing with more serious social, economic, and political problems.

In 1925 Mussolini declared dictatorial powers in Italy. At the same time Adolf Hitler was released from prison, where he wrote his personal memoir, *Mein Kampf*, outlining his future plans for his homeland. Soon after his release, he regained control of the National Socialist Party in Germany. Across the Pacific, Japan and Russia signed the Soviet-Japanese Basic Convention, a doomed treaty designed to stabilize the tense relationship that had developed between the two countries during the war. Although the seeds of turmoil were being planted for another global conflict, it would have to wait out a different type of worldwide catastrophe—one for which the Roach family and millions of others were not prepared.

After moving to Plainview from Memphis, Texas, Rosa Inez gave birth to a second son. Billie Charles Roach was born on June 12, 1927. The infant was another mouth to feed as Stanley, with his limited education and lack of a skilled trade, struggled to find work. The more promising life always seemed to elude Stanley, who never had the resources to purchase property, always relying on farming or working for others, providing little or no security for his own family. This was not lost upon young LaVern.

In October 1929, as Rosa Inez was with child again, the roaring twenties came to an unexpected and abrupt halt. After six straight years of economic prosperity, the stock market failed and, along with it, so did the nation's and most of the world's economic systems. Plainview's economy, based primarily on farming, was not exempt from the repercussions that followed. Land prices dropped overnight from $250 to $25 an acre. Stocks lost all their value in most cases. Mirroring the rest of the country, unemployment rose to 25 percent or higher. All three local banks closed. The Roach family, like many others, was financially unprepared and was swept up in the Great Depression that would last a decade. During this time, on May 18, 1930, Beth Maudell Roach was born, completing the Roach household.

Stanley joined the growing number of unemployed who, from time to time, hired out as truck drivers, sharecroppers, construction workers for the Works Progress Administration, or anything else that came along. With another mouth to feed, Stanley sometimes took desperate measures to provide food for his family, even to the point of sneaking out in the middle of the night and helping himself to a few eggs and milk from some nearby farmhouse.[6]

Adding to the economic woes of the Great Depression, the midwestern states experienced a natural phenomenon never seen before or since in the nation. Texas, along with Oklahoma and Kansas, suffered the brunt of what was to become known as the Dust Bowl. These dust storms often lasted for days due to the lack of any rain or moisture in the air. The water supply shrank rapidly. Crops died in the fields as water was needed more for human consumption. The food supply dwindled due to livestock dying from dust-filled lungs.

The dust was so thick and the sky became so dark that it was difficult to distinguish night from day. Lights were turned on during the day in order to be able to see inside buildings. The simple task of breathing became difficult. Sheets were torn in strips, dampened with water, and placed around cribs to keep the infants and toddlers from choking on the dust. Wet towels were placed around door and window seals to help absorb and keep the dust out of the houses, but to little or no avail. Like the livestock, many infants died as a result of windpipes and lungs being clogged by the dust.

The most conspicuous of these storms occurred on April 14, 1935. Known as Black Sunday, the storm started along the Kansas and Oklahoma border and headed south, gaining strength every inch of the way.

By the time it reached the Texas panhandle it looked like a black blizzard turning day into night. As it quickly approached, many residents thought the world was coming to an end. Among these was Woody Guthrie, living up the road in Pampa, Texas. Thinking he would never see his friends again, he sat down and wrote perhaps his most popular song.

> We talked of the end of the world, and then
> We'd sing a song an' then sing it again.
> We'd sit for an hour an' not say a word,
> And then these words would be heard:
> So long, it's been good to know yuh.
>
> *From "Dusty Old Dust," by Woody Guthrie*

These hard times drove many to give up and move westward to California in hopes of finding, if not a better, at least a less cruel way of life. The populace who remained, determined to survive no matter the odds, developed into a strong and courageous breed of people. Survival required an inner toughness, which benefitted LaVern and his generation in the trials and tribulations yet to come their way.

In addition to being tough, these pioneering men and women were also an honest breed. Locks on doors and windows weren't necessary. Residents left their homes unattended for hours, even days, without the worry of break-ins. An unwritten honor code existed among those who settled there, overlooking minor inconveniences of missing a few eggs and some milk. These were the kind of people who made up Plainview and influenced LaVern's formative years. The blue-collar work ethic served him well all during his life—at school, in the military, and throughout his boxing career.

For some unknown reason LaVern chose to go by his middle name rather than by Raymond. This decision had its drawbacks and brought with it a certain amount of teasing and confusion. An example of the confusion occurred in the taking of the 1930 US Census, where the census taker misspelled his name as Laverne and then listed him as a daughter and not a son. His name was misspelled throughout his life, usually as Laverne or LaVerne. Years later, even on his signature boxing photo, his name was spelled incorrectly.

Growing up in poverty during the Depression left its mark on LaVern and much of his generation. Many of the young people felt that if they ever rose above the poverty level, they would never return to it. He agonized as he watched his dad's constant struggle to make ends meet. He was determined to do better.

He started first grade in Plainview and continued there through elementary school and the first year of junior high. While LaVern was still in grade school, the Mason family moved into town from Arkansas. The twins, Milford and Wilford (who went by Mick and Wick), were a year older than LaVern. Their younger brother Johnny was a year younger than LaVern and a year older than Bill. Right away a friendship was formed, which lasted a lifetime.

Another family, perhaps even poorer than the Roaches and Masons, was the Dean family, who lived a couple of miles outside of the Plainview city limits in the Seth Ward community. Like the Mason and Roach families, George and Ruth Dean struggled just to put a roof over their heads and often didn't know where their next meal was coming from. They had two sons, Jimmy and Don. Jimmy, three years younger than LaVern, and Don, the same age as Beth, grew up with the Mason and Roach kids, none of them really knowing just how poor they were, nor the sacrifices their parents made for them just to survive. Jimmy Dean, an aspiring musician, would later rise out of his meager upbringing and become a country and western music star and sausage magnate. He, like LaVern, never forgot his roots.

LaVern at age thirteen. Courtesy of the LaVern
Roach family.

CHAPTER 3

To Be a World-Champion Boxer

Champions aren't made in gyms. Champions are made from something
they have deep inside them—a desire, a dream, a vision.
—*Muhammad Ali*

As work became more difficult to find in Plainview, Stanley moved his family back to Memphis, Texas, to be nearer to kin. Family units often shared housing and provided financial and emotional support for each other during these difficult times. Memphis, a much smaller town than Plainview, had a population of fewer than two thousand. It was located farther up the panhandle, closer to Amarillo.

Although LaVern left behind his close friends, the Mason brothers, he and Billie soon acquired new chums in Memphis, where LaVern attended his second year of junior high and his freshman year of high school. Their childhood was like that of most kids during that period of time. Activities often centered on family gatherings. Recreation included mainly outdoor and unstructured events such as kick the can, red rover, and sandlot baseball, where neighborhood boys and girls came together, made up their own rules, and played without adult supervision. LaVern and Billie, often guilty of picking on Beth, were nevertheless very protective of their little sister when other neighborhood boys tried the same.

During the Depression, Christmas would often come and go without the exchanging or receiving of gifts. "In 1935," LaVern later recalled, "we were lucky to get one or two presents at Christmas."[1] One year Stanley surprised the boys by bringing a present that proved life-changing for LaVern. He bought each of the boys a pair of boxing gloves. According to his brother, Bill, "LaVern was always interested in boxing."[2]

LaVern immediately fell in love with the sport. Adding to his new fascination was the family talk that he could be related to the great Bob Fitzsimmons, the British boxer who made history as the sport's first three-division world champion and also achieved glory for his victory over Gentleman Jim Corbett (the man who had beaten John L. Sullivan). Although there was no genealogical proof of kinship, family members on his mother's side often spoke vaguely, but in awe, of Fitzsimmons. "It was never proved," LaVern said. "The idea that a great fighter might have been my uncle really was something. It made me dream of being a fighter."[3]

LaVern, much more enthusiastic about boxing than younger brother Bill, always looked for stiffer competition, usually having to settle for bouts with neighborhood kids. The boxing took place in the Roach family's backyard. By age thirteen, LaVern was the best young boxer in Memphis.

One day Cal Farley's Flying Dutchman Circus came to town as part of the ceremonies connected with the Old Settlers' Reunion. This type of reunion, held annually, was an opportunity for locals to get together and celebrate their heritage in a county-fair atmosphere. Entertainment comprised local and traveling shows and the day including a lot of eating and drinking.

One of the sideshows featured a young lad by the name of Gib up on a platform singing a few songs. After Gib finished, Cal Farley, like a carnival barker, yelled out, "Gib can fight as good as he can sing. Anybody in the house want to fight him?" Although this announcement was made everywhere, Gib was hardly ever challenged.

Sitting in the audience with his parents and grandmother, LaVern, not giving it a second thought, blurted out, "Yes, I will." As he headed for the stage, his grandmother, Molly Fitzsimmons Roach, implored Stanley to call him back. LaVern's mother intervened and said, "He won't get hurt. I want to see what he can do."[4] Before Stanley could open his mouth, LaVern's first fight before the public was arranged in a matter of minutes.

Gib appeared to be about a year older and somewhat bigger than LaVern, who at the age of thirteen weighed all of seventy pounds. The youngsters went at it for three rounds, fighting like banty roosters. At the end of the fight, Mr. Farley, who also served as the referee, pronounced a draw. The decision saved face for Gib while bolstering LaVern's local reputation as a young pugilist. Later, while dressing in the basement of the county courthouse, Gib confessed that it was one of the few times he had been challenged. Word of the fight spread like wildfire through the community. Everywhere LaVern went, he was asked, "Aren't you the boy who challenged Gib to fight on Old Settlers' Day?"[5]

In the summer of 1940, the Roach family returned to Plainview, where Stanley got a job hauling hay and produce to market. LaVern enrolled in his sophomore year that fall at Plainview High and was welcomed back by his old friends, the Mason brothers. He introduced them to his love of boxing, and they soon became his sparring partners. They in turn convinced him to try out for the high school football team, their favorite activity.

High school football in Texas was more than just a sport. It became a way of life every fall with nearly everything in town revolving around it. For the community it provided entertainment and business. On Friday nights the opposing team arrived with all of its loyal followers with money to spend on eats, drinks, bets, and gas to fill up their vehicles after the game. Often a community's identity was tied in directly with the success or failure of its football team.

For the participants, it provided competition, an outlet for personal expression, and team involvement. Football players became town heroes, enjoying a celebrity-like status, especially when they won. For those few who were good enough, it could provide a college education. People all over the state, even if they had never been in the towns, were well aware of the Amarillo Golden Sandstorms (Sandies), Lubbock High Westerners, Dumas Demons, and other football powerhouses.

The Mason boys, all considerably larger than LaVern, were naturals at football. They all played in the backfield. LaVern, weighing only 110 pounds, possessed excellent speed, good footwork, coordination, endurance, and most of all toughness, due to his pugilistic training. Even at his size, he had no fear of being hit. He made the squad, joining the Mason boys in the crowded backfield. His sophomore season was spent on the bench alongside Johnny, a freshman on the team. Meanwhile Wick and Mick ran, caught passes, and punted the Bulldogs to a 9-1 record, losing only to their nemesis, the Amarillo Sandies. Since the twins were only juniors, Johnny and LaVern would have to wait a year or so for their chance to get much playing time.

After football season ended, LaVern turned his attention back to his first love: boxing. Plainview at that time had little to offer a young boxer. There was no gym, coach, or trainer. Except for relying on the Mason brothers as sparring partners, LaVern had to teach himself how to box. The library proved to be his best source for information. He often memorized instructional manuals word-for-word. A couple of manuscripts he found most helpful were written by Nat Fleischer, publisher and editor of the *Ring* magazine. They were *How to Train* and *Scientific Blocking and Hitting*. He studied the illustrations and then copied the movements in front of the mirror at home. Mr. Fleischer and LaVern soon met in person, and their paths crossed several times in the following years.

Although Plainview had not produced any championship-caliber pugilists, another West Texan was making a name for himself on the national boxing scene. Lew Jenkins hailed from Sweetwater, a town very similar in size to Plainview and an opponent in football. Jenkins, known as the "Sweetwater Swatter," was small in size but packed a powerful punch.

Like Plainview, Sweetwater had no gyms or Golden Gloves program. A product of the Depression, Jenkins grew up laboring on the family farm. "As a teenager he picked cotton for a dollar a day. He first fought for money in carnivals in a desperate attempt to escape the West Texas cotton fields."[6] Carnivals made their way from town to town, offering local cowboys or other fighters the opportunity to get in the ring with the circuit boxers. Averaging four or five fights a night at five dollars a fight was more than he could make as a farm laborer in a week.

Jenkins soon joined the carnival circuit in West Texas, and after a successful start he moved to the Dallas area, where he could make five to ten dollars a bout, win or lose. He lost as many as he won. As his income increased, so did his penchant for alcohol, cigarettes, women, and the nightlife. From then on he rarely was sober, in or out of the ring. He decided to go to New York to try his skill at the next level. In spite of his drinking, lifestyle, and inconsistent training, he won enough fights to gain the attention of boxing promoters and soon was offered a match with Lou Ambers, the reigning world lightweight champion. On May 10, 1940, while intoxicated, he knocked out Ambers in the third round in Madison Square Garden and became the new world lightweight champ. He was the first world champion boxer to hail from West Texas. After the fight he claimed that he had to knock Ambers out early, knowing that he wasn't in good enough shape to last more than a few rounds.

Six of his next ten fights were held in the Garden, where he averaged twenty thousand to thirty thousand dollars a match, most of which was spent on New York's nightlife. "Jenkins liked whiskey, motorcycles, fast cars, and loose women more than he liked to train and take care of himself. His personal life was a mess."[7] His lifestyle finally caught up with him, as he lost eleven of his next fourteen fights before joining the Coast Guard in World War II. His military duty temporarily turned his life around. As a result of his bravery and actions rescuing injured soldiers behind enemy lines, he received the Silver Star. He also participated in several North African and European offensives, which included the D-Day invasion.

After the war, he resumed his boxing career, winning twenty-one fights while losing thirteen. He retired from the ring in April 1950 after losing consecutive matches to Carmen Basilio and Beau Jack. "By 1950 he was a dead broke alcoholic. When he hit rock bottom he had exactly what he started out with—nothing."[8]

Once again it took a war for Lew to get his act together. "He prayed for another war in which he could be a foot soldier. He got his war in Korea, his Silver Star and his hero's grave in Arlington."[9]

Lew's rise to the top inspired young LaVern in his quest to reach the pinnacle of boxing. His interest in the sport was unlike most boys, who often participated only at the demand of their fathers to help toughen them. LaVern took boxing seriously. He started training in high school as if he were in training as a professional. Several years later in an interview, when asked about his early habits, he responded,

> Every night for as long as I can remember, I was in bed by 10 o'clock. I would never stay up late, and every morning at 6 o'clock I'd get up and I'd do roadwork before school. People thought I was crazy. There were no fighters around there and they didn't know what I was do-ing. I would run at the western edge of town near Wayland College so people wouldn't see me. Sometimes I would overhear people talking about some crazy kid running early in the morning around there. They didn't understand it.[10]

LaVern's concentration and dedication to boxing created some dissent outside of the immediate family. Both Stanley and LaVern received stern criticism from some members who wanted to know why LaVern was not helping his dad after school. It was costing Stanley nine dollars a day to hire someone in his work instead of using LaVern. The question asked was, "Can't that healthy young fist-fighting son of his save him some money?"[11]

LaVern recalled that his dad paid them no mind and told him, "Son, you want to be a boxer, you stick at it. I'll get by without you on the truck." LaVern's mother, Momma Rosa, as she was affectionately called, was just as supportive. LaVern said, "For my roadwork, my mother would fix up an old jersey with a hood, putting zippers on the sleeves. She also prepared separate meals for me so I wouldn't have to eat all of the starches that the rest of the family were having. There was no grease or fried meats, and I had plenty of vegetables."[12] He gave his parents all the credit for giving him the opportunity to box and hoped someday to be able to repay them for their sacrifices on his account.

Like all good athletes, one of LaVern's greatest assets was his competiveness. "LaVern was always ready to try, no matter what the sport. He wasn't very big, but he never quit."[13] Knowing at an early age that he wanted to be a professional allowed him the opportunity to train for his future. How he was going to accomplish this was another thing.

Lubbock, located less than an hour away and considerably larger than Plainview, offered an organized Golden Gloves boxing program under the sponsorship of Collier Parris, sports editor of the *Lubbock Avalanche Journal.* Joining LaVern on the Collier Parris Boxing Team were two other boys from Plainview, Loyd and Roy Belk. Getting to and from Lubbock would have its challenges since LaVern's parents didn't own a car. Determined not to let this opportunity pass him by, he hitched rides with friends, family members, the Belk family, or even complete strangers in order to get to and from Lubbock.

Having grown substantially since his bout with Gib, LaVern now weighed 111 pounds, placing him in the flyweight division. He became an immediate success in the ring due to his regimented training that accompanied his speed and determination. The same ingredients that served him well on the football field proved his main assets in the ring.

After winning the district Golden Gloves meet in the flyweight division, he advanced to the Texas State meet held in Fort Worth, commencing on February 14, 1941, and ending with the semifinals and finals held on February 17. LaVern's first opponent was Elmer Key from Dallas. LaVern knocked him out in the third round. His next opponent, Junior

Hamby from Follett, went the distance, with LaVern winning by a decision. Next up for LaVern in the semifinal round was Jesse Gonzales, boxing star of the Allen Academy of Temple. Only one other Lubbock team member, Rhea Mitchell, made it to the semifinal round, where he was matched against Jay Turner, favored heavyweight and brother of pro football's Bulldog Turner.[14]

The semifinals and finals attended by over seven thousand boisterous fans at Flem Hall were called by a writer for the *Fort Worth Star-Telegram* the best ever staged in the area. In the first bout of the semifinals, LaVern lost in a very close decision to Gonzales, who went on to win the state championship. LaVern had never fought before such a large crowd and seemed nervous and overwhelmed by the noise coming from the fans. Unsettled by the atmosphere during the first two rounds, he came on strong during the third round to make it a close fight. Several years later, when asked about the hardest hitter he faced as an amateur, Lavern singled out Gonzales. Lubbock came up empty-handed in the other semifinal round, with Texas Tech's Mitchell getting knocked out in the first round by Turner, who went on to win the state heavyweight championship.

After the tournament ended, the following report appeared in the *Fort Worth Star-Telegram*: "One of the neatest fights of the night was put on by little Roach of the Lubbock team. He was strong in the first and third rounds. Roach didn't seem to get accustomed to the large crowd until the last round. Most promising youngster for next year's tournament is LaVern Roach." Lorin McMullen continued, "[LaVern] appeared almost too young to be in the ring without his daddy, but he bopped those older foes like he meant it."[15]

The remainder of LaVern's sophomore year passed without a whole lot of fanfare. The summer months came with him working for his dad, doing whatever needed to be done. His physical training included mostly running, shadow boxing, and sparring with the Mason boys whenever possible.

LaVern was given another chance to show off his boxing skills during the first week of August with the Texas Amateur Athletic Federation (TAAF) boxing tournament held in Austin. Fighting again as a flyweight, LaVern knocked out Inez Perez of Killeen in twenty-eight seconds of the second round. The next opponent up was Hubert Gray of Wichita Falls, a southpaw. All of LaVern's previous foes were right-handed, and he had a difficult time trying to adjust to fighting a lefty. Gray outpointed La-Vern in a very close decision. One sportswriter said LaVern was game but lacked in experience. Years later LaVern described his match against Gray as his toughest amateur fight. Gray later turned professional, winning twenty-eight matches while losing only five. Another state boxing championship continued to be just out of LaVern's reach. He and Gray crossed paths again years later.

LaVern didn't have to wait too long for a chance to gain experience. He qualified and was a late Texas entry to the Amateur Athletic Union (AAU) boxing tournament, an eight-state gathering held in Albuquerque, New Mexico, on September 15, 16, and 17. The charitable event sponsored by the Knights of Columbus had Nat Fleischer, wealthy publisher of the *Ring* magazine and famous boxing authority, signed on to referee the event. Fleischer, author of the two books that served as young LaVern's guides to boxing techniques, refereed eighty-four matches that week.

Joining Fleischer at the tournament was the great former boxing champion Henry Armstrong, named the *Ring*'s Fighter of the Year in 1937, and the only boxer to hold world titles in three different weight divisions simultaneously. After Armstrong achieved that feat in 1938, no boxer was ever again allowed to be champion in more than one weight division at any given time. Next to Fitzsimmons, Henry Armstrong was LaVern's greatest boxing idol.

Making it to the finals in the flyweight division, he lost a close decision to John Patrick O'Leary. Although LaVern lost the championship bout, Fleischer was so impressed with his boxing skills that he named LaVern the most promising boxer in the tournament. He did so at the urging of Governor John Miles of New Mexico, an observer of the tournament and an apparent fan of young Roach. In a conversation with Fleischer during the ending ceremonies of the tournament, LaVern said, "I want to come to New York and turn professional."

"Great," Fleischer advised, "but take your time."[16]

At the end of the tournament, when asked by LaVern for some advice on boxing, Armstrong gave him some instruction, which he would adhere to his entire boxing career: "You just run and run. That's the only way you get stamina. Without stamina, you are not worth a dime in a fight that goes over three rounds."[17]

LaVern, previously running two miles a day, returned home and in-

LaVern at age sixteen with former world champ Henry Armstrong. Courtesy of the LaVern Roach family.

creased his distance to four miles. This tournament had a tremendous effect upon LaVern, bolstering his ring reputation, ambition, and confidence.

Except for his excursion to Albuquerque, the fall school year of 1941 started off like most years as LaVern began his junior year of high school. Once more the attention of the town centered on what kind of football team their Bulldogs would field. LaVern again made the football squad as a running back and quarterback, due partially to his sophomore-year experience and to his newly established reputation as a boxer. He received more recognition, respect, and attention than the previous year. Mick and Wick, now seniors, continued to pound out the yardage on the football field, but LaVern and Johnny were used more frequently when one or both of the twins needed a breather. LaVern, due partially to his strong arm, was able to get playing time as quarterback as well as at running back.

Although the headlines in Plainview in the fall of 1941 continued to highlight football, the national media focused more and more on international events, especially the goings-on in Europe. Part of the world, though thousands of miles away, was at war. The attitude of the nation grew more serious as Germany and Japan continued their quests to conquer their respective parts of the world. One only had to pick up a newspaper or listen to the radio to be constantly reminded that the winds of war were swiftly blowing toward America. Many felt it was only a matter of time before the United States would be drawn into this international conflict.

The Plainview Bulldogs finished the season with a very respectable 7-3 record, capped off with a 13-0 upset of the Amarillo Sandies, the only team to beat them the previous year. LaVern and Johnny Mason continued to ride the bench but spent enough time on the field as backups to the Mason twins to letter in the sport. After the football season ended, LaVern and the Mason boys made up the majority of the basketball team. Although short according to basketball standards, LaVern excelled at the sport, even in rebounding, due to his speed, quickness, and natural athletic ability.

On December 7, 1941, as the basketball season was getting under way, LaVern's life along with millions of others around the world suddenly changed and took an unexpected path as Japanese bombs hit their targets at Pearl Harbor. His goal to someday go to New York and become a boxing professional was put on hold.

Suddenly priorities altered. "For once I forgot boxing,"[18] he admitted. Only sixteen and not old enough to join any branch of the military, he set in motion plans to graduate early and join the war effort. During the course of the year he decided that after graduation he would join the Marines. This choice of service was based on his desire to become a Marine Raider, a unit established by an order of President Roosevelt, who wanted the United States to have a counterpart to the British Commandos, an elite fighting force. They were the "toughest of the toughest." LaVern, never one to look for the easy way out, was not afraid to go where the most action was.

Having at least a year to wait before he could enlist, LaVern turned his attention back to basketball and boxing as he prepared for the state

Golden Gloves tournament only a couple of months away. By now, he had gained enough weight to fight as a bantamweight.

Having a year's experience under his belt, LaVern entered the tournament with more confidence than ever. After a first-round knockout of M. J. Lozano of the Lubbock Air Base, LaVern was on his way to the state tournament in Fort Worth for the second time. He advanced to the second round on a default by his opening opponent, Roger Sanchez of San Antonio. Next up was Jack Slaymaker of Beaumont. A victory against Slaymaker set up a semifinal match against Hector Marquez of El Paso. In a hard-fought battle Roach lost to Marquez, who later turned pro and finished with a career record of twenty wins and six losses. Marquez's wins included the USA Texas State bantamweight title in 1947. LaVern was once again denied a state Golden Glove championship.

In addition to entering and winning local area tournaments in Post, Lockney, Slaton, and other small towns nearby, LaVern finished his junior year playing basketball, running track, catching for the baseball team, and boxing. In track he was clocked at 10.5 seconds in the hundred-yard dash. After school he helped his dad haul hay and produce to market while maintaining his strict workout schedule.

Even though he did not win a state title in either boxing organization, he did win the sportsmanship award and was voted most popular fighter in most tournaments he entered. As a sixteen- and seventeen-year-old, the four losses he absorbed at the state tournaments to Gonzales, Marquez, O'Leary, and Gray would make up four of his five losses to go along with over one hundred victories in his amateur career.

LaVern began his senior year at Plainview High in the fall of 1942. Mick and Wick took their gridiron skills up the road to the campus of Texas Technological College in Lubbock, where both received football scholarships to play for the Matadors. It was Johnny and LaVern's time to produce on the gridiron. LaVern became a fixture in the Plainview Bulldog backfield, playing backup quarterback and sharing running-back duties with team captain Johnny Mason. Johnny and LaVern provided a good one-two punch for the Bulldogs. Johnny offered size and speed as a running back, while LaVern was a double threat with his speed and arm strength.

It was a mediocre season for the Bulldogs, who fielded a team for the first time in several years without the Mason twins, and their presence was sorely missed; Plainview ended up with four wins, four losses, and one tie. The Amarillo Sandies and the Lubbock High Westerners, both with a much larger student base, handed the Bulldogs their biggest defeats. The highlight of LaVern's senior season was scoring two touchdowns in the Plainview Bulldogs' 40-13 romp over Borger.[19]

An astute football fan as well as player, LaVern received a six-dollar prize for winning the *Plainview Herald*'s weekly Football Pick'ems contest by correctly selecting the winners of the most games for the second weekend in October.[20]

LaVern was well respected by everyone. One incident involved a new kid in school, Cloyce Terrell. Cloyce, a skinny guy, was continually picked on and bullied by some of the athletes. One day, as Cloyce was sitting on the bleachers in the gym, some athletes started harassing him. LaVern, even though he didn't know Terrell, had seen enough. He approached his classmates and stated, "I am sick of you guys picking on this kid. Don't do it again."[21] Cloyce said no one ever picked on him again.

In school, LaVern had the reputation of being a good, well-rounded student who made acceptable, but not exceptional grades. His favorite subjects were mathematics and history. He also took algebra, advanced algebra, general math, geometry, typing, and woodshop.

In addition to boxing and team sports, he also enjoyed playing tennis and golf and swimming. After school, when not involved with sports, he worked in a tire shop, changing tires, patching tubes, and doing other odd jobs. His extracurricular activities, including team sports, boxing, and work, left him little time for studying or a social life.

LaVern was friendly and well-liked. Friends described him as a good kid, never getting in trouble. Johnny Mason described LaVern as the most disciplined person he ever met. "He didn't drink, smoke, or gamble— habits that were very popular in that day. I don't remember LaVern ever telling or even listening to dirty jokes. He was down to earth, never bragging about his success as a boxer or athlete. He kept his fighting in the ring and did not participate in any street or alley fighting."[22]

The class of 1943 was different from all classes that would follow at Plainview High. This would be the last class to graduate after having attended only eleven years of schooling. The class of '44 and all Plainview High classes that followed would have to complete twelve years of education. The war made the students different in other ways.

Due to the demands of the war effort, everyone, including students, was more serious than in the past. Patriotism and dedication were apparent everywhere, and no more so than in the dedication of the 1943 *Plain View* yearbook, which read,

> The way of life which we in America know is one of unlimited opportunities. To achieve success in such a land as ours, there are but two requirements; namely, talent and ambition. For this is the land where a man is judged on his ability and initiative, rather than on his nationality, religion, or political beliefs.
>
> These things are possible only through our government of, by, and for the people . . . the government which is now fighting for its very existence. It is therefore with a feeling of the deepest concern and loyalty that the "Plain View" staff of nineteen hundred forty-three dedicates this annual to that ideal of government: to UNCLE SAM, the symbol of AMERICA.

These were words written by seventeen- and eighteen-year-old kids, many of whom would go to, but not return from, war. The seniors of 1943 became one of the graduating classes that would make up our nation's "greatest generation." For the yearbook, the graduates of 1943 were asked what they wanted to be after high school. Popular listings included pilot, farmer, engineer, doctor. Under LaVern's name, next to his yearbook photo, were the words, "to be a world champion boxer." Even knowing that his immediate future would be spent in a uniform, he was not giving up on his dream of someday going to New York and fighting professionally.

LaVern earned enough credits to fulfill the academic requirements and graduated at the end of the fall semester of his senior year. In January 1943, one month shy of his eighteenth birthday, he graduated from Plainview High.

Even with the nation at war, the law required one to be eighteen years old in order to join the Marines, except with parental consent. Having graduated, LaVern was anxious to start this new phase of his life. Not wanting to wait a day longer, he talked his parents into giving their consent. Five days before he turned eighteen, the family drove to Fort Worth and LaVern enlisted.

Accompanying the Roach family on the trip to Fort Worth was Wick

Mason, whom LaVern persuaded to join the Marines with him. After finishing out the football season at Texas Tech, Wick decided to give up his football scholarship and join the Marines with LaVern. Due to the military drafting anyone over the age of eighteen, Texas Tech and many other college programs fielded teams with fewer than thirty players. Some colleges, such as Baylor, were even forced to give up football during the war years.

CHAPTER 4

A Few Good Men, Semper Fi

There are only two kinds of people that understand Marines: Marines and the enemy.
Everyone else has a second-hand opinion.
—General William Thornson, U.S. Army

February 17, 1943, Dallas, Texas

After being sworn in and signing an affidavit that he acknowledged
having voluntarily enlisted as a private in the Volunteer Marine Corps
Reserve for the duration of the national emergency and having been in-
spected and certified by the recruiting officer to be entirely sober when
enlisted, LaVern, five days before his eighteenth birthday, took the first
step to becoming a Marine.

The Marine Corps has always taken pride in the fact that it is different from the other branches of military service. The Corps has enjoyed
a reputation for toughness unmatched by the other branches of military
service and is the only service where there is no distinction in labeling its
officers and enlisted men. They are all called Marines, with a capital M.
The navy has officers and sailors. The air force has its officers and airmen.
The army is represented by officers and soldiers. A Marine is a Marine,
period.

By the time of the start of World War II, the famous phrase "A Few
Good Men" had been around for well over 150 years. It was first adver-
tised in 1779 in the Providence, Rhode Island, *Gazetteer* calling for "a few
good men" to engage in a short cruise and has been an invitation issued to
the bravest and toughest ever since.

As of June 30, 1939, two months before Hitler's armies launched their

SGT. H. G. FROWNFELTER   P. F. C. J. K. COPILEVITZ

395th Platoon, US Marine Corps, San Diego, 1943. LaVern, second row, sixth from the left. Courtesy of the LaVern Roach Family.

blitzkrieg, US Marine Corps strength stood at 19,432. By December 7, 1941, the United States entered the war against Japan and Germany with a force of just over 65,000 Marines. By war's end this number had increased to 485,000. While the US Army was the primary land force to fight the Atlantic war against Germany, it was the Marines, along with the navy, that trained to fight the amphibious battles in the Pacific.

Since the attack on Pearl Harbor, the Marines had shown extraordinary bravery in the Battles of Wake Island and Guadalcanal. These engagements marked the first combat test of the new amphibious doctrine and also provided a crucial turning point of the war in the Pacific by providing a base to launch further invasions of Japanese-held islands.

LaVern was always fearless and ready for battle, whether it was against Gib in his first fight in Memphis, or running head-on into the mammoth linemen on the Amarillo Sandies football team. He was ready to answer the call and join the brotherhood of the Corps.

After his swearing-in, he returned to Plainview to take care of any unfinished business before reporting to the May basic training class. On May 12, 1943, as his former classmates prepared for graduation, LaVern returned to Dallas where he and other enlistees boarded a train headed for California. Instead of heading east to New York to achieve a lifelong dream in boxing, he was shipped west to San Diego to fulfill his military duty for his country. He arrived on May 14 for seven weeks of basic training, better known as "boot camp." Once he got off the train and was met and escorted to the base, he became the property of the US Marines and would remain so until after the war ended.

Under the seven-week schedule, recruits spent three weeks in the recruit depot, two at the rifle range, and the rest back at the depot. The objective is to turn a civilian into a fighting machine. "The purpose of Marine boot camp is to instill the discipline that will cause a Marine to stand and fight, when every inborn instinct tells him to run."[1] This mentality served LaVern well as a Marine and a boxer.

LaVern, along with fifty-nine other "boots," were assigned to the Ninth Recruit Battalion, Recruit Depot, 395th Platoon, US Marine Corps under the Third Marine Division. Over half of the platoon had southern roots, with twenty being from Tennessee and fifteen from Texas. Joining this group were seventeen Yankees from Michigan. The other eight represented the states of California, Ohio, Colorado, and South Dakota. Their drill instructor was Sergeant H. G. Frownfelter, who was assisted by Private First Class J. K. Copilevitz. For the next seven weeks, these two men spent twenty-four hours a day with the recruits, teaching them to be Marines.

The regimental life of boot camp didn't faze LaVern. Without knowing it at the time, he had been training for boot camp since he was a youngster. At the age of eighteen he became a drill instructor's dream of what an ideal recruit should look and act like. The physically challenging and mentally demanding aspects of boot camp didn't intimidate him at all. The self-discipline and the physical rigors he had been putting himself through for boxing now paid large dividends for LaVern and Uncle Sam.

PT (physical training) played an important role in boot camp, with the obstacle course being the most dreaded event for the new recruits. With his quick footwork, speed, and coordination, LaVern became the fastest in his platoon to complete the intimidating obstacle course.

Another area in which he excelled was the boxing pit, where boots are not necessarily matched against someone their own size. When the call came for volunteers to put on the gloves, he was the first to put up his hand, just like in Memphis. At the weight of 145 pounds, he wasn't aware that his opponent would be a 200-pounder. The fight was on, as they stood in the ankle-deep southern California sand. "He threw a right, I pulled my head to the side and countered with a right. He went down and over on his back."[2] The fight was over. LaVern, at only eighteen years of age, quickly gained the reputation as being one of the best fighters on the entire base.

His boxing skills in the pit were soon noticed by the military command and put to test under the watchful eye of actor John Wayne. Wayne, on base to help boost morale while making "The Fighting Seabees" in the area, was asked and agreed to referee a boxing match between LaVern and an opponent to be picked out. A fellow Texan from Austin was selected as his adversary. LaVern wasn't excited about fighting another Texan but had no say in the matter. The fight was on, as Wayne watched the two young men exchange blows. LaVern's reward for being the last man standing was a silver Marine bracelet presented to him by Wayne.[3] The bracelet became one of his most prized possessions.

LaVern proved a good Marine. "I never took a crooked step," he later admitted. "I knew that the Corps was out to teach a fellow how to take orders. I wanted to be the best. Honest, I kind of imagined myself trying to win a competition."[4] LaVern loved the challenge of physical competition, whether it was in the boxing ring, on the football field, on the basketball and tennis courts, running track, or on the golf course. He excelled in all.

Nearly half of the time spent in recruit training was devoted to weapons. LaVern shined in this endeavor also. Most young boys growing up in the Texas Panhandle are used to handling the family .22, either shooting at rabbits or tin cans set up on fence posts as targets. On the rifle range, he scored 322 out of a possible 340 in preliminary firing. In the record firing, the official one that counts, his score slipped to 302. He just missed becoming an "expert rifleman," which required a score of 305 and would have meant an extra five dollars per month bonus pay. He did score enough to be a "rifle sharpshooter," which added a three-dollar bonus to his fifty-dollars-per-month salary. He also qualified as a pistol sharpshooter. He rated as an expert in both the machine gun and bayonet. In

LaVern's Marine scroll, medals, and dog tag. Photo by author.

the automotive training he qualified for driving light trucks, heavy trucks, and tractors.[5]

As boot camp was winding down, it was time for the recruits to fill out their requests for their next assignment. The Marine Raiders, one of the main reasons that LaVern chose this branch of service, were in the process of disbanding. The Marine outfit that introduced "Gung ho!" into the American lexicon was not taking any more recruits, in part due to the criticism of the rest of the Marine Corps, which considered all members part of an elite unit. No doubt LaVern would have been ideally suited for this group in spite of his young age. With being a Raider no longer an option, aerial gunnery became his first choice.

LaVern's platoon, along with five others, graduated from boot camp on July 6, 1943. LaVern became Private First Class Roach. He had made the grade and joined the brotherhood. These new private first class Marines would become part of that group of fighting men to whom Sir Winston Churchill gave tribute: "I am convinced that there is no smarter, handier, or more adaptable body of troops in the world."[6] Admiral William "Bull" Halsey stated, "The Marine Corps has just been called by the *New York Times*, 'the elite of this country.' I think it is the elite of the world."[7]

After boot camp graduation, LaVern was eager to return to Plainview for a brief visit. He had never been away from family and friends this long before. The local newspaper carried the story: "Pfc. Lavern Roach, USMC, is home on a 10-day furlough. He is to leave Thursday for San Diego where he finished eight weeks of boot camp July 7. He has been assigned to the aviation branch of the Marine Corps and hopes to be an aerial gunner."[8] The eighteen-year-old boy who had left home just a few short months earlier now returned to his hometown as a Marine.

LaVern ultimately would be sent east, but Wick Mason was assigned to the Fifth Marine Division, which was headed west. They said their good-byes, not knowing when, where, or if they would see each other again. While home on furlough, LaVern was given a warm welcome by the local residents. After the brief visit, he returned to California. On July 21 he reported to the base located at Kearney Mesa for ten days of basic aviation training, where he scored a grade of excellent.

Private First Class LaVern Roach received orders to "Aviation Gunnery Duty," Cherry Point, North Carolina. First he was sent to the Marine Aviation Detachment located at Norman, Oklahoma, to attend combat air crewman training school. This was a fourteen-week course where he received basic training in aviation ordnance as well as guns, cannons, ammunitions, bombs, and fuses, including their installation on aircraft. He graduated from this school on November 13 with a mark of 87.24, ranking 104 in a class of 211.

Upon completion, LaVern was transferred to the Ordnance School at the Aberdeen Proving Ground in Maryland for a three-week course on aircraft armament at the Small Arms Section. He completed this course with a rating of Excellent, finishing eighth in a class of twenty-nine. He was now classified as a semiskilled weapons mechanic, aircraft. This course also included twenty-seven hours of concurrent military training and physical conditioning. As a semiskilled weapons mechanic, LaVern was able to perform general repair, overhaul, and maintenance work under the supervision of a skilled mechanic.

With all of the training schools behind him, LaVern reported for duty to his new home at Cherry Point, North Carolina, to receive further training before being shipped overseas to the war zone. In the short period of time from January 1, 1943, to December 31, 1943, LaVern went from being a seventeen-year-old high school senior to a fully trained eighteen-year-old Marine ready for battle.

The Cherry Point Base, located in Craven County between New Bern and Morehead City, was the largest Marine air base in the country. Cherry Point was a new facility, with construction having begun seventeen days before the Pearl Harbor attack. The Japanese attack on Pearl Harbor resulted in it being finished ahead of schedule and commissioned on May 20, 1942. The base also served as an antisubmarine base for the army air corps and the navy. Each of these units was credited for sinking German U-boats off of the North Carolina coast in 1943.

As the young private first class settled into his new home in the base barracks, he began receiving letters from home with disturbing news, informing him that the Roach clan was in a desperate financial situation. Stanley, suffering from a back injury in January, was now even more limited in finding work. It was becoming increasingly difficult to provide for his family. Feeling helpless to do anything about it, LaVern learned that he could set up a portion of his military pay to send back home. He chose to keep only five dollars a month for toiletries and bare necessities and was able to send thirty-seven dollars a month back home. On the weekends when his buddies headed to the movies and bars in the nearby towns, LaVern stayed on the base and took in the free base movies as his entertainment.

After getting used to his daily work routine and finding extra time on his hands due to the extra hours he was spending on base, LaVern sought out the base gym to work out. He found a makeshift facility attached to the back of the PX. While working out one day he noticed a posted sign calling for boxing tryouts for the Marine team. He inquired about the posting and was informed that the base was organizing a squad to compete against other military units and amateur organizations, including in the Golden Gloves.

LaVern, out of interest and curiosity, returned the next day and asked the sergeant in charge if he could try out. This chance encounter began a lifelong relationship for LaVern and John Abood that would transcend the Marine Corps and end up being a professional business relationship as well as a father-son-like bond between the two.

John Abood and the Fighting Leathernecks. LaVern, fourth boxer from the left.
Courtesy of the LaVern Roach family.

CHAPTER 5

John Abood and the Fighting Leathernecks

Ta-ta-ta-ta-ta
I thought it was a machine gun.
The sound rattled from the gym,
a boxer practicing on a speed bag.
The sound changed my life forever.[1]
—*Johnny Kostas*

John Abood was anything but a typical Marine sergeant. He was born in Lebanon on July 7, 1910, and his family moved to the United States when he was a child. His father started a knitting mill business, but Johnny, who was always expected to go into the family enterprise, had a different set of plans. Despite parental disapproval, he pursued his first love, boxing. In the late 1920s he went to the National AAU lightweight finals and turned professional soon after.

Listing Bakersfield, California, as his hometown, he fought under different aliases, including that of Johnny La Mar, to keep his parents from knowing that he was boxing. He fought several good fights against some reputable pugilists during his short career before quitting the ring, rejoining the family business, and returning to the good graces of his parents. In spite of the broken nose he received along the way, a badge of honor among the boxing ranks, Johnny maintained his good looks and kept in boxing condition, always looking years younger than his age.

After returning home, he took over the family enterprise and in just two years doubled production and profitability. Although his participation in boxing appeared to be over as he settled into the corporate life, he never lost interest. He soon married, and he and his wife, Eleanor, much to the delight of his parents, started a family. The lessons learned as a boxer and as a businessman helped him in the following years as he applied these skills to his profession in the boxing world.

The day of December 7, 1941, changed Abood's life, just as it had LaVern's and everyone else's. John, thirty-one years of age and married with a child, insisted on going into the military. He joined the Marines and applied for aerial gunnery, which he was denied due to his age. At the Marine Corps Recruit Depot in Parris Island, South Carolina, he was involved in a conditioning program that included boxing. A new opportunity opened for him to transfer to the Cherry Point Air Base as boxing coach and instructor. In 1943 he started making plans to form a competition boxing team for the base.

As in World War I, the different branches organized their own boxing squads to compete against the others and also to go against willing civilians. The rationale was to build morale for the men in uniform and provide entertainment for both the military and civilian population. It also became a successful vehicle for promoting the sale of war bonds, which the nation badly needed.

Morale on the battlefield and on the home front has always been important in winning battles and wars. The US government and military learned this lesson in World War I. As a result, President Franklin D. Roosevelt wrote his "green light letter" at the start of 1942 to the baseball commissioner, urging the continuance of baseball in some form or fashion. He reasoned that men and women having to work longer hours needed some sort of an outlet to take their minds off work and the war, even if it was only for a couple of hours.

As a result, baseball continued, even if it meant using older players, since the younger ones were off to war. Women baseball leagues even came into play. Baseball games were relatively inexpensive and took only a couple of hours or so to watch.

The same logic applied to military boxing teams. Baseball and boxing, along with horse racing, had been the three most popular sports in the country at the start of the war. The war effort depleted the ranks of professional boxing, with over four thousand young fighters joining the service. Professional boxing championships were frozen at the start of the war, not to be continued until after the end of hostilities.

Amateur pugilism thrived under these conditions. Military teams and local Golden Gloves squads joined to provide good entertainment for the troops as well as the civilians. The natural competitiveness of the inter-service rivalry would ensure boxing at its best.

Although Cherry Point's boxing team was officially named the Fighting Leathernecks, other records indicate they were called the Flying Leathernecks or the Lethal Leathernecks. Flying, Lethal, or Fighting, they soon became a force to be reckoned with along the eastern seaboard.

The word "leatherneck" had its origin in the wide, stiff leather neck-piece that was part of the Marine Corps uniform from 1798 until 1872. This leather collar, called "the stock," was roughly four inches high and had two purposes. In combat, it protected the neck and jugular vein from an opponent's sword slashes, and while marching in a parade, it kept a Marine's head erect. The term is so widespread that it has become the name of the Marine Corps Association monthly magazine: *Leatherneck.*

Early on, Sergeant Abood knew he had discovered someone special in the young Texan. The kid from Plainview possessed raw talent and en-thusiasm, but more important, a desire to learn. After a few workouts, Johnny was amazed at LaVern's level of skill, especially considering his lack of formal training. He liked what he saw in LaVern and welcomed him to his team.

LaVern wasn't just a good boxer but also a good Marine. Thus, he would follow orders, regardless of what they were or where they led. Johnny convinced LaVern, ready to go overseas, that he could be more helpful to the Marine Corps and his country by staying home and helping build morale for the troops here and abroad with his boxing talent. He explained there were many Marines who possessed his same skills on the battlefront, but few if any had his boxing abilities.

Reluctant at first, the convincing factor was mentioning former Ma-rine Gene Tunney's military service during World War I. Tunney, an idol of LaVern's, had fought on the Marine boxing team and was named the best fighter to come out of World War I. Abood challenged LaVern to serve his country in the same way.

Prior to continuing his amateur boxing career as a fighter for the base team, LaVern was granted a ten-day furlough and returned home to Plainview to visit family and friends. He left in the middle of May and re-turned on May 30, well rested and ready to resume his place on the newly formed team. While he was gone, Johnny had been busy forming the rest of the squad.

The members of this soon to be powerhouse included Marines primarily from the eastern seaboard states. Among these were Harold Anspach, nicknamed "The Farmer," and John D. Kelly, III, known as "Stoutheart," from Pennsylvania. Edsel Martz hailed from the Washington, DC, area. Corporal Joe "Frenchy" LeBlond was a former boxing champion from Maine. From the state of New York were J. E. Lawson, Jr., Howie Brodt, and Al Highers. Others included James McFadden from nearby New Jersey; Joe Rindone, also known as "Dynamite Joe," from Massachusetts; and Ray Klingmeyer of Maryland. From inland came Ernie Charboneau of Detroit and Frankie Rich of Cleveland.

The oldest team member was Johnny Byrnes, who was in his midtwenties and already a well-seasoned fighter as a featherweight. "I used to love to fight," Byrnes said. "Sometimes I took such a beating that I had to look in the paper the next day to see that I won."[2]

The last to join the team was Johnny Kostas of Ambridge, Pennsylvania, a 146-pound welterweight. Corporal Kostas, at the age of twentytwo, had already been a Marine drill instructor. The war had interrupted his college career at Indiana University of Pennsylvania. "I was originally in the navy reserves, but my older brother told me the Marines were the biggest and baddest boys around, so I joined," he remarked.[3]

LaVern was the only boxer from the South and, by far, the farthest from home. His friendly, outgoing, charismatic personality made it easy for LaVern to make friends. Although younger than several of his boxing teammates, all looked up to and admired him.

His esteem among his peers, as well as his reputation on base, gained a new height on a hot and muggy July day in 1944. LaVern and teammate Frankie Rich, a featherweight, were standing in line waiting to get a haircut when a husky two-hundred-pounder cut in line in front of the much smaller Rich. Heated words were exchanged. The featherweight, not one to back down, challenged the heavyweight to settle the matter behind the building. LaVern, figuring that his friend might have chewed off more than he could handle, followed. Before the first punch was thrown, LaVern stepped forward and pushed his buddy aside and quickly put his larger opponent down before returning for the haircuts. This was the only time that LaVern was known to use his boxing skills outside of the ring.[4]

Cartoon by Corporal Johnny Inglis. Official US Marine Corps photo. Reprint by the permission of the US Marine Corps. Courtesy of the LaVern Roach family.

Sergeant Abood soon realized that Private First Class Roach, in addition to his boxing skills, was a natural-born leader. Needing an assistant, he enlisted LaVern's leadership talents to help him train the team. John soon recommended a promotion for LaVern as a boxing instructor. On July 25, 1944, Private First Class Roach was promoted to corporal. This was his first promotion since his departure from boot camp. At the same time, Sergeant Abood was promoted to the rank of staff sergeant.

The bedrock of character for all Marines consists of honor, courage, and commitment. It made no difference if a Marine was on the battlefield or not; these were still the standards they lived by, and living by the code was one of them. The Marines instilled in each of these individuals the traits that made Johnny Abood's job much easier. Each of these young men devoted their all to the boxing team.

The young combatants numbered about twenty. At the age of thirty-three, Sergeant Abood was old enough to have the respect of his young fighters and physically fit enough to match most in the ring. He and La-Vern both gained the respect of the entire team. They jelled into a formidable fighting force. Of all the boxers, LaVern became Johnny's favorite. Roach had that special something that set him apart. A few years later, Johnny would comment, "I had boys on that team who could learn faster than Roach, but none who worked harder to learn. I will never forget one time he got so mad at himself that he stuck his head in a water bucket."[5]

LaVern adjusted well to his new position. He summed up his feelings about his current military service in a letter to relatives back home:

> I don't do anything except instruct boxing and fight on the station boxing team. Guess I'm lucky to get to stay in the states so long. I wanted to go overseas about a year ago but they wouldn't let me, so now I don't want to go. But if they ever say the word, I'll be ready. I don't think I'll have to go over for quite some time now. They need boxing instructors so they probably won't let me go. I kinda hope they keep me here for I know mother and daddy would worry about me.[6]

Not one to ever brag about any of his accomplishments, he failed to mention that the week before he had participated in the Marine base track meet, finishing third in the mile run. Not bad considering he had never run the mile in a race before.[7] His boxing training, roadwork, and natural competitive spirit paid off for him once again.

LaVern performed his duties so well in his new capacity as boxing instructor that he received another promotion. On October 26, 1944, at the age of nineteen, Corporal Roach was promoted to Sergeant Roach.

Amateur boxing was quite glamorous during the war years and often dominated the sports pages as the Fighting Leathernecks traveled the East Coast. In the Carolinas, everyone knew when the boys from Cherry Point came to town to contest their local challengers.

During the 1944 season, the Marine team didn't lose an interservice team competition, often going toe-to-toe with professionals who were serving in the military. On an individual basis, LaVern won fight after fight and gained quite a reputation. Up next for LaVern and his team was the Carolinas Golden Gloves welterweight championship held at Charlotte, NC. The tournament covered South Carolina as well as North Carolina.

LaVern easily fought his way to the semifinals, where he was matched against a very tough paratrooper, Billy Tiger from Oklahoma. Tiger, a Native American, was representing Camp Mackall, a US Army Air Force training base in North Carolina. To his credit, Tiger had already won three titles as an amateur, including the Golden Gloves. He would make it a fourth in a very close, hairline decision over LaVern, who lost another opportunity to be a state Golden Gloves champion. LaVern was never knocked down during the match, keeping intact his record of never having been sent to the canvas in a fight. It was the last amateur fight that LaVern lost.

Once again, LaVern was named the most popular boxer in a tournament. Sportswriter Dan Magill, Jr., in an article written for the *Atlanta Journal*, stated, "It was uncanny how LaVern always won the most popular award at various Golden Gloves tournaments—the first time in this tourney's history that a non-finalist achieved this distinction."[8]

On December 4, 1944, LaVern, still over two months short of his twentieth birthday, was promoted to staff sergeant. At the same time he turned down his first of two appointments to the US Naval Academy.[9] His decision for not accepting the appointment was financial. A navy midshipman received less pay than a staff sergeant, which meant less money to send back home to his family in Plainview.

The year 1945 would be the crowning achievement for LaVern's amateur boxing career, as well as for the Marines' Cherry Point Fighting Leathernecks boxing team he captained. LaVern and his teammates were ready for the big challenges ahead. First up was the Twelfth Annual Golden Gloves Tournament, sponsored by the *Washington Times-Herald*, to be held at Uline Arena. The finals were held on Wednesday, January 3, 1945. Seven boxers represented the Cherry Point team. Unfortunately, two from the team were faced off against each other.

Representing the Fighting Leathernecks was Jim McFadden in the 135-pound class in the Novice Division. Also in the Novice Division facing each other were Cherry Point's Joe Rindone and Harold Anspach in the 160-pound class. The Senior Division was represented by Ernie Charboneau in the 118-pound class and Joe LeBlond in the 135-pound class. Howard Brodt in the 160-pound class and LaVern in the 147-pound class rounded out the unit.

Both McFadden and Anspach won championships in the Novice Division. The winners for Cherry Point in the Senior Division were LeBlond, Brodt, and LaVern. The Cherry Point team won the Senior Division team championship.

The awards banquet was held at Washington's Mayflower Hotel in the Chinese Room on January 11, 1945. During the awards presentation, LaVern garnered another personal award, the Mrs. Eleanor Patterson Trophy, named after the publisher of the *Washington Times-Herald*. Frank "Buck" O'Neill, *Times-Herald* sportswriter, made the presentation to the "Outstanding Senior Boxer."[10]

Coach Johnny Abood, now a tech sergeant, was presented the team award. Johnny's and LaVern's reputations skyrocketed. For his victory, LaVern received personal congratulations from Brigadier General Lewis G. Merritt, commander of the Ninth Marine Aircraft Wing. LaVern, as assistant trainer to Abood, felt a deep sense of pride in the part he had in the training of his teammates.

John Abood's team, now the number-one military boxing team in the United States, headed to the Eastern National Golden Gloves Championships held in New York City from March 12 to March 14. The quarter-finals and semifinals were to be held at the Ridgewood Grove in Brooklyn, with the finals being showcased in boxing's premier venue: New York City's Madison Square Garden.

New York City, considered the center of the boxing world because of Madison Square Garden, held what it called the National Golden Gloves

Championship each year. Teams were sponsored by large newspapers along the East Coast from Florida to New England. The New York newspapers called it their national tournament, producing national champions. Chicago, New York's perpetual rival, held its own "national championship" comprising teams from California, Texas, and other western states, including Illinois. The tournament was called the Inter-City Golden Gloves Championship, and Chicago considered its winners national champions as well. Starting in 1928 the two groups met each year, rotating between New York and Chicago. Years later they consolidated. Newspapers sometimes referred to the matches as the eastern and western championships.

Having never won a state Golden Gloves championship, LaVern now had the opportunity to win at a national level. The next day he clipped his headlines out of the Washington paper and sent them back home to Plainview, with a note that read, "I finally got my chance to go to the national tournament in New York. Please tell all the folks hello and to wish me luck."[11]

The Cherry Point boxing team was highly regarded in the DC area. As the *Times-Herald* stated, "It is believed that Washington has one of the best balanced teams ever entered in the New York Golden Gloves." LaVern was partially realizing his dream. He was fighting in New York City, but as an amateur, not a professional.

Unlike professional matches, which were scheduled as six, eight, ten, or fifteen rounds, amateur fights lasted no more than three. In the quarterfinals, LeBlond, Anspach, and Highers each won, outpointing their opponents. Brodt gained a second-round TKO. It took LaVern only one minute and seven seconds of the first round to knock out his competition, Curtis Moore. After the war, Moore turned professional and chalked up a 24-17 win/loss record before retiring in 1955. As a professional he twice fought LaVern's teammate, Joe Rindone, splitting the fights. John Byrnes suffered Cherry Point's only loss.

The semifinals, an old nemesis for LaVern, were held the next day. Anspach defeated his opponent on points. Brodt scored a second-round TKO, and Highers scored a first-round TKO. LaVern for the second day in a row scored a first-round knockout, this time over Woodson Speirs, finally overcoming the semifinal jinx. The only casualty of the day for the Leathernecks was LeBlond, who lost his decision on points. LaVern was the only boxer in the tournament to score first-round knockouts in his first two fights.

The next day, March 14, the championship finals took place in the Garden. Every boxer's dream, amateur or professional, was to compete in this venue. At the age of twenty, LaVern was fighting in the Garden for a national title.

In the fourth bout of the evening, Cherry Point's Highers would go the distance but lose in the lightweight division. The next fight was the welterweight bout, matching LaVern Roach representing Washington, DC's *Times Herald* against Mike Koballa of Pittsburgh, representing the Miami (FL) *Daily News.* On hand to watch the event were 19,177 fans. With LaVern's reputation preceding him, most came to see this good-looking, young, and upcoming boxer from Texas.

Since both of LaVern's first two contests lasted such short periods, he was fresh and well rested. He came out in the first round with the composure of a veteran. LaVern gashed Koballa's left eye and slowed him with body punches. Most of his blows landed as targeted, and Roach took Koballa's best punches in stride. It wasn't as easy as his previous two fights, but at the end of the final round, LaVern was finally a Golden Gloves champion, and at the national level. Along with the title, he won the diamond-studded outstanding fighter trophy.

His opponent, Mike Koballa, turned professional the next year and won his first nineteen fights as a welterweight. He fought until the end of 1952, compiling a record of 29-14-3. One of his draws was against Al Highers, one of LaVern's teammates. Koballa's most impressive win occurred on March 27, 1950, against Carmen Basilio, where he was a three-to-one underdog against the Cuban. Angelo Dundee worked in Koballa's corner that evening. After the fight Angelo visited Basilio's dressing room. "Great fight, Carmen. I'm glad my guy won, but I am sorry that you lost. You got a lot of talent."[12] Five years later on June 10, 1955, Basilio became Angelo Dundee's first world champion.

Although a lot of talent was displayed on center stage, LaVern made the biggest headlines of the tournament. One New York writer summed it up in the newspapers the next day with the headline, "Plainview Boy Is a Comer." The writer went on, "Several fight managers were angling today for 'connections' with Sergeant LaVern Roach of the Cherry Point (NC) Marines, who stood out as the classiest, all-around boxer in the Eastern

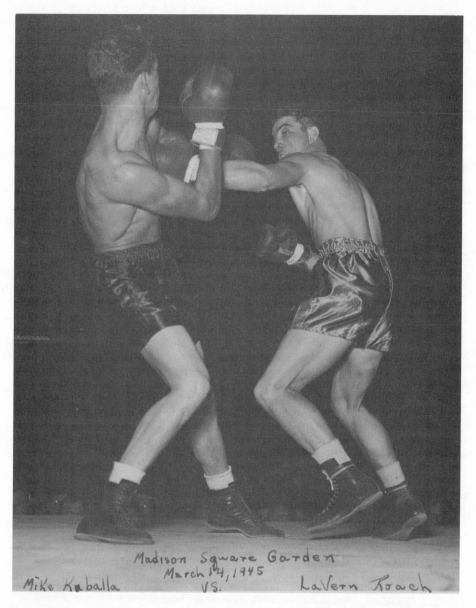

Koballa and Roach (l–r) fight for the Eastern National Golden Gloves Championship. Madison Square Garden. Courtesy of the LaVern Roach family.

Seaboard championships staged at Madison Square Garden. Managers with mouths watering said of LaVern, 'a regular picture fighter.'"[13]

LaVern and the Fighting Leathernecks weren't finished yet. The winners of this tournament would next meet the Inter-City Golden Gloves champions in Chicago on April 4. The excitement and celebration for LaVern and his teammates were short-lived. While they prepared for the Golden Gloves championship tournaments, a very different type of battle was shaping up for their Marine brothers in the Pacific.

After boot camp, as LaVern headed east to Cherry Point, North Carolina, Wick's Fifth Marine Infantry Division stayed at Camp Pendleton, California. It was a division made up of both hardened war veterans as well as new Marines. Among the veterans were former members of that select group known as the Raiders, the outfit that LaVern had earlier wanted to join. The Fifth Division was being trained to be the spearhead in an attack on a small, remote, yet strategic island in the Pacific, the name of which was being kept secret even from the troops for security reasons.

The Pacific Front

On September 19, 1944, after six months of intensive amphibious warfare training at Camp Pendleton, California, the Fifth Marine Division boarded troop transport ships for their two-week voyage to Hawaii. The beaches, greenery, and overall scenic landscape of Hawaii provided a stark contrast to that which Wick and his fellow Marines left behind in San Diego. For Wick, it was a far cry from Plainview, Texas.

The Marines soon learned that this trip was going to be anything but a vacation. They came here only to train further for their assault on a small Japanese island in the Pacific known as "X." For four months they continued training in amphibious warfare. Hour after hour was spent embarking and disembarking transport ships, climbing down the webbing of the cargo nets into the beach crafts, carrying only their heavy backpacks, rifles, and ammunition into the small craft that would take them to the enemy shore. Once ashore they were to repel the enemy and capture the small island.

In December 1944, orders were given to ship out to the secret destination. Before leaving the islands, the Marines and the sailors aboard the transports were given liberty at Pearl Harbor and Honolulu. For so many, this would be their last.

In January 1945, at the same time that LaVern and the Cherry Point boxing team were preparing for the Golden Gloves championships, the large armada of American warships was under way for its destination. After leaving Honolulu, there would be no more communication with friends or family back home for weeks, unless the identity of "X" was made known. LaVern received his last letter from Wick as the Fifth Division headed for Iwo Jima, a small, remote Japanese island located 650 nautical miles south of Tokyo. Iwo Jima was no larger than eight square miles in size, about two-thirds the size of Plainview, Texas. On its southernmost tip rose a small mount with a peak of a little over five hundred feet above sea level named Mount Suribachi. It would take the fleet of ships several weeks to reach the destination.

After nearly nine months of air bombardment by the army air force to soften the enemy, the US forces were set to take the island. On February 19, 1945, these US forces included over 450 American ships with the Marines numbering around seventy thousand, including Private Wick Mason.

At approximately 0900 hours on the morning of February 19, 1945, the first wave of Marines from the Third, Fourth, and Fifth Divisions began to storm the beaches of Iwo Jima, with Mount Suribachi seen in the background. By the end of day one, nearly thirty thousand Marines landed on the small island.

The battle over Iwo Jima was the most costly engagement that the Marine Corps ever endured. One staggering fact is that one-third of all the Marines killed during three and a half years of war lost their lives in one month on this tiny Japanese island.

At the end of the first day, the Marines had secured the two-mile beach on the south side of the island, but not without a costly price. In addition to the 1,755 Marines wounded, there were 566 men killed, among whom was Private First Class Wick Mason. Wick and the other fallen comrades were buried on the island, becoming the largest cemetery in the Pacific for American forces. Wick's parents weren't notified of his death until a month later. On March 15 a telegram from the War Department was delivered to the Mason home. On January 15, 1949, nearly four years later, Wick's remains were removed from his Pacific grave and shipped back to the States for interment in Plainview.

Back in the USA

A few days after winning his coveted Golden Gloves championship, La-Vern received the devastating news of Wick's death. His lifetime friend, whom he had talked into joining the Marines with him, died on an overseas battlefield while LaVern was safe in the States fighting for a Golden Gloves championship.

LaVern enjoyed writing letters, but he also had a penchant for writing poetry and short stories. After receiving the sad news of the loss, he wrote two poems expressing his feelings on war and the sorrow of losing a former sparring partner, football teammate, fellow Marine, and most importantly, a lifelong friend.

The Ones Who Pay
Lives are lost and much blood is shed,
some don't know if their boys are dead.
They are fighting for land and fame,
thousands fall but "WAR" goes on just the same.
They count the lives that they have lost,
then over their heads they place a cross.
The machine guns spat and the cannons roar,
above the clouds the airplanes soar
If this would stop and all was quiet,
this world would be a better sight

Why Are They Fighting
Why are they fighting so much over there?
No one knows and some don't care.
But we will learn the truth someday,
why so many lives are taken away,
from their children and their wives
when they could live such happy lives.
Someday they'll speak peace near and far,
for then they'll know the wage of "WAR."[14]

LaVern and his teammates weren't given much time to grieve over the loss of their fellow Marines. The consolidated East/West National Golden Gloves Championships were scheduled for Chicago on April 4, only

Wick Mason's grave marker.
Plainview Memorial Park
Cemetery. Photo taken by
Sandy Lindeman.

a couple of weeks away. As important as the eastern National Golden
Gloves Championship, these matchups were even more so. East meets
West for the ultimate amateur championships. The championship started
in 1928 rotating from New York's Madison Square Garden to the Chicago Stadium. During its eighteen-year history the East team never won in
Chicago. Five leathernecks made up the twenty-seven-man East squad;
LaVern was one of them. The East coaches, including Abood, felt this
was the best chance for their team to win in Chicago in its fourteenth
attempt there.

Bear Mountain, New York, was selected as the training camp for the
East team. The team arrived on March 24 and set up camp in the historic
Bear Mountain Inn. After three days of training and getting to know each

other, LaVern was unanimously elected captain of the East team. "Roach has made a great hit with the other youngsters in training at the Inn. They admire his fighting ability [the general opinion is that he is the surest bet New York has against Chicago] but they admire even more his quiet demeanor and readiness to assist the coaches."[15] Once again, his leadership skills were put to good use.

After a week's training at Bear Mountain, the team broke camp and headed to Chicago. There to meet LaVern were his mother and dad, whom he hadn't seen for several months. John Abood, knowing that Stanley couldn't afford the trip, paid all of their travel and hotel expenses out of his own pocket. He was always anxious to help LaVern and his family in any way he could. In all of the excitement, Stanley's heart condition flared up and he wasn't able to attend his son's fight. Thereafter, he would limit his support and enthusiasm to listening on the radio.

Chicago Stadium, built in 1929, was a state-of-the-art indoor arena. It was home of the Chicago Black Hawks and later home of the Chicago Bulls. It held national conventions for both political parties as well as rodeos and boxing events. It was the site of the first NFL playoff game in 1932. The game between the Chicago Bears and the Portsmouth Spartans (two years later they became the Detroit Lions) was moved from the outdoor Wrigley Field to the indoor Chicago Stadium due to extremely cold weather. It was the first indoor stadium with air conditioning. The stadium was built to seat as many as twenty thousand or more.

LaVern's opponent was Gilbert Garcia from Houston, the reigning welterweight Golden Gloves champ of Texas. LaVern, by winning this match, could ease some of the pain of not ever winning a Texas State title. Over 20,752 boxing fans (surpassing the 19,177 that witnessed his victory at the Garden the previous month) watched the hard-fought battle, settled by a decision in LaVern's favor. This victory would be LaVern's last official fight as an amateur, and it firmly established him as the top amateur in the nation. He finished his first boxing cycle in style; he was a national champion, joining a select group of previous and future Golden Glove winners, including two-time winners Sugar Ray Robinson and Cassius Clay as well as Joe Louis, Floyd Patterson, Sonny Liston, Ernie Terrell, Emile Griffith, Barney Ross, and Tony Janiro. After being denied the championship by LaVern, Gilbert Garcia won it the following year.

LaVern's victory announcement appeared in the *Plainview Herald* the same day as Wick's obituary.

For the record, the event ended in a tie between East and West. After a disputed disqualification decided weeks after the event, the East team was declared the winner, much to the disdain of the West team.

LaVern's achievements as an amateur boxer may never be surpassed. Beginning with his Golden Gloves success on the Lubbock team as a flyweight and finishing as the national Golden Gloves welterweight champion, LaVern won over one hundred fights while losing only five. Four of those were suffered before reaching the age of eighteen. Perhaps the most remarkable statistic was that, even in the defeats, he was never knocked down in the ring. By being named the best fighter to come out of a war, he joined Gene Tunney as the only other recipient of such an award.

A week later, on April 12, 1945, the nation mourned the death of Franklin Delano Roosevelt. President Roosevelt died three weeks before the Allies claimed victory in Europe on May 8. As the GIs slowly returned home, the Marines fought on. But now, with the Germans defeated, all of our military power could be focused on defeating the Japanese. A two-front war had been reduced to just one, with the navy and Marines left to shoulder much of the burden.

LaVern turned to pursuing his ultimate goal: professional boxing, with his sight on fulfilling his childhood dream of becoming a world boxing champion. Just four years after expressing to Art Fleischer his desire to come to New York and become a professional boxer, what seemed then just a fantasy now became a reality.

Staff Sergeant LaVern Roach. Marine Corps Air Station, Cherry Point, North Carolina. Courtesy of the LaVern Roach family.

CHAPTER 6

Fighting Marine to Professional Boxer

When you're fighting, you're fighting for one thing—to get money.
—Jack Dempsey

There were hurdles to clear in order for LaVern to turn pro. LaVern was about to discover that it was much more difficult getting out of the military than getting in, even though the war was ending. As the war in Europe ceased, fighting still raged in the Pacific, with the Japanese showing no signs of giving up. Family news from Plainview was also discouraging as Stanley continued to be without work and the family had little income except what LaVern sent home. The elder Roach's heart condition prevented him from doing any kind of manual labor, which is all he was qualified to do. LaVern, for the first time, was torn between loyalty to his country and the Marine Corps and the love of his family. Stanley and Rosa desperately wanted LaVern home, especially after the Masons lost Wick in the war. Word was coming out of Washington, DC, that an all-out invasion of Japan might be needed to win, which meant that all of the Marine forces available might be needed, including LaVern.

LaVern decided to take a fifteen-day furlough and left for Plainview on May 14 for a much needed rest. The previous three months had been a physically and emotionally charged period of time, from the high of winning a national boxing championship to the low of losing a close friend. This furlough allowed him to check out his family's financial situation in person.

Upon his return to Plainview, LaVern's concerns were confirmed. Stanley was out of work with no prospects for employment. The family

LaVern Roach signature boxing card. Courtesy of the LaVern Roach family.

was behind on their bills, having to rely on borrowed money to get by. After his visit with friends and family, LaVern returned to Cherry Point to discuss his family situation with mentor John Abood. John, who looked upon Roach as a son, immediately loaned him three hundred dollars, providing a quick fix but not a permanent solution.

The answer agreed upon by Johnny and LaVern was to seek a dependency discharge for LaVern. LaVern could turn professional and, with his potential earnings, help out his family and pay Abood back.

On June 15 LaVern submitted an official request for a dependency discharge that was forwarded to the chain of command of the Marine Corps, starting with his commanding officer. Upon receiving the request, LaVern's commanding officer forwarded it to the commandant of the Marine Corps, Washington DC, with his strongly recommended approval. His endorsement included the following statement:

> It is a matter of personal knowledge that this request entails great personal sacrifice on the part of Staff Sergeant ROACH as his interest in a military career and pride in the Marine Corps is outstanding. This was clearly demonstrated, not only by his exemplary conduct and attention to duty, but also during a personal interview when Staff Sergeant ROACH was informed that he was to be recommended for appointment to the US Naval Academy Preparatory School, and was compelled to request that no recommendation be made because of his impending request for discharge. It is considered that this request was not originated until it became apparent that no other course of action was feasible. It is further believed that all statements as made by Staff Sergeant ROACH are honest and sincere and that the conditions as outlined in the supporting documents are absolutely correct.[1]

LaVern, having done his part in applying for a dependency discharge, focused his attention back on boxing. With the Golden Gloves championships behind him, he and Johnny headed to Houston for an exhibition. The purpose of the bout was to boost the Seventh War Loan Drive. Ringside seats sold for a five-thousand-dollar E bond. Two million dollars in E bonds were sold at the event. Gilbert Garcia, the fighter LaVern beat for his national championship, was selected as his opponent. This time Garcia would be fighting in front of his hometown fans.

The fight took place on June 26. The results were the same as in Chicago. LaVern polished off the highly regarded state champ in five two-minute rounds. The Houston sports critics went so far as to call LaVern "perhaps the finest amateur to ever box in a Houston ring."[2]

When asked about his young charge, Johnny replied, "Yes, sir, this Roach has got it. He's got everything. Can he punch, you say? Sure he can punch. Left hand? Wonderful. Speed afoot? Yes, sir, he can move. He wastes no effort. He can fight when he's hurt."

LaVern, quick to reciprocate, gave credit where credit was due. "Johnny taught me everything."[3]

Back in North Carolina, after a review of the dependency discharge situation, a second endorsement from the commanding general of the Cherry Point Marine Base was forwarded to the commandant of the Marine Corps with approval. Upon receiving the endorsements from the Cherry Point Marine Base, the US Marine Corps Headquarters Personnel Department turned the matter over to the Selective Service System. On July 7, the following instructions were given to the Selective Service director:

> Please investigate the circumstances in this case through the facilities afforded by State Selective Service Headquarters and the Local Selective Service Board having cognizance, in order to determine whether, in the opinion of the State Director, the circumstances in this case are sufficiently serious to warrant discharge from the Marine Corps.[4]

On July 10 the request was sent to the state headquarters Selective Service director in Austin. Having received the request the next day, the deputy state director of the Selective Service, Colonel John Banister, forwarded the matter to R. A. Jefferies, chairman of the Hale County local board.

On July 20 Stanley Roach was asked to appear before the Hale County Local Selective Service Board. Although the interview would last less than thirty minutes, the results would decide if LaVern would receive his early discharge. The interview went well for the first ten questions, which required simple answers establishing Stanley and Rosa's inability to work and provide for their family. With the following questions, the tone of the interview suddenly turned south for Stanley:

Question: "You have another son?"

Stanley: "Yes sir, he registered here the other day."

Bill, LaVern, and Beth.
Courtesy of the LaVern
Roach family.

Question: "Does this 18-year-old son work?"

Stanley: "During the summer."

Question: "Where?"

Stanley: "Right now he is working at Peerless Pump."

Question: "You and Mrs. Roach and the girl are able to take care of your-
selves other than finances?"

Stanley: "That's right."

Question: "You say the other boy just registered?"

Stanley: "It was the 12th of June" (Billie's eighteenth birthday).

Question: "Do you think he will pass his examination?"

Stanley: "I couldn't tell, his feet are like his mother's."

Question: "How much is he making at Peerless Pumps?"

Stanley: "I think it is approximately $35.00 a week. He has been helping me pay up."

Question: "Is he working full time?"

Stanley: "Yes sir."

Question: "In the event the Marine doesn't get his discharge, what would be wrong with the younger one staying out of school and making a living for the family until the other one got back?"

Stanley: "He could, I guess, but if the other one could get out it would help."

Question: "Is there anything else you think of?"

Stanley: "No, sir."

Question: "Then, that is all, thank you."[5]

Stanley's sworn testimony helped seal the fate of LaVern's early discharge. The local Selective Service Board recommended that LaVern, with all of his military experience, stay in while his younger brother receive an exemption, allowing him to continue to work to and contribute his income of thirty-five dollars a week to help the family.

The local board chief recommendation of a denial to LaVern's request for a dependency discharge was upheld by the state director, Brigadier General J. Watt Page. A memorandum dated July 30 to the Washington headquarters of the Selective Service stated, "1. Based upon the records in the case and the national situation, discharge is not favorably considered. 2. The evidence fails to disclose that soldier's dependents are suffering any undue critical hardship in excess of that being imposed upon hundreds of thousands of other service men. 3. Factual information shown in a letter from the Hale County Local Board No. 1 and statements of Mr. Stanley J. Roach, attached."[6]

On August 6 the Selective Service Liaison Section in Washington informed Marine Headquarters of its findings, resulting in a recommendation of disapproval of the request. That day the first atomic bomb was dropped on Japan. Three days later the second bomb was dropped on the enemy. The Japanese finally surrendered on August 15, 1945, ending World War II.

With the war officially over, Stanley felt sure that LaVern could soon come home. Yet on August 30, fifteen days after the war ended, the Office of the Commandant of the Marine Corps officially issued the following memorandum to the commanding general, Ninth Marine Aircraft Wing, Fleet Marine Force: "Reference: (a) Request of S/Sgt. Roach, dated 6-15-45, w/encl. and ends. thereon. 1. Please inform the subject-named that the request for discharge as contained in reference (a) is not approved."[7]

This was an unexpected blow to LaVern and his family. World War II was over, and he was to remain on active duty while many military personnel were being discharged and sent home. Many who left Plainview during the war never returned. Sparsely populated Hale County, with most of its populace located in Plainview, suffered a death toll of ninety-nine young men, including Wick Mason.

Disappointed with the results of the appeal, Stanley lost no time in preparing a second appeal to the Marine Corps for LaVern's release, considering the war's end. Stanley once again solicited letters from members of the Plainview community, but this time he selected different influential supporters than he used in his initial request. One letter was from a farmer friend named Daw Nix, guaranteeing work for LaVern on his four-hundred-acre farm in Plainview. This was a clear indication of differences between LaVern and his family regarding his future.

While Stanley was working for LaVern's release from the Marine Corps, John Abood and LaVern decided to waste no more time in starting his professional boxing career. With all of his success managing the Fighting Leathernecks, Abood's love for the sport intensified to the point that he wanted to continue managing boxers after his military service was completed. He sought and received permission from the Marines for LaVern to start boxing professionally while waiting for the outcome of his discharge procedures.

Over four thousand boxers left the boxing ranks to join the war effort. Many of these returning veterans, with no idea what to do with their lives after the war, returned to the ring. Initially there was no shortage of fighters and no problem finding opponents for LaVern. Although the postwar job market appeared wide open with a booming economy, for many, their prewar work skills became obsolete due to the technological advances that had taken place. Boxing provided an opportunity for countless young men to continue what they had been doing for the past few years: fighting.

Boxing and baseball, the two most popular sports of the day, provided the quickest way for those without college degrees or specialized work skills to make a decent living. Due to the limited number of professional teams, the players going into or returning to baseball were few in comparison to those who could enter the sport of boxing. There was big money to be made in boxing, especially for managers and promoters, always looking for the next Joe Louis.

Starting out his pro career, LaVern had two important advantages over most of his opponents. First of all, he didn't have to worry about a place to sleep or where his next meal was coming from. Uncle Sam was still his provider. Next was his training. Until his release, LaVern would continue to train at the base facilities. He was already in top shape after having fought as many as one hundred boxing matches as an amateur.

Since his arrival at Cherry Point in the late summer of 1943, LaVern never needed to get time off for training. When first asked for permission for LaVern to fight, his squadron commander replied, "Roach? Sure— he's a fine lad. Tell him to shove off any time he pleases. And let me know when he fights—I want a ringside seat."[8]

Besides the level of competition, one of the biggest differences that exists between fighting as an amateur and as a professional is the length of the match. An amateur match is usually limited to three rounds, whereas the format for a professional match usually requires six or more rounds. This greater length of time requires more stamina on the part of the boxer, and stamina required conditioning. Like the advice that young LaVern heard four years earlier, the best way to build up stamina is to run. Distance running, a big part of the boxing team's daily training routine, came easy for LaVern.

Johnny Abood's game plan for LaVern initially centered on fighting relatively unknown professionals in local arenas. The competition would be similar to what LaVern had been accustomed to, and most likely he would have the crowd advantage.

His first professional fight took place on September 26, 1945, against Don Ellis. The event was held at Uline Arena, Washington, DC, where

LaVern had won a Golden Gloves tournament. Ellis came into the fight with a record of seven wins, four losses, and two draws. LaVern won on points after five rounds of fighting for his first professional win. He and Johnny learned quickly that, due to LaVern's excellent conditioning, he could easily go the few extra rounds if necessary.

The extra rounds weren't necessary for LaVern's second fight. Two nights later, LaVern took on Jackie Alexander, who was fighting just his third fight, having lost his first two. The bout was held in Norfolk, with LaVern winning easily with a third-round knockout, cheered on by a large navy backing. His success in his first two fights in a short span of just two days provided what Abood wanted to see in his young charge.

Before his next fight, LaVern received a very important letter of recommendation for his release from active duty from an unusual but welcomed source. Nat Fleischer, publisher and editor of the *Ring* magazine, placed his support behind LaVern's effort to be released from active duty. Fleischer's relationship with LaVern went all the way back to 1941 in Albuquerque when LaVern fought in the seven-state tournament. Fleischer's letter, dated October 17, 1945, read,

TO WHOM IT MAY CONCERN:

As a friend of long standing of Staff Sgt. Raymond L. Roach, a Marine stationed at Cherry Point, North Carolina, I am writing this letter in the hopes of aiding him to obtain his discharge in order to pursue his chosen profession, that of professional boxer.

Staff Sgt. Roach has written me informing me of the distress of his family in Plainsville [sic], Texas and I have likewise received word from his family requesting that I write this message to the Marine Corps Headquarters, with the hopes that it will enable their son to receive his release so that he may enter the business for which he feels that he is best suited and from which he can earn, during the first year of his professional career, upwards of $5,000.

This amount has been guaranteed him by those who are willing to handle his professional affairs and from my personal knowledge of Sgt. Roach's ability, I feel confident that his earning capacity will be far beyond that.

I regard Sgt. Roach as one of the world's outstanding welterweights and that his release from the Marine Corps at this stage will bring credit to the outfit to which he has been attached for three years as did Gene Tunney to the Marine Corps after his discharge in the last World War.

Trusting that my little effort on behalf of Sgt. Roach will aid in bringing about the discharge which both he and his family so eagerly await, I remain

Sincerely yours,
Nat Fleischer, Publisher and Editor[9]

Upon receiving the request, LaVern's commanding officer, E. B. Diboll, immediately forwarded it to the commandant with his strongly recommended approval. In his endorsement dated October 23, Diboll stated, "In view of the urgent nature of this request and the demobilization program which has been activated since Staff Sergeant ROACH's previous request, favorable consideration is highly recommended."[10]

With the dependency discharge still in process, LaVern faced his next opponent, Hugh Stell, for his third professional fight, on October 24 in Uline Arena. Stell, with a very respectable record of twenty wins, six losses, and two draws, presented the most significant competition to date. LaVern easily rose to the challenge with a second-round knockout. LaVern had now won all three of his first professional fights, two by knockouts, with none going past five rounds.

Two days later, on October 26, the commanding general of the Cherry Point Marine Base approved the second endorsement for LaVern's dependency discharge and forwarded it to the commandant of the Marine Corps, Washington, DC.

On November 2 LaVern squared off against Baudelio Valencia in his fourth bout, held in Norfolk. Valencia came into the ring with only three victories against twenty-six losses, one of those boxers whom opposing managers loved to line up for their young guys. LaVern knocked out Valencia in the fourth round, handing him his twentieth loss by knockout while moving his own record to four wins and no losses. After the Valencia fight, LaVern took a fifteen-day furlough. He returned home to spend the Thanksgiving holiday with family and friends before returning to Cherry Point.

Upon receiving LaVern's resubmission for a discharge, the Office of the Commandant of the Marine Corps chose to take a different route for investigation of the matter. Instead of choosing the Selective Service, they chose the American Red Cross to investigate the circumstances. The expedited request was sent to the Hale County Chapter of the American Red Cross on December 6, the same day that LaVern fought his fifth bout.

Fight number five for LaVern was against Jimmy Grimes, held in the City Auditorium, Norfolk, Virginia. Grimes was fighting only his second professional fight. He lost his first fight against LaVern's former teammate Howie Brodt in the professional debut for both fighters. While it took two rounds for Brodt to knock out Grimes, LaVern accomplished the task in one. After these two losses to the Marine duo, Grimes hung up his boxing gloves. LaVern was undefeated in his first five fights, four by knockouts. From the time that he fought young Gib in Memphis, Texas, and throughout his amateur boxing career, LaVern now extended his streak of never being knocked to the canvas to include his first five professional fights.

Unlike the Selective Service, it took the Red Cross only two days to investigate and return their findings to their Washington headquarters. On December 8, Mrs. Ina Thornton, home service secretary of the Hale County Chapter of the American Red Cross, sent her findings to headquarters, verifying the facts that Stanley and LaVern presented. The request, which had been expedited up to this point, got caught up in the Christmas season. Experiencing its first Christmas without a war in five years, Washington basically shut down until after the first of the New Year.

Having confidence that his discharge was imminent and having accumulated extra furlough time, LaVern requested a leave to go home for the Christmas and New Year's holidays. Granted furlough, LaVern returned home to Plainview on December 20 and returned to Cherry Point on January 11, 1946.

Prior to LaVern's return to Cherry Point, the commandant of the Marine Corps issued a memorandum discharging Staff Sergeant Raymond L. Roach from military service. On January 16, 1946, LaVern received his honorable discharge from the US Marine Corps, returning to civilian life one month shy of his twenty-first birthday. His mustering-out paycheck in the amount of $232.12 was forwarded in care of Mr. John Abood, 568 Broadway, New York, New York.

In less than three years LaVern had advanced from an eighteen-year-old private to a staff sergeant in the US Marine Corps. From a Golden

Gloves semifinalist in the state of Texas, he had become a national Gold-en Gloves champion and professional boxer with a record of five wins and no losses. From a little-known boy from small-town Plainview, Texas, he had become the top amateur boxer in the country, making headlines in all of the New York City newspapers.

The boxing record left behind by the Fighting Leathernecks would never be matched. One by one the boxers of the Fighting Leathernecks left the service to return home. LaVern was one of the first to leave. Others followed, and the last was Johnny Kostas. He stayed in and replaced Johnny Abood as the new manager of the Fighting Leathernecks and con-tinued the unbeaten tradition.

LaVern's former teammates returned to civilian life. Ernie Char-boneau enrolled at Michigan State and went on to be the 1948 NCAA flyweight boxing champion. Joe Rindone turned professional under the management of Johnny Abood and was ranked as high as number sev-en at one time. He twice fought Sugar Ray Robinson, losing both times. Rindone hung up his gloves after his last fight against Sugar Ray. He died of lung cancer in late 1998.

Ray Klingmeyer had a professional boxing record of 39-8-3. He later became a professional boxing referee and judge. He once was a judge in an Ali fight and twice for Sugar Ray Leonard. In 1976 he was inducted into the Maryland Boxing Hall of Fame. At the end of his career, he said, "I enjoyed the excitement of the arena, yet am disturbed by the clutter of too many champions caused by a proliferation of associations, plus con-trived weight classes. It makes for confusion and distraction."[11] This was a sentiment later shared by Angelo Dundee.

Joe LeBlond had a four-year professional boxing career, finishing with a 16-17-1 record. Al Highers's professional boxing career culminated with a winning record of 22-9-4. He fought his last bout on February 9, 1950. Edsel Martz had three professional fights and then became an am-ateur baseball coach. He died April 9, 2006, at his home in Arlington, Virginia.

Under the leadership of Johnny Kostas, the Cherry Point boxing team continued the winning tradition started under Abood. After his release from the military following the 1946 boxing season, Kostas returned to Indiana University at Pennsylvania, where he rejoined his college boxing team and posted thirty-nine victories in forty-three bouts, including one draw. He had fought three professional fighters while in the Marines, including future welterweight champion Marty Servo. At the age of eighty-six, in the year 2007, he became the world's oldest active boxing coach. Through his sixty-five years in boxing, Johnny was inducted in four sports hall of fames: the IUP Athletic Hall of Fame, the Pennsylvania Golden Gloves Hall of Fame, the Indiana County Sports Hall of Fame, and the Ambridge Boxing Hall of Fame. Kostas died in 2008 at the age of eighty-seven.

Wanting to continue in the boxing profession, John Abood developed a plan that included not only LaVern but also four other teammates to stay together and continue their boxing careers under his management once they left active duty. The way he wanted to do it was unheard of in the boxing world, but Johnny was known for doing the unheard of and had the personal resources to back it up.

The headline in the *Stars and Stripes* on January 23, 1946, read, "Champion Marine Boxers Join to Assault Pro Ranks": ". . . A fantastic post-war experiment will be attempted soon at South Orange, New Jersey." Johnny Abood was quoted by United Press International as follows:

> I plan to buy a large house in the South Orange area, and have the five boys live and train there when they are not on the road fighting. I'll build a special gymnasium near the house. It will be patterned after the fine boxing gym we had at Cherry Point. Out of their earnings, the boys will share the upkeep costs.
>
> I plan to bring Lavern Roach's mother and father to South Orange from Plainview, Tex. They will run the show. This Roach boy is one of the grandest chaps I ever met. Although only 20 now, he has been supporting his mother, father, sister and brother during the three years he was in service. Each pay day he would keep only five dollars for himself, and send the rest home. His father has a weak heart, and can do but little work. He is providing for his 15-year-old sister and sending his 17-year-old brother through school.
>
> Roach, an exceptionally promising combination boxer and puncher, has had five professional bouts since emerging from service. He won all five, scoring four knockouts. He is campaigning now as a middleweight and may grow later into a light heavy. Meanwhile,

middleweight Brodt of Chadwicks, N.Y. also has had five pro starts, winning three by knockouts and two by decisions. Roach fights next on the 8th at Nicholas Arena in a six-round preliminary Monday night; and Brodt is slated for a six-rounder at Brooklyn's Ridgewood Grove Club Saturday night.[12]

John Abood was faced with a new problem. All of LaVern's previous bouts were held in and around Washington. Managing boxers in New York required a state boxing license. The ever resourceful John befriended Chris Dundee, who was already managing a group of young fighters. Dundee, having been in the business for a few years, had a New York manager's license. LaVern, Howie Brodt, and Al Highers joined the select group of young boxers known as Dundee's Dandies, forming the largest number of boxers under one management team.

John's arrangement with Chris allowed him to personally take care of the day-to-day management of his former Marine outfit, apart from the fighters whom Chris already had in his camp. Johnny, with his wealth, did not need to rely on Chris for any funding. The housing arrangement would allow the young fighters to concentrate on boxing and not worry about living expenses. This also allowed him to provide them with the best food fit for a boxer. The boxers would pay John back from their ring earnings. Chris would be involved in arranging fights, making contract decisions, and handling publicity for the fighters.

Rookie boxers were often pushed into fights that they weren't ready for in order to have a payday to help cover living expenses. This wasn't the case for John's young men. His passion for the sport of boxing, which preceded his military days, and his private resources allowed him to take care of his men as he had done in the Marines.

LaVern and Howie Brodt were the first two fighters to receive their discharge from the Marines. Both had already fought five professional bouts. Howie, like LaVern, won all of his matches. Three of their teammates were expecting their release from the Marines soon. They were Sergeant Al Highers, the national Golden Gloves lightweight champ; Corporal Harold Anspach, middleweight runner-up in the New York Eastern Golden Gloves finals; and Corporal James McFadden, featherweight winner in the Golden Gloves sectional final in Washington, DC.

Of the five, LaVern was the most likely to go all the way to the top, according to Nat Fleischer.

Even before he launched his professional career, some big-name celebrities and boxing enthusiasts, including Bing Crosby, Bob Hope, Jack Dempsey, and Billy Conn,[13] were interested in LaVern's services. Crosby, an avid sports fan, was actively involved in partial ownerships in race horses, racetracks, and baseball and football teams. LaVern received a telegram from boxing great Billy Conn asking to serve as LaVern's manager. Conn, who had defeated the likes of Tony Zale and Gus Lesnevich, was a former light heavyweight champion. His boxing lore skyrocketed when he gave up the title to challenge Joe Louis for the heavyweight crown.

Conn attempted to become the first light heavyweight champion in boxing history to win the heavyweight title. He fought Louis on June 18, 1941, at the Polo Grounds in New York City before 54,587 fans. Conn outfought Louis for the first twelve rounds. Instead of coasting for the next three rounds and winning on points, Conn, against the advice from his corner, decided to go for a knockout. In the process, he opened himself up and was knocked out by Louis in the thirteenth round. After the fight Conn told reporters, "I lost my head and a million bucks."[14]

The start of the war prevented a rematch, with both boxers serving in the military. After the war was over, a rematch was set for June 19, 1946, to be held in Yankee Stadium. The fight was the first heavyweight championship to be televised nationally, with an audience of 146,000 being the most ever to witness a heavyweight championship. Over 40,000 saw the fight in person. Prior to the bout, it was mentioned to Louis that he might have trouble with Conn's foot speed. Louis responded with the famous line, "He can run, but he can't hide."[15] Although it was apparent that inactivity caused by the war had diminished the boxing skills of both fighters, Conn's suffered most. Louis won by knocking out Conn in the eighth round. Conn fought two more times, winning both in the ninth round, and then retired from boxing.

Even with LaVern idolizing Conn, his loyalty and allegiance remained with John Abood. The two had bonded in an almost father-son-like relationship over the previous couple of years, and not even well-known celebrities could put a chink in that armor, although the telegraph that he received from Conn would be one of LaVern's most prized possessions.

John's original plans were altered due to Stanley and Rosa's refusal to leave Plainview to come to New York, an area where they had never set foot. Even without their involvement, Johnny continued with his plan. He purchased a house, but only LaVern and Anspach moved into it. Instead of LaVern's parents, John's sister Nora served as house mother for the boys as they settled in their new home in Millburn, New Jersey.

CHAPTER 7

A Rising Star

It was the best of times, it was the worst of times.
—*Charles Dickens*

The year was 1946. The war was over. LaVern, after serving his country
for three years in the Marine Corps, returned to civilian life for the first
time as an adult. Ironically he ended up where he wanted to be before the
war started—the New York area—and doing the thing that he had always
dreamed of doing: professional boxing. LaVern and the nation grew up
a lot during the war. American troops returned home in droves to find a
nation that had changed. The men and women of the armed forces had
changed. Going off to war as boys and girls, they returned as men and
women. The realities of returning to civilian life weren't always an easy
transition for the veterans. While some returned to the rural life of farming or small-town living, others sought something different. It was an opportunity for many to seek a change in their way of life.

LaVern fell into the latter group. A country boy and proud of his Texas heritage, he always planned on someday returning to his roots in the
Lone Star State. In the meantime he sought to take advantage of what the
military had provided him. He had acquired a skill that few possessed and
even fewer could make a good living at. He was a professional boxer. Having grown up in poverty, he did not want to follow the same path as his
father, where struggle for survival was the way of life. Other than boxing,
he found himself without any other marketable skill, but he did not have
to make the transition alone. John Abood, who became a father figure to
LaVern while in the service, was there to help guide LaVern to his next

Stillman's Gym, New York City. Courtesy of the LaVern Roach family.

step. There was no better teacher to show the young Texan how to be a financial success while achieving his lifelong dream.

During the war years, Abood's family textile business continued to blossom into a very profitable endeavor. He was not lacking the resources to help LaVern and his teammates continue what they built up in the Corps. This was his one chance in life where LaVern was in the right place at the right time to pursue his dreams, and John provided him the encouragement, opportunity, and financial means needed. Plainview would have to wait. LaVern's plan was to win the championship, return home with enough money to buy a ranch, and raise cattle.

The start of the 1940s, in many ways, represented the glory days of boxing. Boxing, baseball, and horse racing were the biggest box office draws, with boxing and baseball the favorite sports of the working class. Both offered the possibility of someone to better himself without a college education. Boxing represented big money for up-and-coming pugilists, especially if they were successful. Even the unsuccessful ones made a better living than the average hourly worker.

The advent of World War II changed the face of sports in America. All able-bodied men between the ages of eighteen and twenty-six were expected to serve in the military. This took its toll on boxing. As many as four thousand professional boxers joined the military, including some of the best in each division. In fairness to the boxing champions who joined the military, a hold was placed on the major boxing titles until after the war.

The three most popular boxing divisions at the time were the heavyweight, middleweight, and welterweight. The heavyweight champion at the start of the decade and the start of the war was Joe Louis. Not only did he enlist, he donated over one hundred thousand dollars and fought exhibitions to help the war cause. He held the world title in each year of the decade of the 1940s.

In the welterweight division, Henry Armstrong (LaVern's Albuquerque acquaintance) came into the decade with the title but relinquished it on October 4, 1940, to Fritzie Zivic. He in turn held the title for a little over a year before losing it to Freddie "Red" Cochrane on July 29, 1941. The title holder at the start of the war, Cochrane held the frozen title until February 1, 1946, at which time he lost to Marty Servo. Servo suffered an injury to his nose in a nontitle fight with Rocky Graziano and vacated the crown in September 1946. In December Sugar Ray Robinson edged Tommy Bell in fifteen rounds to claim the vacated title. Robinson kept the welterweight title for most of the remainder of the decade.

This left the middleweight division to provide most of the boxing excitement in the 1940s. Al Hostak entered the decade with the middleweight title. He lost the title on July 19, 1940, to Tony Zale, who joined the navy and was the holder of the frozen title until after the war.

Big money attracts those people wanting to take advantage of the situation and claim their share legally or illegally. Boxing was no different. The underworld of gambling was ruled by the Mafia element, headed by gangster Frankie Carbo. With a record longer than his real name of Paolo Giovanni Carbo, Frankie represented the undesirable element that entered the boxing profession. He had been arrested dozens of times, charged with more than a half dozen murders and other crimes, but repeatedly got off due to witnesses not wanting to testify or conveniently disappearing. Realizing that a lot of money was to be made fixing fights, he became a promoter and was known as the czar of boxing. The sport suffered one of its worst periods during this time. Although some fighters caved in to his requests, there were many who refused to play his game—at their own peril.

One who played it straight was the middleweight champion of the time, Tony Zale. The war ended with Zale, nicknamed the "Man of Steel," as the world middleweight champion. Tony was born in the slums of Gary, Indiana, on May 29, 1913. His birth name was Anthony Florian Zaleski. His father, a steelworker, was killed in a bicycle-car accident when Tony was only two. Tony, like his other brothers, was sent to work in the steel mills at a very young age and hated it. Boxing proved to be his only way out. He started fighting as an amateur at the age of fifteen. "Alternately working in steel mills in between fights he forged his toughness and earned his nickname, 'The Man of Steel.'"[1]

Like LaVern, Tony got his start in the Golden Gloves, compiling a record of eighty-seven wins and eight defeats in a three-year span. On reaching the age of twenty-one, he turned pro. After winning his first nine bouts, he lost eight of his next twenty fights, including being knocked out in one fight. Discouraged, he quit boxing and returned to the mills for a couple of years. His return to boxing in 1937 was more successful. Although he lost a few more fights, including another knockout, he made his presence known with seven straight victories. This culminated with a triumph over Al Hostak on July 19, 1940, for the world middleweight championship.

Zale then spent the next year and a half fighting mostly nonchampionship bouts. He was very careful about putting his championship on the line, as LaVern later discovered. Then on February 13, 1942, Tony fought his last fight until the war ended. Billy Conn beat Tony in a disputed nontitle fight, his last fight for four years. Zale joined the Navy Coast Guard and spent his tour in Puerto Rico. Much like LaVern, he spent most of his time on base training and sparring, not joining sailors in the bars and brothels.

Due to his military service, the boxing authorities placed Zale's championship on hold until the war was over, when he returned and continued his pattern of nontitle fights, compiling an impressive stream of knockout victories. At the age of thirty-two, he was well past his prime as a boxer.

LaVern, not yet twenty-one, was a few years away from reaching his full potential as a boxer. John Abood and Chris Dundee were in no hurry to rush LaVern into fighting big-name pugilists. His time would come soon enough. The plan worked, with five straight victories as proof. The remainder of 1946 would primarily be spent in training and conditioning for the longer-round fights and occasionally taking on some more no-name fighters.

With the letdown of not having his own gym for his boxers, Johnny decided to train his charges in Stillman's Gym. Stillman's wasn't just a gym; it was an institution. According to Angelo Dundee, "The center of the boxing world was not, as one would have thought, Madison Square Garden. Instead it was a walk-up gym at 919 Eighth Avenue called Stillman's Gym—as imaginative writers would have it, 'the Mecca of Mayhem,' 'the Emporium of Sock,' or, in the immortal words of A. J. Liebling, 'the University of Eighth Avenue.'"[2]

The gym occupied two stories of a three-story building. On the first floor of the gym section of the building were two boxing rings. One was for the headliners, the champions, and the contenders for whom the public would pay fifty cents admission, often giving up their lunch hours, just to watch the boxer spar. In the other ring were the journeymen, the wannabes who were there hoping to be discovered or picked as sparring partners for the fighters in ring one. The second floor was used for jumping rope and the punching bags.

Lou Stillman seemed to take pride in the grime that covered the floors, walls, and ceilings, as well as the overwhelming stench that permeated the gym. The gym was only for the brave at heart, seldom seeing the presence of females. Lou, whose real last name was Ingber, ran his facility like a tyrant. He had the reputation of mistreating everyone the same, whether a champion or a bum. He spent most of his time sitting on his stool chewing on his cigar while announcing the comings and goings of boxers as they entered the main ring for sparring sessions. He was usually armed with a pistol just in case things got out of control.

Johnny paid for LaVern, Howie Brodt, Hal Anspach, and a few of his top fighters to train there for both experience and exposure. Roach soon became a favorite at the gym, partially due to the selection of Charley Goldman as his trainer. Abood, sparing no expense, hired the services of

LaVern and John Abood at Stillman's Gym. Courtesy of the LaVern Roach family.

Goldman, who had produced a few world champions to date. Goldman, already fifty-seven years old, trained his first world middleweight champ in 1914 and several since. He spent six hours a day at Stillman's training LaVern and company.

A short time after he started training LaVern, Goldman discovered another young fighter and war veteran. One day Goldman confided to Angelo, "Ang, I want you to see this guy. Not too tall, slightly balding, stiff shoulders, two left feet, and he throws punches from behind. But, oh, how he can punch."[3] Goldman chose to train the new find at the Twenty-Third Street CYO, where he could keep him under wraps until he felt it was time for him start fighting professionally. From then on, Goldman split his time between Stillman's training LaVern and the CYO Gym training his new find, Rocky Marciano.

LaVern's first fight in the New Year was scheduled for January 28, 1946, at St. Nicholas Arena in New York City. LaVern's wish made known to Nat Fleischer four years earlier ("I want to come to New York and turn professional.") was finally coming to fruition. Although he had been a professional fighter for four months, he now was having his first pro fight on the soil of New York City.

Johnny's plan of bringing his fighters up slowly by scheduling fights with more inexperienced pugilists ran aground as LaVern's next scheduled opponent, Verne Lester, backed out of the scheduled bout due to a hurt thumb. This was okay with Johnny and LaVern because the Texan was anxious to take a few months off and return to Plainview before continuing his career.

The promoter, determined to have LaVern on the preliminary ticket to help draw a larger crowd, assured Johnny that he had another fighter of equal caliber as Lester. Johnny and LaVern, though not familiar with the replacement, reluctantly agreed. His new opponent was named Henry Johnson. The fight would be a six-round match, preliminary to the main event.

The fight went the distance, with neither athlete able to score a knockdown. At the end of the hard-fought battle, Johnson was declared the winner in a very close decision. LaVern had lost his first professional bout. Afterward, it was discovered that Johnson had fought under an alias, his other boxing name being Arte Towne. Towne, born with the name of James Tufts, had been fighting professionally for two years with a professional record of twenty-two wins, four losses, and one draw. He had already fought Jake LaMotta, losing in a ten-round split decision. Towne went on to be a top-ten middleweight contender, retiring with a professional boxing record of 92-14-1.

Johnny and LaVern had been duped. Johnny said, "Had I known that it was Towne, I wouldn't have taken the match. I thought Johnson was just another 'bloke.'"[4] True to his character, LaVern never gave his inexperience as an excuse for his loss. If anything, he used his first professional loss in a positive way, not wanting to experience it again. He hoped for a rematch with Towne down the road, after he had a few more matches under his belt.

With no more fights on the horizon, LaVern used this time to take a vacation. He returned home to Plainview to spend time with family and friends and to check on his parents' health and finances. Johnny took this time to arrange for some permanent housing arrangements for members of his boxing team whom he persuaded to continue as professionals under his tutelage.

CHAPTER 8

Evelyn

It is difficult to know at what moment love begins; it is less difficult
to know that it has begun.
—*Henry Wadsworth Longfellow*

Evelyn Joyce Ogden was born on June 4, 1927, to Vera and Harold Ogden
in a rural area south of Plainview. Her parents divorced early on in her life,
and she and her mother went to live with Vera's parents, the Churchwells,
near the rural community of Snyder, located six miles south of Plainview.
Snyder consisted of a school and a few other scattered buildings. It was
a five-mile bus ride for Evelyn as she started first grade. A few years later the family moved closer to the rural community of Bellview, situated
about nine miles southeast of Plainview. Her bus ride to her new school
was shortened to three miles.

In 1937 Vera married Herbert Castleberry. The family thought it
best for Evelyn to remain with her grandparents while Herbert and Vera
got settled in. Vera, the next to the oldest of the Churchwell clan, had six
younger brothers and sisters. Evelyn fit right in with her aunts and uncles,
several just a few years older than her. Mavis, only seven years senior to
Evelyn, was more like a big sister than an aunt.

The nation was deep in the Depression with no end in sight. The rural
areas often were hit the hardest. Without electricity, they had to depend
on carbide lights, kerosene lamps, and a wind-charger. They farmed the
land using horses and plows. The only news they received came over a
battery-operated radio. Without reliable transportation to go into town
and separated from other farmhouses by a few miles, the Churchwell
family became a close-knit group.

MOST BEAUTIFUL GIRL

Evelyn Ogden

1944 Plainview High School yearbook. Courtesy of the LaVern Roach family.

After Herb and Vera settled in, Evelyn went to live with them. With the onset of World War II and the Depression winding down, transportation became more accessible, allowing for many of the rural communities to consolidate with the larger urban schools in Plainview. The transition was not without its problems. "The city kids looked down on the country people as country bumpkins," Evelyn recalled. "But our country boys, strong and healthy from performing farm work, soon took over the athletics and showed the city boys a thing or two."[1]

Evelyn skipped her freshman year and started Plainview High as a sophomore. It didn't take her long to be accepted, as she was named sophomore class favorite. Overnight she became very popular because of both her looks and personality. By the time she graduated in May 1944 she was a cheerleader, named "the girl with the best figure," and selected "the most beautiful girl" of Plainview High her senior year, though her strongest asset remained her friendly and sincere personality.

One of her first recollections of LaVern occurred as she was driving the family truck from the farm into town. LaVern passed her at a high speed and waved at her trying to get her attention. It got her attention all right but alarmed her more than anything. Their paths seldom crossed, even with her on the sidelines performing her cheerleading routine for the Bulldogs. She wasn't even aware that he graduated at midterm of her junior year and joined the Marines.

Evelyn graduated from Plainview High in May 1944. On June 7, three days after turning seventeen, she married her high school boyfriend, who was from the same class. Soon after the honeymoon, he enlisted in the navy without consulting her. With the war going on and knowing that the military needed all the men they could get, she took the decision in stride and decided to make the best of it. He headed to San Diego for boot camp, and she was on her own. In September, upon completion of boot camp, he asked Evelyn to come to San Diego for a few days prior to him shipping out. Evelyn left for California, spent a few days with him before he left for his new assignment, and then returned to Plainview. Nine months later, on June 12, 1945, a year after getting married, she gave birth to a beautiful blonde-haired girl and named her Ronnie. She moved in with Vera and Herb and started raising Ronnie on her own. Vera and Herb had bought a house in town as well as keeping the farmhouse. She and Ronnie split time between the two, although the farm was always Evelyn's favorite.

Things did not work out for the young couple as he returned to Plainview after the war. He had experienced too much freedom and wasn't ready to settle down and be a devoted husband and father. Evelyn was not willing to live on the terms presented and a divorce soon followed. She became a single parent, which was somewhat of a rarity during that period. The divorce became final in January 1946 as she and Ronnie continued to live with Vera and Herb.

About the same time that Evelyn's divorce was finalized, LaVern returned to Plainview for a three-month visit. All LaVern was looking for was just a little rest and relaxation and to check on the health and financial situation of the Roach family. His return was well publicized in the local newspaper, the *Plainview Herald*. He received a warm welcome as a military hero and a professional boxer. As the word got out about his return, the handsome young pugilist immediately became the most eligible bachelor in town.

All of the single girls flocked around LaVern, hoping to be the lucky one who might be asked out on a date. LaVern was flattered, but he didn't seem overly interested in any of them. This is not why he came home. That changed after he was told about Evelyn's divorce.

In high school LaVern had always admired Evelyn but felt she was beyond his reach socially. The incident of trying to get her attention by passing her on the highway didn't work, and neither did his exploits on the gridiron. Although he noticed her as a cheerleader, she perceived him as just another football player.

LaVern soon asked her out on a date. Unlike his high school days he now had money, a relative's borrowed car, and more importantly, the confidence to pursue her. But to his dismay and the astonishment of her friends, Evelyn turned him down. LaVern, not one to give up easily, asked her out a second time. His request was turned down a second time. Her friends, who would give anything to go out with LaVern, were bewildered. She explained to them that the only reason a single divorced mother would be asked out was that the suitor would figure she was "easy." She had not gone out with anyone since her courtship, marriage, and divorce and wasn't ready for another relationship, especially if she thought it involved being a one-night stand with a big-shot boxer.

After finding out the reason why she was turning him down, LaVern decided to pay a visit to her mother. In his plea to Vera, he stated (almost begged), "I just want to take her out for a date, that's all."[2] His honesty and politeness won Vera over. She told Evelyn that she thought LaVern seemed like a nice, well-mannered young man, and it would be okay for her to go out with him.

Playing matchmaker behind the scenes was the wife of Herbert Hilburn, editor of the *Plainview Herald*. Having a fondness for both LaVern and Evelyn, she arranged a small dinner party, inviting the two of them. This provided the opportunity for LaVern to pick Evelyn up and escort her to the party. She accepted his invitation.

The two hit it off immediately. He thought she was a knockout beauty in high school and motherhood made her more even so. Her pleasant personality had not changed even with what she had been through since graduation. He enjoyed her company more than any other girl's he had ever been with.

In him Evelyn saw someone who was not only strong and handsome, but polite, sincere, and a true gentleman, features not expected of someone who made boxing their profession. "He had piercing blue eyes, a gorgeous physique, and a certain charisma about him. When he entered a room, he immediately became the center of attention. I was instantly swept off my feet. More importantly he had not let his fame go to his head."[3]

Evelyn and LaVern's romance soon became the talk of the town. They were a perfect match. As Evelyn's family came to know LaVern, they adored him. According to Evelyn's Aunt Mavis, LaVern was polite and well mannered. "He was good to play with the younger kids in the family and they loved it. One of the favorite things the kids enjoyed was LaVern flexing his arm muscle and letting them hit it as hard as they wanted to."[4]

More importantly, any concerns about Ronnie being a hindrance to the relationship were laid to rest. While it would have been a problem for some men, LaVern was not a bit concerned about her previous marriage and having a child. He spent as much time as he could with both of them. Entertainment in Plainview was limited for young couples. Too old to "drag Broadway," they occasionally took in a movie at the Granada or Fair Theaters while Mavis or Vera took care of Ronnie. They were content staying home and spending time with Evelyn's family.

Once people knew that LaVern was back in town, his services in refereeing bouts was in big demand. Not wanting to miss any time with them, he asked Evelyn to accompany him to these events and to bring Ronnie. If the matches were outdoors Evelyn would bundle Ronnie up, and the three of them took off. It was apparent to everyone that the young couple was falling in love.

As Vera got to know LaVern, she had no problem with her daughter falling for a boxer. From the devotion he showed to both Evelyn and Ronnie to his unusually good manners, she was extremely impressed. This is not what she expected from one who made his living as a prizefighter. LaVern was quick to credit Johnny Abood for what he learned outside the ring as well as inside. Abood took pride in not only training his young men to be good Marines and good boxers but also to be gentlemen. John, who could afford the best of clothing and was always appropriately dressed for any occasion, taught LaVern to do the same.

The weeks and months passed quickly, and soon it was time for LaVern to return east to his new life as a boxing pro. It was a difficult departure for LaVern and Evelyn. From then on, it was understood that neither would date anyone else, and at the right time, they would marry.

Upon arriving back east, LaVern had a new home located at 470 Elmwood Avenue, Maplewood, New Jersey. Johnny Abood had found the perfect housing setup for his boxing team. LaVern and Hal moved into it. In place of Stanley and Rosa, who would never consider the possibility of leaving Plainview and moving east, John Abood's sister Nora became their housekeeper and cook. LaVern and Evelyn continued their long-distance romance courtesy of the postal and telegram service.

During the summer of 1946 LaVern resumed his boxing career primarily by training and conditioning. His next opponent, according to personal records given to Choc Hutcheson, friend and sportswriter for the *Lubbock Avalanche Journal*, was Buddy Newby. LaVern recorded winning the fight with a KO in six rounds. The fight is not recorded anywhere else. Although LaVern never listed a date for the fight, he had it chronicled after the Towne fight and prior to the Hearold fight. For purposes of record keeping and due to lack of an official acknowledgment, this victory is not included in LaVern's official win-loss count in this work.[5]

LaVern fought Billy Hearold on October 1, 1946, at Park Arena, Bronx, New York. Hearold sported a record of five wins and two losses. Failing to score a knockout, LaVern outpointed his opponent in six rounds, moving his record to six wins and one loss.

Up next for LaVern was Charlie McPherson, a seasoned boxer from Brooklyn with a 36-59-4 record. LaVern was McPherson's one hundredth professional fight. His most notable fights to date took place in 1943 when he fought Rocky Graziano three times. His record against Graziano was two losses and one draw. One of the busiest boxers in the ring, he had the distinction of fighting thirty-four times in 1943, often on two days' rest.

The fight with McPherson took place on October 14 at St. Nicholas Arena. For this bout, McPherson, not having fought for over six weeks, was better rested than Roach. Only two weeks had passed since LaVern's fight against Hearold. The fight went the full six-round distance with LaVern winning on points, flooring McPherson in the process. After absorbing this loss, McPherson was back in the ring four days later.

LaVern's next fight took place ten days later on October 24 at Hamid's Pier Ballroom, Atlantic City, New Jersey. His opponent was Manuel Rosa

LaVern's and Hal Anspach's living quarters, 470 Elmwood Avenue, Maplewood, New Jersey. Courtesy of the LaVern Roach family.

from Baltimore. LaVern, the underdog, didn't waste much time in finishing off Rosa, scoring a tremendous upset. With a third-round knockout, he recorded his eighth win. LaVern left Atlantic City heralded as one of the "finds of the year" in boxing.

Roach then returned to the Washington, DC, area, squaring off against Arthur Bethea on November 4. It was sort of a homecoming since he had fought in the area while in the Marines and it was the location of his first three professional fights. LaVern was a six-to-five favorite to beat the eighteen-year-old Bethea, fighting in front of a hometown crowd. The location of the bout was Turner's Arena. This was LaVern's first ten-round match, which was not a factor, as he needed only three rounds to score a knockout.

One more bout was scheduled prior to taking a break for the holidays. On November 14 at Hamid's Pier Ballroom in Atlantic City, LaVern entered the ring against Joe Tate of Philadelphia. Tate, considered one of the best fighters to come out of the Quaker City during the past year, was a last-minute substitute for Stanly Sims, who had been placed on an ineligible list because of a suspension in New York. The Atlantic

City newspaper on the day of the fight wrote, "Laverne [*sic*] Roach, the good-looking scrapper from Plainview, Tex., who is being acclaimed as the middleweight find of the year by New York fistic experts, is the 2 to 1 favorite in Hamid's Pier Ballroom tonight."[6]

Tate, with a record of three wins, four losses, and a tie, was ready to test his ring skill against the Texan. He proved more difficult to take down than LaVern's two previous opponents. The fight went the full eight rounds, with LaVern winning on points. Newspaper headlines read, "Roach Hangs Up Another Scalp." That was LaVern's last fight in 1946. With five fights in a six-week period, he welcomed the break.

The year ended on a successful note, winning five straight bouts since his return from his Plainview vacation. He finished the year with a record of ten wins and the lone loss. LaVern took the Thanksgiving and Christmas holidays off, returning to Plainview and Evelyn. While home LaVern couldn't make himself stay away from the sport he so loved. The Lubbock District Golden Gloves tournament was scheduled for the month of January. He now umpired the matches that just a few years earlier he was participating in.

CHAPTER 9

1947, The Perfect Season: A Star Is Born

They are the greatest athletes in the world.
—Sylvester Stallone

After spending the holidays at home with his family and friends, LaVern was eager to get back to work. Abood and Chris Dundee felt LaVern was now ready for stiffer competition, but seeking out quality competition had drawbacks. LaVern had built such a reputation that many pugilists were not willing to fight him. Several times bouts were scheduled only to have the opponent back out at the last minute.

Before his next fight, LaVern celebrated his twenty-second birthday. Two weeks later, on March 3, after nearly a three-month layoff, he returned to the ring. The opponent for his third fight at St. Nick's was Joe Agosta, who with fifty-three bouts under his belt brought a considerable amount of experience. Next to the Towne fight, this was LaVern's toughest bout to date. Agosta had faced some good competition, including Herbie Kronowitz, Norman Rubio, Sonny Horne, and Rocky Graziano, all with commendable win/loss records. The fight went the full eight rounds with LaVern winning on points.

Next up was journeyman Leroy McQueen of Harlem. Prior to Jackie Robinson's breaking the color barrier in baseball, boxing had done so nearly from its start. Although racism often reared its ugly head outside the ring and sometimes in the ring, Joe Louis's victory over Max Schmeling in 1938, along with Jesse Owens's 1936 Olympic feats, gave America its first black American national sports heroes. LaVern was color blind in-

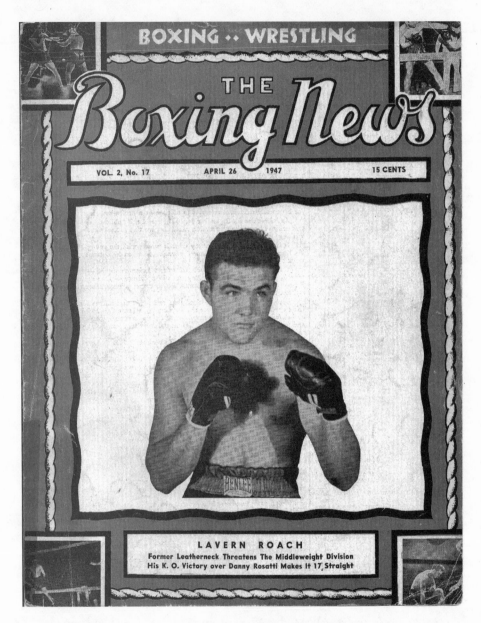

Cover of *Boxing News*, April 26, 1947. Courtesy of the Roach family.

side and outside the ring. He had no animosity toward any of the fighters he faced. In fact, except for a couple of hometown sportswriters, he was never known to have anything bad to say about anyone.

The McQueen bout took place on March 11 in White Plains, New York, at the Westchester County Center. McQueen came into the fight with a record of six wins and seventeen losses. LaVern handed him his eighteenth loss with another solid performance, going the full six-round distance. It was LaVern's second win of the year and twelfth overall.

There was little rest for LaVern as his third fight of the month was also scheduled in White Plains. A crowd of nearly four thousand fans paid a gate of fifty-eight hundred dollars on March 25 to see the former Marine fight Danny Rosati, an ex-sailor from Newark, New Jersey. Rosati's best performance to date was his fight against the undefeated Sonny Horne five years earlier, which ended in a draw. Three months earlier, he lost a ten-rounder to the up-and-coming Billy Arnold. Rosati had a respectable record of 29-10-3.

LaVern, cool and confident from the start, won the first three rounds with his quick left jabs, scoring more hits than his opponent was able to deliver. In the second round LaVern threw a quick right that landed square on Rosati's jaw and sent him reeling. By the end of the third, Rosati had a slight cut over his left eye, but he recovered to score his best round in the fourth by getting in some good punches against LaVern. In the fifth La-Vern regained his composure and landed a barrage of unanswered head and body blows. One of LaVern's hard rights landed in Rosati's left rib cage, causing Rosati to gasp for breath and retreat for the rest of round.

At the end of the round, Dr. Thomas Bockner, the ring physician, quickly examined Rosati. He discovered Rosati had suffered a broken rib and ordered Referee Anthony Mealfe to stop the fight. After the tilt it was discovered that Rosati had suffered two broken ribs. The three-month layoff didn't seem to slow LaVern, finishing the month of March with three wins.

Working on just two weeks of rest, LaVern returned to Hamid's Pier to face his toughest competition of the new year, Irish Billy Cooper from Paterson, New Jersey. Cooper, an experienced fighter, had won thirty-seven fights, more than anyone LaVern had fought to date. He had lost only four times and had six draws. LaVern won a solid ten-round decision.

As a result of his win over Rosati, LaVern appeared on the April cover of the *Boxing News*. The write-up on the inside front cover of the magazine stated,

> The Marines have landed and have the situation well in hand. You can apply this well-known saying to the boxing success of former Marine LaVern Roach. Chris Dundee represents Johnny Abood in the handling of Lavern Roach. Chris has decided to test the leatherneck leather pusher against the capable Vinnie Rossano at Fort Hamilton on the first of May. A victory over Rossano will move LaVern Roach one step nearer to the goal of all contenders—a crack at the middleweight title.[1]

At the last minute Rossano backed out of his fight with LaVern but was quickly replaced by Andres "Indian" Gomez. It was LaVern's first professional fight against a foreign-born opponent. Gomez was born and reared in Cuba. His first two years of professional fighting took place in his homeland. Among his early accomplishments was winning the middleweight championship of Cuba, before he started fighting in the United States. He had a winning record while fighting on the island. Once he started fighting in the States, his record began to slip. A busy fighter, he brought a 25-35-9 record into the ring.

The fight took place in the Fort Hamilton Arena in Brooklyn, New York, on May 1 before a crowd of twenty-five hundred. The eight-round bout failed to go the distance. LaVern scored a knockout in the sixth round. To his credit, Gomez continued to fight some of the best fighters in the business, losing twice to Tony Janiro, three times to Lee Sala, and once to Herbie Kronowitz and Joey LaMotta (Jake's brother). With the win over Gomez, LaVern chalked up career win number fifteen while remaining unbeaten in 1947.

After an extra week of rest and training prior to his next fight, it was back to Fort Hamilton to face Victor Amato in a ten-round match to be held on May 22. Amato had twenty-six victories while losing fifteen, along with three draws. After the full ten rounds, LaVern was awarded the victory on points. Victory number sixteen was in the bag.

The Texan returned to the ring on June 12 to square off against Sal Richie, who had a respectable record of 18-9. Nine months earlier Richie lost a ten-round decision to Arte Towne, their only common opponent.

Forty-five hundred fans packed into the Fort Hamilton Arena. Prior to this fight Richie had never been knocked out in his professional career. This changed when LaVern scored with a right cross at 1:05 of the fourth round. Fort Hamilton was becoming a favorite venue as LaVern scored his third victory there, with two of the three being knockouts. Roach's momentum and reputation continued their upward spiral.

John Abood was so impressed by the victory over Richie that he referenced it three years later in a letter to Choc Hutcheson. After witnessing the Sugar Ray Robinson / Steve Belloise fight on August 24, 1949, at Yankee Stadium, Abood wrote, "Robinson looked great in beating Belloise. I still totally believe the Roach of the Sal Ritchie fight would be the only one to beat Robinson."[2] To be mentioned in the same company as the great Sugar Ray Robinson was quite a compliment for LaVern.

Things were proceeding well, and his boxing was now turning a profit. He used his earnings from the Richie fight to set his father up in an O.K. Rubber Welders store, a tire repair shop, in Quitaque, Texas.

LaVern wasn't the only one making news in the boxing world. On July 16 Rocky Graziano dethroned Tony Zale of the middleweight title with a six-round TKO. This was sweet revenge for Graziano, who was beaten by Zale the previous September.

During the months of July and August, LaVern had a half dozen fights cancelled. His reputation and victories caused opponents to have second thoughts about getting into the ring with the upstart Texan. The Roach camp was looking forward to a ten-round matchup with Bill Poli, the Italian middleweight, scheduled to make his second bout on American soil on August 26 at MacArthur Stadium in Brooklyn. With the borough's large Italian population, the fight was expected to a big draw. It was cancelled the day of the fight. The respect was welcomed, but the idleness became a big concern, putting a damper on LaVern's morale.

LaVern never used a layoff as an excuse to get out of shape. He knew training was the most essential part of boxing. Always looking forward to that day when the call would come for him to face a great boxer, he would be ready. "I can't afford to get out of training; sure as I do that's when the opportunity I am waiting for will come. When I get a crack at a big-name fighter and the reward that goes with it, I'm going to be in as perfect physical condition as I can."[3]

It was time again for LaVern's camp to step up his competition. His chance came against Norman Rubio. Although the match wasn't a main event, it was the next best thing to it. On July 30, an outdoor championship bout was scheduled at Ebbets Field in Brooklyn between the current light heavyweight champ, Gus Lesnevich, and Tami Mauriello. LaVern and Rubio were featured in an eight-round preliminary. Ringside seats were priced at only ten dollars. The evening matches were expected to gross two hundred thousand dollars, of which fifty thousand dollars would go to the Damon Runyon Memorial Cancer Fund. Damon Runyon, the famous and popular New York newspaperman and writer, died of throat cancer the previous December.

Norman Rubio, sporting a very respectable 45-18-7 record, held his own in the ring with the best. Two of the losses were against Sugar Ray Robinson, the second one going the distance. It took LaVern eight rounds to come out on top. "I was ill going into the bout, but won handily."[4] He then contributed his entire purse of twelve hundred dollars (a year's salary for the average American worker) to the Damon Runyon relief fund. This generous gesture elevated his all-American image among fans and the media. In the main event Lesnevich won his bout on his way to an undefeated year. LaVern's undefeated year also remained intact.

Anxious to see family and friends, especially Evelyn, LaVern took a break from boxing and returned to Plainview in the middle of August. With his new celebrity status, it became more difficult to come home without the notice of the local paper. His comings and goings became newsworthy. When asked, LaVern was never one to turn down an interview. The *Plainview Herald* reported,

> Plainview's contribution to professional boxing is here for a visit with friends. He has just finished a long training stint interspersed with an occasional match and marred by numerous fight cancellations. . . . Roach trains with almost religious fervor. The night spots and myriad other metropolitan attractions have their lure but the "country boy" so far has not succumbed. He trains, goes to bed early, eats properly, doesn't smoke or drink, and trains some more. As a result, his stamina is such that he is going stronger after the fifth or sixth round than when he started.[5]

In the interview, when questioned about his manager, John Abood, La-Vern answered, "Johnny takes a fatherly interest in us. He wants us to succeed and sees that we toe the mark."[6]

LaVern had to once again cut his visit short and return back east to begin training for his next fight. Upon his return, he wrote Choc, apologizing for not being able to get to Lubbock. He used the lack of transportation as an excuse, but his desire to spend more time with Evelyn was also a factor. Up until now he had never mentioned her to him. Since their romance seemed to be blossoming, he felt it was time to share the news of his good fortune with his buddy:

> I'm fighting Billy Arnold Sept. 26th so be sure and listen in. If I can get by him I may get the Cerdan shot in Dec. or Jan. so keep your fingers crossed & wish me luck. I think I can beat him, but he's a tough baby.
>
> I guess you've heard from Chris Dundee's brother by now for he's supposed to send you a story every other day, & also one to Plainview. They perked up their ears when they read your story before. Thanks Choc, for the plug, for it was really a good story. Hope I can live up to all the nice things you said.
>
> I have 9 more days to train so I'll be sharp for this one. That two weeks rest did me a world of good & my girl was a good sight to look at. I get in the dumps when I'm away from her too long, so I feel better now. Her name is Evelyn Winkels & we plan to get married in Dec. or January. She was married before so don't put Miss if you mention her anytime. I'll tell you the story sometime Choc, for she's a wonderful girl.
>
> Did you hear the broadcast last Friday? I was interviewed on the Gillette Sports Cavalcade. Say hello to the folks in Lubbock for me.[7]

LaVern's star was rising. Behind the scenes, Gene Tunney, former Marine and former world heavyweight champ, helped spread the hype for the young lad. For his own service to his country along with his boxing skills and performances, Tunney was awarded the "Fighting Marine of World War I." On September 23, the Marine Corps, in a show of support for his boxing achievements and in appreciation for his service to his country, honored LaVern with a scroll representing the "Fighting Marine of World War II." Presenting the award was Tunney himself. Along with this honor, LaVern was appointed a permanent "honorary" recruiting sergeant in the US Marine Corps by the direction of the commandant of the Marine Corps. He was given the award by Major Sidney Altman. The award presentation ceremony took place at Stillman's Gym. LaVern joined one of his idols as the only two men in American history to receive such an award.

Gene Tunney presenting award to LaVern. Photo by Herbie Scharfman © 1947
KING FEATURES SYNDICATE INC., WORLD RIGHTS RESERVED.

LaVern's next opponent's fan base included President Harry Truman.
The familiar venue of St. Nicholas Arena was the setting for the bout
against Billy Arnold, a favorite of the president. The ten-rounder was being broadcast on the Gillette national hookup sponsored by ABC.

Arnold, a year younger than LaVern, sported a very respectable 37-5-
1 record. According to Chris Dundee,

LaVern is rounding into shape at Stillman's Gym boxing daily with the best middleweights in the country in preparation for the most important bout in his career with Billy Arnold at St. Nicholas Arena—in New York. Arnold is a boy rated one of the toughest in the country. He won his first 30 bouts straight—28 by knockouts. He has lost only to the likes of Rocky Graziano and Fritzie Zivic. The bout will be over a nationwide radio hook-up and also on television. You will all be able to listen to how Roach performs.[8]

LaVern, in peak condition, was in charge from the opening bell through the end of the bout. Never relinquishing the momentum, the fight actually turned out to be one of his easier wins. LaVern, not accustomed to fighting a ten-rounder, said after the fight, "I didn't want to finish him particularly. I paced myself along because I wanted to get the feel of ten rounds. I was stronger at the finish than the start. I don't smoke, and that smoky air bothered me the first few rounds. Besides, guess I was just a little shaky."[9] Sportswriter Lewis Burton, in describing the fight in his column, wrote,

> Roach did everything but knock out Arnold. He won a unanimous decision, from which there couldn't be a dissenting vote among the 3,624 fans that paid out $8,852 for the entertainment. One of the wonders of it was that Arnold was on his feet at the finish. He was never knocked down and the only person on the canvas any time, was—oddly—Roach. He threw himself out of the ring missing a left in the second. Donovan counted "one" before Roach scrambled back.[10]

Referee Art Donovan scored the fight in LaVern's favor, eight rounds to two. Judges Arthur Susskind and Frank Forbes both gave LaVern nine of the ten rounds. Burton added, "Roach's appearance and style are similar to Billy Conn."[11]

Excitement was building in the Roach camp. Just as the year 1947 was coming to an end, so were his days of battling the so-called journeymen of the trade. Abood and Chris Dundee started looking for legitimate contenders to test LaVern's skills, and apparently some contenders started looking his way also. In a letter to Choc, LaVern wrote,

> Well it looks like things will start popping soon for I've had a feeler

from Marcel Cerdan. Boy, I'd give anything to fight him, for a win there would put me in line for a title shot. I think it would draw from 80 to 100 thousand dollars in the Garden, I hope. Don't mention this though Choc, for if I know my luck, I'll not get that kind of break.

Say Choc, when there's anything in the Lubbock paper, I'd appreciate it if you'd send it to me. I always like to keep things like that for my scrapbook.[12]

A Cerdan fight in December or January failed to materialize. With no big-name boxers on the immediate horizon and wanting to keep LaVern fresh, Abood scheduled Jackie Kenny for his next bout.

It would be the headliner at Broadway Arena in an eight-round match to take place on October 14. Kenny, a journeyman fighter, had a record of 24-10-4. He last suffered defeat two weeks earlier to LaVern's roommate and former Marine boxing teammate, Harold Anspach, who had scored an eight-round decision to bring his professional record to eleven wins with only one loss and a draw. LaVern matched Harold's victory over Kenny by scoring a unanimous decision in eight rounds for his tenth win of the year.

A few days later, in a letter to Choc, LaVern wrote,

The eye isn't bad and didn't bother me any. I made the fight harder than it should have been by trying to knock him out early. I got off wrong and it took me 4 or 5 rounds to settle down again. I'll learn someday I guess and these fights help a lot. Right now I'm booked for Nov. 21st with Herbie Kronowitz in St. Nicks, so if it works out you'll hear me in action again. Boy if I can beat him it will help a lot toward getting that Cerdan bout. Maybe things will work out okay and I'll have that go in the Garden in Jan. or Feb. Hope so anyway. Keep your fingers crossed & wish me luck. Hope someday you can come out and see me fight a good fight.

LaVern continued the letter, revealing a softer and somewhat insecure side that he seemed only to be able to reveal to Choc:

Say Choc, it makes me feel good to think you have a good opinion of me. I only hope I don't have you fooled and give you cause to change it someday. It's funny how you meet a person and know right away that they're just the kind of guy you like. That's the way it is for me and I knew all along Choc that you were a right guy. I'm not just saying this because of what you said about me. I mean it and I know that we'll always be good friends.[13]

With the Cerdan fight still out of reach, up next was Kronowitz. Bill Corum, announcer and sports editor of the *New York Journal-American*, made the announcement on the *Cavalcade of Sports* program. He stated, "I predict this boy from Plainview, Texas will go far if nothing happens to him. He is a good, clean, hard fighter."[14]

LaVern, while focused on boxing, never lost interest in keeping up with his high school football team, the Plainview Bulldogs. LaVern wrote in a letter to Choc,

> Say, what do you think of that Plainview, Pampa game? The way things sound it must have been some game. Sure wish that could happen against Amarillo, but I doubt it. Boy I am anxious to read the results & see what happened. This Kronowitz deal is set for Nov. 28th so be sure and tune in. It means a lot to me for if I can do good, I may get a fight with Tony Janiro. That will be okay with me for I think we would draw pretty good in the Garden. Guess I'd better concentrate on Kronowitz for it's just as you said about taking them one at a time. That is important Choc, for there are no easy ones. I was planning on going out to play some golf today but it's cloudy and damp. The sun just came out. Maybe if I come home Christmas we can get together for a couple of rounds.[15]

The Plainview Bulldogs scored an upset win over their panhandle rival, the Pampa Harvesters, by a score of 20-19 as Plainview's future NFL All-Pro Bill Howten caught a touchdown pass in the last minute. Afterward, Plainview lost its game to Amarillo High School.

While LaVern was training and preparing for the bout with Kronowitz, a major boxing scandal was in the making. On November 14 Jake LaMotta lost to Billy Fox by a TKO in round four of a scheduled ten-rounder. The immediate reaction of ringsiders was that the fight was fixed. There had long been rumors of an underworld or "mob" element in the boxing industry under the control of Frankie Carbo. Up until now they had remained rumors. Out of fear, self-preservation, or both, many chose to look the other way. It appeared that LaMotta was a much better boxer than an actor in taking the dive. The widespread reports of the fix now received official recognition from the boxing authorities, at least temporarily robbing Fox of the acclaim of becoming the first boxer ever to knock out the tough LaMotta.

Boxers everywhere were concerned about the aftermath of the LaMotta/Fox match, including LaVern as he wrote to Choc:

> The farmer [Anspach] and I played football Sunday, so you can imagine how sore I am today. Should have my rear kicked but I'll be okay in a day or so. I'm in good shape and should be plenty sharp by fight time. Keep your fingers crossed and wish me luck for a lot depends on this one. Say Choc, I'm getting all the Marines in New York to follow me or rather I'm trying to. If I can do that I'll be able to get fights in the Garden pretty easy. I hope. Sure would like to get a good bout there in Jan. or Feb. for just one would make me an independent man. I still owe John Abood so you know how anxious I am to get out of debt. Things are looking good and if that LaMotta-Fox fight doesn't ruin boxing, I may make some money. You can never tell about things like that so I don't know what to think. Some say it is crooked but you can't tell. Angelo said he'd send you a story as soon as he could and informed me to inform you he'd like a clipping or two of each write-up you use. Also remember me for I'll never see the ones he gets.[16]

The New York State Athletic Commission, suspecting that the fight between LaMotta and Fox was fixed, froze the earnings and suspended LaMotta. Years later LaMotta, testifying at an FBI hearing, confessed to throwing the fight for the mob in return for a chance at the middleweight title. That and a twenty-thousand-dollar payment got him that chance.[17]

The Kronowitz fight took place in St. Nicholas Arena. It was the biggest fight in New York City that week, being broadcast over the nationwide ABC radio network's *Cavalcade of Sports*. It matched the ruggedness of Kronowitz, from Coney Island, against the speed and skill of LaVern. Kronowitz was LaVern's toughest opponent to date. His forty-seven victories included several over fighters whom LaVern had faced—Agosta, Valencia, Gomez, and Amato. More impressive were his wins over Johnny Greco, Sonny Horne, and Harold Green. These wins propelled him to the number-ten middleweight ranking in the world by the *Ring* magazine.

A crowd of 3,602 packed the house for the Friday night headline fight. The purse of eleven thousand dollars represented the largest gate that La-Vern ever fought for at that time. LaVern, known in the boxing circles for being a "stickler" for conditioning, was in excellent shape for the fight.[18]

The crowd cheered loudly for LaVern while Kronowitz was greeted with catcalls along with some boos.[19] LaVern fell behind early with Kronowitz knocking him into the ropes. Although suffering from a cut above the eye in the seventh round, LaVern was able to land more and harder punches throughout the fight, rallying to win a close but unanimous decision in ten rounds. Art Donovan, once again refereeing one of LaVern's fights, had each winning five rounds but favored LaVern 14-13 on points. Judges Barnes and Swartz scored the fight 6-4 and 5-4-1, respectively, for LaVern.

LaVern gave his assessment of the fight to Choc after the fight:

> Guess you heard the fight so you know I made out okay. Didn't get started until the 6th round for some reason so I didn't do as good as I expected. It was a real good fight and I thought I had 6 rounds at least but two judges had it close. He only hit me two good punches for I was blocking all the body punches. I wouldn't have a mark on me if I hadn't got butted in the 7th round. I guess I'm satisfied since I won.[20]

Four days later Lavern added,

> Say Choc I'm leaving tomorrow and will be home Saturday the 6th. You can call 452-M in P.V. Sunday morning early and catch me, okay. I don't know where to call you & I won't be able to get to Lubbock for a few days. I'll be happy though to drop down and see the kids at the club, so you can arrange things.[21]

The Kronowitz victory gave LaVern his eleventh win of 1947 with no defeats and extended his string of wins to sixteen, with an overall professional record of twenty-one wins and only one loss. To date, LaVern had still never been knocked down during a professional fight.

LaVern returned to Plainview for Christmas. He closed the tire store in Quitaque and with some of his earnings set up his dad in the same tire business in Plainview. It was an exceptional year, with Lavern winning all of his matches and gaining some financial independence. However, the greatest moment was Evelyn accepting his marriage proposal as he presented her a diamond engagement ring. Life was good, but about to get much better.

Word of his next match cut his Plainview visit short. Still not able to line up Cerdan for a fight, Abood landed the next best opponent: Tony Janiro. The fight was to take place on January 16 at Madison Square Garden. After getting the word from Abood, LaVern immediately returned to New Jersey on Christmas Day and was met with fifteen inches of snow, with more to come.

Upon his return, the *Ring* was announcing its 1947 annual boxing awards. In his twenty-third annual review of the world's boxers, Nat Fleischer, editor and publisher, surprised the boxing world in naming light heavyweight Gus Lesnevich Fighter of the Year over heavyweight Jersey Joe Wolcott. Wolcott, a few weeks earlier, had scored a victory over Joe Louis, and many had expected Wolcott to receive the award. Fleischer defended his decision by giving credit to Wolcott for being a "one-night sensation," but contends "that Lesnevich in coming back from a long hitch in the Navy and winning four important fights during 1947 did more than any other man to improve the standing of the sport."[22]

Along with the news that Lesnevich was awarded the Fighter of the Year award, LaVern was greeted with a post-Christmas present. Headlines of the New York newspapers read, "LaVern Roach Named 'Rookie of the Year.'"

This was a new award given out to a young boxer who had made the greatest advancement during the year. In an article that appeared in the February 1948 edition of the *Ring*, Jersey Jones wrote this about the new award:

> It seemed an excellent idea when Nat Fleischer suggested it.
>
> "What do you think," he asked, "of *The Ring* adding to its awards a prize for the year's outstanding 'new face' in boxing?"
>
> "You mean a sort of 'Rookie of the Year'?" we ventured.
>
> "Yes," he replied, "though he doesn't necessarily have to be a rookie in a strict sense. After all, how many boys become headliners in their first year of boxing? No, I mean some lad who may have been fighting before 1947, but was practically unknown to the world at large on January 1, yet earned a place in his division's top ten by December 31."
>
> "It's a swell idea," he said, with something more than a touch

of enthusiasm. "An award of that sort will give ambitious kids an added something to shoot for during the year."

"Okay, then," Nat continued. "See if you can figure what youngster was the standout of 1947, and we'll award a new prize. We will call it 'The Rookie of the Year' trophy."[23]

Although this description fit LaVern to a T, nowhere is it written that Fleischer had him in mind when this conversation occurred. His staff, after combing through the records of more than one hundred newcomers over the past couple of years, narrowed it down to four candidates. They were Livio Minelli, an Italian welterweight; Maxie Docusen, a lightweight; Jackie Darthard, a welterweight from Kansas City; and middleweight LaVern Roach.

LaVern's resume included the following:

Fighting chiefly in the New York area, the youngster, a smart, clever, heady boxer, put together an impressive skein of wins, capped by a decision over a ranking middleweight, Herbie Kronowitz, at the St. Nicholas Arena. LaVern's earlier accomplishments included a knockout of Danny Rosati, and verdicts over Billy Cooper, Vic Amato, Norman Rubio, and Billy Arnold.

Jones concluded the article,

The final selection of the outstanding "new face" uncovered during 1947 settled down to a choice from among Minelli, Roach, Docusen and Darthard.

And those were the four names submitted to a round-table gathering of *The Ring* staff for ultimate decision.

The voting was close, as it figured to be. But the final score, in what horse-race enthusiasts would call a photo-finish, gave the edge, by the narrowest of conceivable margins, to Roach.

So, for the first winner of what will become an annual award by *The Ring* to the year's outstanding development, we give you: Laverne Roach, late of Plainview, Texas, and the United States Marine Corps, now of Millburn, N.J., and a lad who, during 1947, rose from boxing's preliminary ranks to the status of a ranking big-time middleweight.[24]

With 1947 finishing up on a high note, LaVern now set his sights on his childhood dream—the world championship. It was back to work.

Although the snow put a damper on his daily roadwork, it didn't take LaVern long to get into fighting condition because he never let himself get out of shape. He revealed his secret to Choc in a letter written on New Year's Eve:

> Happy New Year! Thanks a lot for the pictures and clippings. I'll show them to Angelo & see if he wants to make any copies. Well pal, I'm getting back on the ball again and sure do feel good. I weighed 159 when I got back and everybody is wondering how I can hold my weight down and stay in condition the way I do. People seem to think a guy has to get drunk and eat a lot of junk when he isn't training. As long as the other fighters do that, it's okay for that only helps me. Choc I want to thank you for what you're doing for me and I hope I can do you a favor someday. All that publicity back there will help me a lot if I ever settle down in that country.
>
> This fight means a lot to me and if I beat him I'll really get the breaks. Most people think that I'll be the biggest drawing card out here if I do real good. Don't mention that I said anything like that, but I thought that I'd tell you. Boy I sure hope so for I'd like to get another Garden bout and make some money one of these days.[25]

CHAPTER 10

Roach versus Janiro, Battle of the Most Handsome

The two best-looking fighters in the business are meeting.
— *Angelo Dundee*

The difference between small-time and big-time boxing is often as simple as where the bout takes place. A fighter has made it big when his next match is the main event at Madison Square Garden against a ranked opponent. This was the scenario as LaVern was set to fight Tony Janiro on January 16 of the New Year.

For the sport, it could not have come at a better time. It followed the LaMotta/Fox fiasco by only two months. At the same time LaMotta's friend Rocky Graziano, the reigning middleweight champ, was suspended by the New York State Athletic Commission for failing to report a bribe. His AWOL charge while serving in the army also came to light. Boxing was still reeling from the negative effect these two great fighters had on the coverage of the sport. The Janiro/Roach tilt could provide some redemption since both had clean reputations.

The underworld was more apt to go after fighters with tarnished backgrounds such as LaMotta and Graziano than someone like Roach, who was managed by Abood and Chris Dundee, both beyond reproach. Messing with hoodlums was one thing. Meddling with someone who had the backing of the US Marine Corps was another.

Several differences and similarities existed between Janiro and his upstart challenger from Texas. Both entered the "sweet science"[1] at an early age.

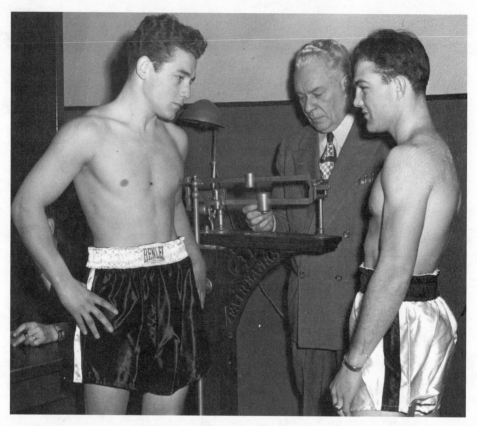

Tony Janiro, Dr. Nardiello, and LaVern at weigh-in. Courtesy of the LaVern Roach family.

Janiro was born Anthony Gianiro (later shortening his first name while changing the spelling of his last name) on February 2, 1926, in Springdale, Pennsylvania, to parents of Italian American descent. At the age of four, his family moved to Youngstown, Ohio, which Tony always considered home. At the age of sixteen, Tony left Youngstown to pursue a boxing career in New York City.

Manager/promoter Frankie "Jay" Jacobs, despite being on the receiving end of ridicule from many of his rivals suggesting he was wasting his time on the baby-faced kid, recognized potential in the youngster. He took the teenager under his wing, and soon the jeering turned to jealousy as Tony skyrocketed to the top.

Tony made his professional debut at the age of seventeen against

Charlie Jeffries, a no-name boxer with only three fights under his belt—all defeats. The fight was held at Scott Hall in Elizabeth, New Jersey, in which Tony outpointed his opponet. For the next six months, Jacobs limited Tony to small arenas in New Jersey, where his ring talent blossomed into a fighter to be reckoned with. After winning his first seventeen fights against primarily rookie opponents, only five of whom had winning records, he was awarded his first fight at the Garden.

At the age of eighteen he defeated Tommy Mills in a preliminary six-round bout at the Garden in his first fight in New York on June 23, 1944. After winning his first twenty-three bouts, he finally lost to Al Guido. After the loss, he would put together another string of victories, this time sixteen straight. Tony, in a return match, beat Guido two months later. The streak was broken in a loss to Johnny Greco, the welterweight king of Canada. Then in his next three fights he would beat Greco and Guido and then lose again to Greco. Tony finally strung together another sixteen straight victories, including impressive wins against Tony Pellone and former world boxing champion Beau Jack, a fight for which Tony received twenty-one thousand dollars.

By the age of twenty-one, he earned the right to face Jake LaMotta as his next opponent in the featured ten-round bout to be held on June 6, 1947, in Madison Square Garden. The press played up Tony's attractiveness in an effort to heighten boxing's interest among females. Sportswriter Leonard Cohen dubbed him "Tony the Beautiful."[2] Another writer chose to use a Betty Grable label, by nicknaming him "Pin-up" Tony.[3]

This publicity soon proved detrimental. Prior to the fight, Janiro had attracted the attention of Jake's young teenage wife, Vicki. Her simple remark about how good looking he was landed Tony in some hot water with LaMotta. The remark, along with his playboy reputation of scoring outside the ring, sent the jealous husband into one of his well-known rages. When the two met in the ring shortly thereafter, LaMotta vented his pent-up feelings in a brutal beating of the Youngstown product. Tony lasted the full ten rounds against the tough LaMotta but lost a unanimous decision. It appeared that LaMotta prolonged the fight in order to inflict more punishment. Graphic scenes of the pounding Tony received are featured in the movie *Raging Bull*. The young boxer from Ohio then won his following six fights, and up next was LaVern Roach.

Although LaVern was the new kid on the block, the former Marine was nearly a year older than his opponent. LaVern was a little over a month away from his twenty-third birthday while his counterpart was a couple of weeks away from his twenty-second.

Youthfulness wasn't the only similarity. Angelo, now with the newly acquired title of "sports promoter," used their good looks as a promotional tool as he wrote his press release. "This promises to be one of the most interesting matches of the year, the two best-looking fighters in the business are meeting. Both are young and ambitious—eager to get ahead in their profession."[4]

As a general rule, handsome faces and boxing don't go together. The countless pounding a fighter takes to his face often results in disfigured features, including cauliflower ears, broken noses, missing teeth, and scars. Both young men had been able to avoid this downside. Dark, wavy hair and handsome features described both.

Each shared a similar style of boxing, using speed and savvy. LaVern had the edge in pure skill while Tony was given the nod in ruggedness. Neither was known for his dynamite punches.

Having entered the ranks of professional boxing much earlier than LaVern, the pride of Youngstown sported an eye-popping 63-4 record. LaMotta was the only loss in which he had not settled the score. To his credit, he had already appeared in fourteen pro fights in the Garden. His manager, Frankie Jacobs, also served as vice president of the New York Boxing Managers' Guild, which helped his chances of using Garden bouts for his fights. Even though Garden bouts took place frequently, Jacobs never forgot those little clubs where Tony got his start. He would still schedule fights at such locales. LaVern's only previous experience in the mecca of the boxing world was winning the Golden Gloves champion as a Marine pugilist.

Due to his greater experience as a professional, Tony started the week of the fight as a two-to-three favorite, but at post time the odds had shifted, making him only a slight six-to-five choice over the Texan.

Major differences existed in each athlete's preparation. Tony, living up to his playboy reputation outside the ring, was known for his lackadaisical approach to training, which tended to drive his no-nonsense trainer, Ray Arcel, crazy. On the other hand, LaVern was known for his ability to always stay in fighting condition. Arcel would have rather trained LaVern. Another big advantage for LaVern, according to trainer Goldman, was that LaVern had brains, a commodity not always found in fighters.

A funny incident occurred with Tony a few years earlier, causing his manager to question either Janiro's intelligence or lack of knowledge on current affairs. The story goes that on March 9, 1945, then vice president Harry Truman was in attendance at Madison Square Garden for the featured fight between Rocky Graziano and Billy Arnold. Truman, an avid boxing enthusiast and Arnold fan, had been in the audience for the preliminary bout which featured Janiro. Mr. Truman had been so impressed with Tony's fighting that he had asked to meet him. Tony obliged, and after an introductory "Nice to meetcha," a handshake, a few photos, and a concluding "Nice to meetcha," Tony continued on his way to his dressing room. His manager asked him how it felt to shake the hand of the vice president. The now duly impressed young boxer asked, "You mean that man is the vice president of Madison Square Garden?" "Naw, ya dope," replied his manager, "he's the vice president of the United States." "Gee," said Tony, "I didn't know that."[5]

With only two weeks of preparation before fight night, LaVern and his team of John Abood, Charley Goldman, and Chris and Angelo Dundee had their work cut out for them. They all knew the importance of this event. A victory over Janiro would guarantee a top-ten ranking, with the possibility of a title bout on the horizon.

The most suitable sparring partners were brought in for LaVern to train with in preparation for the fight. LaVern expressed his prefight feelings to Choc:

> Say Choc I'll be training with all of the top boys out here so use your own judgment and write what you want to. It won't matter much what you say so you do what you think is best. Use Randy Brown, Sonny Horne, Georgie Small, Herbie Morris, Harold Anspach or anybody you can think of as these guys I'm working with. The more you put in the [Lubbock] paper the wider awake Plainview will get. I'm in good condition and will be real sharp for the fight. I'm working on speed and counter punching mostly.

LaVern continued,

> Choc, this fight is really important to me and if I beat him I'll really be set. He's a good boy and I'm really going to have to put out to beat him, but I think I can do it. Guess we'll all know more about that the 17th. Keep your fingers crossed.[6]

This letter expressed three aspects about LaVern's state of mind as he approached this fight. One, he was not taking his opponent lightly. Two, it was evident through this letter and others he wrote that he felt largely ignored by his hometown folks and newspaper. Three, as with many sports figures, he had a certain amount of superstition and routinely used the statement, "Keep your fingers crossed and wish me luck."

Choc, after writing his articles about LaVern for the *Lubbock Avalanche Journal,* sent him copies along with words of encouragement. LaVern, a prolific letter writer to family and friends, always responded. Three days before the fight, he wrote,

> Dear Choc, thanks for the clippings and the encouragement. Just hope I don't let all of you down Friday night, for this is my big break. I'm in top shape so if I have the ability I think I'll do O.K. Just keep your fingers crossed and say some prayers, for everything depends on this fight. Choc, I can't get my mind on writing now, for I'm on edge and kinda jumpy. Just bear with me this time and I'll try to do better next time. Keep your fingers crossed and please send me all the clippings you find.[7]

Even though he continued the training routine he had started as a kid in Plainview of getting up at six, putting in three to four miles of roadwork in the morning, two meals a day, boxing and exercise in the afternoon, and getting ten hours of sleep, LaVern always found time to write his family and friends, often as many as ten letters a day.

His training was going well, and he was in top form. In a letter to Choc, on the day before the fight, he wrote,

> Well, Buddy, thanks again for the clippings and I hope when you get this you've heard me beat Janiro. I'm in perfect condition and really feel good so if I don't beat him, it will be because I don't have the ability. Maybe the Good Lord will give me the strength to win, for I sure do need this win.[8]

LaVern had an unassuming confidence in his own ability and felt he could win any fight, even though he exposed a certain amount of insecurity to Choc. He also felt it wouldn't hurt to have a little help from above.

As the night approached, the New York press was doing everything it could to promote the fight. Hollywood could not have written a better script. There was LaVern Roach, the small-town boy from Plainview, Texas: clean-cut, handsome, with that all-American look and smile who served his country proudly as a Marine. He was known not to drink, smoke, womanize, or even curse. According to Angelo Dundee, "He was a breath of fresh air to a sport in trouble."[9]

Even though the oddsmakers had Tony picked to win the battle of the two young stars, it was a slim margin and not everyone agreed. One reason had to do with respective weights. All except five of Tony's fights had been in the welterweight division, and Tony was not accustomed to fighting in the middleweight division. Earlier in the week a sportswriter for the *New York Enquirer* wrote, "If he continues at the pace he set last year, Roach will probably send Tony whimpering back to the welts for cover."[10]

At the prefight weigh-in with Dr. Vincent Nardiello, a look of concern or nervousness was detected on Janiro's face as he tipped the scales at 153¼ pounds. LaVern, on the other hand, appeared to be calm, relaxed, and jovial as he weighed in at 155½, giving him a slight edge in the weight category.

The day of the fight, LaVern's confidence was bolstered by a couple of dozen telegrams wishing him good luck. Among the senders were his aunts and uncles from Plainview, former teammates Johnny Kostas and Howie Brodt, former Marine skippers, and Choc Hutcheson.

Tony Janiro, LaVern's toughest challenge to date, was clad in dark trunks. The referee for the main attraction of the evening in the Garden was Art Donovan. The two judges were Arthur Susskind and Harold Barnes. The ring announcer was Don Dunphy. On hand to witness the fight were 11,924 fans. The gate was $47,702.

The opening bell rang, and the fight began with Tony landing the first blow, a glancing left hook to the side of LaVern's head that did no damage. LaVern countered with a short left to Tony's jaw. LaVern continued scoring both body and head shots. One of the head shots drew first blood from Tony's nose. Round one went to LaVern as he set the pace for the rest of the fight.

The second round continued with LaVern as the aggressor, offering combination body and head shots. Tony backpedaled for most of the round. Round two easily went to LaVern.

Janiro came out swinging in the third, landing more punches and even staggering Roach momentarily. It appeared Janiro was going to make a

fight out of it after all. Even though LaVern drew more blood from Tony's nose, the round went to Tony on all scoring cards. The momentum
had shifted to Janiro while LaVern hung on with a minimum amount of
damage.

With solid lefts and rights to the face, LaVern regained control as
round four progressed. By the end of the round, more blood was oozing
from Tony's nose as Roach continued as the aggressor. Janiro had trouble
escaping the barrage of body shots; LaVern won the round.

Tony once again tried to bring the fight to LaVern, but each time he
attacked, LaVern did a good job of tying him up. There was a lot of hitting
and missing with both fighters. Being on the defensive for most of the
round, LaVern ended the round chasing Janiro into a corner. Both judges
gave the round to Janiro, although Donovan saw it differently and awarded the round to the Texan.

Barring a knockout and with half the fight over, the advantage clearly
belonged to LaVern. With LaVern's history of taking control of a fight in
the later rounds, the outcome was not looking good for Tony.

Momentum continued for the Texan, as he started the sixth with a jar-
ring right that landed on Janiro's jaw and quickly followed up with several
left jabs. "Roach rattled Janiro's molars with the first good punch in the
sixth and from that point there was little hope for Tony."[11] After six full
rounds, it was apparent to Janiro's handlers that their fighter was in trouble.

Leading the fight by a comfortable margin, LaVern tried to speed up
the action in round seven. He was successful landing hits with his left and
throwing effective rights. Tony began showing signs of tiring. The round
went to LaVern.

Tony started round eight by throwing two left hooks. LaVern deflect-
ed both. Then twice Roach beat him to the punch with left jabs followed
up by a left and a right that seemed to shake any confidence that Janiro
might have left in him. As the round progressed, LaVern seemed to be
getting stronger. It was another round for him. Obvious frustration was
building in Janiro.

As round nine started, a knockout was Tony's only chance of winning.
Somehow able to gather every ounce of energy left, he stood toe to toe
with the Texan and exchanged blow for blow. Both landed and took lefts
to the jaw, but neither was able to take the other out. His impressive re-

Janiro, Roach, Referee Art Donovan. Courtesy of the LaVern Roach family.

bound was enough to convince both judges in scoring the round in Tony's favor, but the referee awarded it to LaVern.

LaVern led eight rounds to one on the referee's card and seven to two on the judges'. This is the moment he had been training for since the first time he boxed. Only three minutes separated him from contender status and perhaps even a shot at the world championship. On the other side of the ring stood the disappointed pride of Youngstown, knowing what he had to do to win but not feeling good about his chances. He hadn't suffered defeat since his loss to LaMotta.

The bell rang as the two fighters battled evenly through the last round, with LaVern taking a slight edge with his counterpunching, able to keep Tony off balance for a good part of the round. Neither was able to knock the other one down, and both fighters were still standing at the end of the fight. LaVern looked fresh but was tired. This was only the fifth time he had gone a full ten rounds in the ring. The referee and both judges gave him round ten. Tony was much worse for wear, sporting a bloody nose to show it.

They flung their arms around each other, as was the custom of fistic warriors at the end of a battle. Instead of celebrating, LaVern walked Tony back to his corner, consoling him.

The near capacity crowd, upon hearing announcer Harry Balogh proclaim LaVern the winner by a unanimous decision, gave both men a tremendous ovation as the two headed to their respective locker rooms. For the victor, the atmosphere was one of joy and celebration. For the loser, it was a locker room full of anguish and silence.

It was a shocking defeat for Janiro. In one sense, it was even more devastating than the defeat at the hands of Jake LaMotta. This was a fight he was expected to win. In his locker room, Tony seemed to be talking to himself: "I knew what I wanted to do, but I couldn't do it. He licked me, that is all." He was then asked by a reporter, "Do you think your showy mode of living between fights caught up with you?" Tony answered quite candidly, "If great trainers [alluding to Ray Arcel] know what they're talking about, it's so."

With the reality of the loss sinking in, Tony finally turned to his trainer and asked the question to which he feared the answer: "You're not going to quit me, are you?" Arcel was quick to assure Tony that he wouldn't, but then issued a stern warning: "You can't play and fight though." Tony seemed to get the message.[12]

The only consolation for Tony and his handlers was their take of the gate. In order to get the fight, LaVern's brain trust of Chris Dundee and Johnny Abood had to guarantee Tony fifteen thousand dollars. LaVern, after expenses and taxes, walked away with somewhere between three thousand and four thousand dollars. From the excitement and celebration in LaVern's locker room, you would have thought he had earned a million.

Over in the winner's dressing room the Texan beamed. "This was the one I had to make a good showing in," LaVern said quietly. "It was the chance that I dreamed about since I began fighting back in Texas as a schoolboy at the age of twelve as a sixty-five-pound kid. I knew I had to look good in the Garden if I wanted to get anywhere as a fighter and I'm very happy I won as I did."

And then his mind flashed back to the folks back home. "I guess my mother and dad, my girlfriend Evelyn, and my relatives are all pretty happy right now. They were all listening in at my girlfriend's house—she lives out in the country in Plainview and there is no static out there."[13]

LaVern continued to hold court in his dressing room as he was handed telegram after telegram congratulating him on his performance. Many of his fans listened to the fight on the radio and were quick to send the congratulatory notes. Most came from friends and relatives from Lubbock and Plainview, including those from Choc and O. R. Stark, the boys of Texas Tech, and one from tiny, remote Comanche, Texas. He made no move to rush to the showers, taking advantage of his moment to shine. As manager John Abood rubbed his chest down with alcohol, LaVern told his story to the press, in his soft and modest way without any signs of arrogance in his voice. New York sportswriter Lester Bromberg described the scene: "The former leatherneck staff sergeant, obviously a thinking fighter, dazzled interviewers with a crystal-clear analysis of how he made Tony, a fast puncher, look slow." As LaVern assessed the fight,

> He hesitated after punching and my hands were generally in proper position to counter. He stands too stiff, too much arm in his punching. He hits from the hip. He's too wide to hit at because he doesn't pivot and turn his body in." Then LaVern gave an imitation of Tony that was much more than a reasonable facsimile. Thereupon Roach, like an instructor in mass boxing, a job he held at the Marine Air Station, Cherry Point, N.C. submitted a critique on the tactical situation as it worked out, to wit: "I had him coming to me in the first two rounds

but he gave me a going-over in the third (Janiro's best round) because I was going for his feints and coming in. So I met his feints with feints and he began coming to me again. It was no trouble after that.[14]

Bromberg then summed up his observation: "It was so remarkable an impromptu lecture that Janiro should have been in the room to hear it. Roach, a 155½ pounder, with a full middleweight's height and reach, clicked solidly with the crowd. And with good reason. The Rookie of 1947 may well become the Fighter of 1948."[15]

The press did not let up on Tony. Bill Corum, a noted columnist, praised LaVern for his training techniques and condemned Tony for his. His advice to Tony:

> Take a vacation away from the bright lights, and then return to try again. He has so much to offer in the way of boxing. It seems a shame to see him go to pot by the time he has come of age. I take nothing away from Roach, who is coming even faster than Tony is backing up, and who fights with the dash of the Marine Corps in which he served, and the determination of a true Texan, Texas being his home state. The difference is the 22-year-old Roach makes a job of his job. Whereas Janiro finds it only an easy way to make more money in order to have more fun. Roach in his first "main" in the Garden was much cooler and smarter than Janiro, who'd been in that spot nine times before. The Texas thumper won it from here back to Plainview, Texas, and that dear Plainview is a long "fur piece" away.[16]

Leonard Cohen of the *New York Post* all but wrote an obituary for Tony in his newspaper column, saying that Tony was all washed up and if he were smart, he would quit now:

> Tony the Beautiful was a rather sorry-looking mess most of the way, as the blood from his nose was smeared over his classic features. At times he stopped and spat blood in the ring canvas. It wasn't pretty to see—and it isn't a pretty thing to write. It isn't pretty to look at. All the world loves a winner in sports, especially when he's a good, clean-cut lad such as LaVern Roach proved himself to be at the Garden last night.[17]

Lewis Burton added the finishing touch to an already mounting barrage of criticism for Tony: "The District Attorney should investigate who stole the fists out of Tony Janiro's gloves."[18] Tony didn't hang up his gloves, but he took the next three months off. Whether he took trainer Ray Arcel's or sportswriter Bill Corum's advice on his life outside the ring, or LaVern's critique of his fighting style inside the ring, is unknown, but Tony went on to win seven of his next eight fights and became a legitimate contender for the middleweight crown.

LaVern's biggest reward for his victory over Janiro was being cited as a "top-ten" challenger for the middleweight crown by the *Ring*. Roach had reached that level of professional boxing to which so many aspire, but few succeed. Unlike the fictitious Terry Malloy played by Marlon Brando in the movie *On the Waterfront*, who complained to his brother, "I coulda had class. I coulda been a contender. I coulda been somebody,"[19] LaVern was now a contender. He was already a somebody. More importantly, he exhibited class, inside and outside the ring.

One reporter wrote, "Lavern Roach, Texas' current gift to the boxing big-time, has apparently breathed new life into the professional fight game—which for several years now has needed a breath of fresh air badly."[20] Another echoed the praise: "It took a World War to bring LaVern Roach and Johnny Abood together. The association has been good for both, to say nothing of the badly wounded fight game and the Roach family. With a demand to drive the underworld characters out of the business, it is refreshing to have a pair of Marines like Roach and Abood. It has been quite a spell since Cauliflower Alley has had a team as good looking as Roach and Abood, and they look enough alike to be brothers. Both are blue-eyed, sandy-haired, five-foot 10 and just under 160 pounds."[21]

Even the *New Yorker*, not known for its sports coverage or love of boxing, wrote, "He has class and confidence and poise and he ought to stick around a good while and earn himself a tidy stack of chips."[22] The sport of boxing had apparently found its next golden boy.

The newspapers continued analyzing the Roach/Janiro fight for several days after the event. LaVern became the talk of the town. In one article titled, "Latest Hit on the Talent Parade," the writer called the young man from Texas, "the hottest thing in the boxing world." He described Roach not as a modest man, but one who recognized his ability and was confident in his future. He was a guy who was quick to give someone else all the credit for his success. The man who brought him to the top, taught him all he knows was Johnny Abood."

The article continued with praise of Abood, relating how the wealthy businessman took care of his young prizefighters with good living quarters and surroundings, knowing from his personal experience in the trade how they were easy prey for the gangsters, has-beens, and pugs that are associated with the sport. "Roach insists that Abood has been like a father to him, has never and will never exploit a fighter for personal gains, and is the reason for his being where he is today. With that kind of back, how can a guy lose?"[23]

Another journalist was just as quick to give LaVern star quality. "What does make a fighter? If LaVern is to be taken as an example, it takes will power, guts, perseverance, intelligence, and above all, confidence in one's own ability to win both in and out of the ring. His is the life of a story-book athlete; the next idol of the nation's kids. LaVern Roach presents that rare picture of the 'all-American,' fighting a tough racket, in and out of the ring, and winning his battle with spectacular ease."[24]

Lavern's rise to stardom coincided with the sport's fading reputation due to the antics of Graziano and LaMotta. At a time when boxing had received a black eye, a real-live Joe Palooka was in the offing. Although it didn't seem like it to LaVern, who had been training for this moment for over a decade, the media looked at his victory as an overnight success story.

Although the Janiro fight failed to produce the monetary rewards LaVern hoped for, it was the catalyst that opened the door for his next fight and pushed him to the forefront of a quest for the world championship. the *Ring* named him Boxer of the Month for January along with his new status as a "top-ten" contender. The Texan felt that Cerdan could no longer avoid him. A bout with Cerdan could possibly determine the championship or at least set up a championship bout for the winner. LaVern climbed the next fistic ladder of success, that of a contender.

After having time to digest his victory over Janiro, LaVern wrote Choc,

> Well, I finally made the grade, it looks like. Thanks anyway Choc for
> that nice letter. I'll save it, for there'll be a day. Guess all of you were
> excited for they say it sounded pretty good. We have it recorded, so
> when I come home we'll be able to listen to it. Say, Plainview is giving
> me some kind of a home coming, I think. Don't mention it unless you

Gus Lesnevich, LaVern, and Jersey Joe Wolcott receiving awards at the Annual Boxing Writers Association Awards Dinner, January 18, 1948. Lesnevich received the Edward J. Neil Memorial Plaque and Boxer of the Year award. LaVern received the Rookie of the Year award. Wolcott received the Outstanding Performance of the Year award. Courtesy of the LaVern Roach family.

> find out for sure, cause I'm not certain. That will be nice if they do want it. I was voted "Rookie of the Year," so I guess they are giving me a baseball home coming. Only kidding for I'll be a happy guy if they do. Of course I won't get a big car like the baseball players, but it would be nice just to know that the people are interested.[25]

Once again, LaVern expressed his insecurity and the desire for hometown recognition that he longed for.

The reference to baseball players was due to the surge in popularity that the sport had experienced in 1947 at boxing's expense. Jackie Robinson broke the color barrier, and baseball joined boxing as an integrat-

POLICE GAZETTE GALLERY
MIDDLEWEIGHT STARS

LAVERN ROACH (right)—The best Marine fighter to come out of World War II has shown much of the ambition which made a great fighter out of Gene Tunney, Marine star of World War I. He labored long to correct his faults. And he made conditioning a ritual. He has become a remarkably clever boxer as well as a fine judge of pace and distance. His victory over Tony Janiro showed him at his best, to date.

LAVERN ROACH

TONY ZALE (left)—The Man of Steel from Gary, Ind., will be remembered for all time as one of the most durable and bravehearted men ever to hold the middleweight championship. He invariably takes a beating to hand out one, but his determination carries him beyond the limits of ordinary endurance. His first title match with Rocky Graziano saw him come back from a near-knockout to win by a knockout. His second produced a thriller in which he nearly pulled the title out of the fire.

TONY ZALE

LaVern Roach, Tony Zale (above), Marcel Cerdan, and Rocky Graziano (on the following page), Middleweight Stars. Reprinted by permission of the *National Police Gazette*.

MARCEL CERDAN (right)—The spectacular North African is a picture-book action fighter. He comes weaving in, low and ready to punch from all angles. He doesn't pack a knockout wallop in a single punch but overwhelms an opponent with a series of smashes. Cerdan, a Free French sailor in the last war, long has been a popular favorite in Paris. He made his reputation in America by defeating Georgie Abrams and went on to further conquests in the U. S.

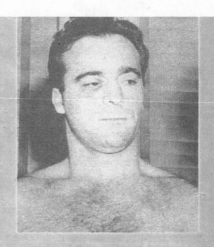

MARCEL CERDAN

ROCKY GRAZIANO (left)—The middleweight champion has run afoul of regulations after a comeback saga that thrilled the ring. Rated a has-been a couple of years ago, Graziano catapulted to fame on his knockout of Billy Arnold and parlayed that success into a capture of the title at Chicago last summer after a rebuff in New York the previous summer. He is a deadly puncher with his right hand and, in shape, combines the fury of Jack Dempsey with Luis Firpo.

ROCKY GRAZIANO

ed sport. The World Series between the Yankees and Dodgers was the first to be televised. War hero Ted Williams, despite winning the Triple Crown, was edged out by Joe DiMaggio for the American League MVP Award by one point. With Joe Louis passing his prime and the disgraces of Graziano and LaMotta, baseball players replaced boxers as the top sports figures.

On Sunday evening, January 18, the Tenth Annual Boxing Writers Association Award Dinner was held at Ruppert's. Restricted to two hundred, only the elite connected with the world of boxing were invited. LaVern was in attendance to receive his Rookie of the Year award, presented to him by Nat Fleischer. Other award recipients included Gus Lesnevich (Ed Neil Memorial Plaque), Jim Farley (James J. Walker Memorial Award), Jersey Joe Wolcott (the *Ring*'s medal for outstanding performance against Joe Louis), and Al Buck (for long and meritorious service as president of the BWA). Guest speakers included District Attorney Frank Hogan, Mayor William O'Dwyer, New Jersey boxing commissioner Abe J. Greene, former New York City police commissioner Edward P. Mulrooney, Milton Berle, and Joe Louis. The toastmaster of the event was James P. Dawson, boxing editor of the *New York Times*.

Represented at the event were six of the eight current world champions: Louis, Lesnevich, Graziano, Robinson, Ike Williams, and Willie Pep, in addition to former champs Jim Braddock and Gene Tunney (all future Hall of Fame members). The kid from Texas was not only rubbing elbows with the best of the best, he was one of them. Fresh off of his victory over Janiro less than forty-eight hours earlier, he was a hit at the event, with everyone wanting to meet the newcomer.[26] Receiving the Rookie of the Year award and fraternizing with boxing's elite was the crowning event for the perfect season, yet it never went to his head and he never even mentioned the occasion in his letters to Choc.

Since his Christmas and New Year holidays were cut short, LaVern made plans to return home, awaiting his next bout. On January 26, he wrote Choc,

> I am anxious for the 12th to come for I may get to go home for a week. Hope so for I'm sure lonesome for that little woman of mine. She and I will run down to Lubbock & chat with you for a while, as soon as I get there, if we possibly can. Someone said something about a home coming for me, but that's the last thing I'd ever get in PV. Guess I

should have been a baseball player, for then I'd get big cars and everything. It doesn't matter to me though, for I know who my real friends are.

Contrary to his written words, it did matter what people thought, and he yearned for hometown recognition. LaVern then quickly changed the subject as he related to Choc his talent in yet another sport:

> Say, I bowled 19 games the last two days and averaged 181. Not bad is it? I've just found out how to bowl after so long a time, & I actually believe I can average close to 200 if I keep bowling. Guess I need 3 arms to pat myself on the back, don't you? Ha!
>
> P.S. I have a complete recording of the fight, and it's pretty good. Dunphy favored Janiro the first 7 rounds, didn't he? "Off the record."[27]

The future had never looked brighter for LaVern. His fight with Janiro received more media coverage than the previous month's fight between Joe Louis and Jersey Joe Wolcott. In their February edition, the *National Police Gazette*, in a two-page article, highlighted four middleweight stars of the day with individual photos and a short write-up of each. LaVern was listed first, followed by Tony Zale, Marcel Cerdan, and Rocky Graziano. No mention was made of Jake LaMotta.

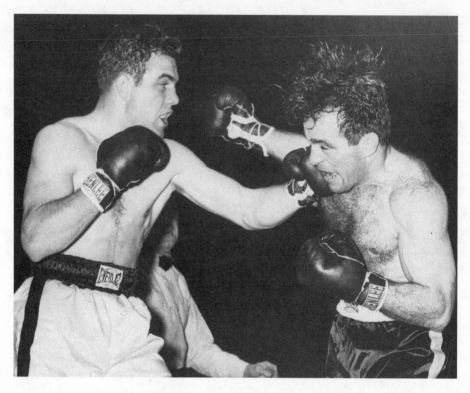

LaVern landing a left to Marcel Cerdan, March 12, 1948, at Madison Square Garden, New York City. Reprinted by permission of AP Images.

CHAPTER 11

Marcel Cerdan, the French Connection

A champion is someone who gets up when he can't.
—*Jack Dempsey*

The middleweight boxing division was in a state of confusion. It was recently disclosed that Rocky Graziano, the reigning champ, was a known AWOL army offender. Even before this news hit the stands, he was suspended by the New York Boxing Commission for failing to report offers of money to throw a fight. It was still up in the air if he could keep his crown. Among the leading contenders for the crown were Cerdan; Tony Zale, who had lost the championship to Graziano; Jake LaMotta, who was suspended and may have disqualified himself since he was under investigation for possibly throwing his recent fight against Fox; and LaVern.

Sol Strauss, in the absence of boxing promoter Mike Jacobs, was now calling the shots at the Twentieth Century Sporting Club, the syndicate that controlled big-time boxing promotion in New York City. Strauss suggested a Cerdan-Roach fight in the Garden. Upon hearing this, Chris Dundee, willing to think it over, responded, "One thing is certain; Roach isn't going to give Cerdan all the money. We gambled at the gate with Janiro and just about broke even. I'd rather he'd fight Rocky Graziano for the title, or maybe Tony Zale. He's willing to fight Cerdan, but not for nothing."[1] A fight with Zale was doubtful as he had a reputation of being very selective on who he got in the ring with. LaVern had previously served as Zale's sparring partner and had more than held his own with Zale. Word got out that Zale didn't want to fight the much younger Roach.[2]

Twentieth Century Sporting Club was founded in 1933 by Mike

Press ticket to the Roach/Cerdan fight. Courtesy of the LaVern Roach Family.

Jacobs. Jacobs, a protégé of the legendary Tex Rickard, the sport's first great promoter, secured the rights to promote live events in Madison Square Garden in 1925. Rickard died in 1929, leaving his operation to Jacobs, who proved to be as shrewd a businessman as Tex. His biggest coup was a business deal with Joe Louis in 1935, giving him the rights to promote and stage all of Louis's championship bouts. This arrangement provided the influence needed to control all title bouts for all divisions. No championship match took place in the Garden without his blessing. Jacobs suffered a cerebral hemorrhage in 1946, giving temporary control to Sol Strauss, a relative of Jacobs.

As usual, the Twentieth Century Sporting Club got its way. Even though the contract was not signed by both camps until February 10, word leaked out. On January 28, the headlines in New York City and Paris papers read, "Roach to Fight Cerdan March 12th." European middleweight champion and the former Marine champion were scheduled to fight a ten-round main event in Madison Square Garden, with the winner getting a shot at the world middleweight crown or possibly even being crowned champion as a result of this match, depending on the results of the boxing commission investigation of the Graziano debacle.

Prior to signing the contract and before financial arrangements were agreed to, Chris Dundee and Johnny Abood were working behind the scenes to see if a championship fight with Graziano was possible. They were informed by boxing authorities that a championship bout with Graziano was out of the question for LaVern or anyone else until Graziano's championship status was cleared up. "LaVern could have had Graziano this spring. It would have been a nontitle fight in Washington where Sonny Horne fights Rocky April 25. Instead they chose Cerdan in the Garden."[3]

Based on both boxers' previous histories in the Garden, the fight was expected to gross one hundred thousand dollars at the gate. The Roach-Janiro bout drew a crowd of almost twelve thousand. Both of Cerdan's wins in the Garden over Georgie Abrams and Harold Green also were good draws. Financial agreements were made and contracts signed, with Cerdan receiving 30 percent of the gate to LaVern's 25 percent. Win or lose, each would walk away with a good chunk of money. Both money and a step closer to the coveted championship were motivating factors for LaVern. The prize for Cerdan was the step closer to the championship. Money was not an issue. "Cerdan turned down an offer of 16 million francs ($160,000) to stay in Paris for five fights under Jo Longman's promotion. The Casablanca clouter has millions of francs. What he wants before he retires is the world 160-pound crown."[4]

LaVern's plans to go home and see Evelyn, family, and friends were put on hold. His handlers had a different idea for their boxer:

> Choc, I'm sorry I won't be able to come home before March, but when I do I'll be able to stay awhile. From what I hear a bunch of businessmen are coming out for the Cerdan Fight & I wish it was so you could make it. Maybe next summer you and Stark can come out if I'm lucky enough to get a Yankee Stadium fight. If I beat Cerdan, it's practically a certainty. Keep your fingers crossed and wish me luck for I'm going to need a lot of it.
>
> Choc, I'm fighting Al Thornton in Miami, Fla. Feb. 18th. It's going to be a good fight but I should beat him alright if nothing happens.[5]

Whether a calculated risk or a gutsy call, scheduling a warm-up fight prior to the Cerdan bout raised more than a few eyebrows. Neither Abood nor Dundee seemed to have second thoughts, however. They originally wanted a fight in New York City, but plans changed at the last minute as they signed for LaVern to fight Thornton in the featured bout at Flamingo Park, Miami Beach, to take place on February 20. LaVern did not protest, as he had complete confidence in his brain trust. His biggest concern was not being able to see Evelyn.

This disappointment lessened as he got word from home, which he relayed to Choc:

> Say, I think Evelyn is coming out here for the fight & I'm hoping she does. She's never seen me fight & besides it will be nice for her to meet John and everybody out here. If she doesn't get to come out, I'm

going to be terribly disappointed for I am sure planning on her. Her mother, Mrs. Herbert Castleberry may come with her & I sure hope she can, for neither of them have ever been out East.[6]

LaVern was set to depart for Miami the following week, when he received news that Evelyn wasn't going to be able to come after all. His upbeat mood quickly shifted upon hearing the news. A couple of days later, still prior to his departure for Miami, some welcomed news came:

> Choc, I heard from Forrest, "my uncle," & he said they have decided to let her come out. Boy I hope so for I really miss that little devil. She's a wonderful girl Choc, & didn't deserve the tough break she got, but everyone is entitled to a mistake. Hope I can make her a good husband, for I know I could never find one who will make a better wife.

In the same letter, LaVern mentioned that his stock was rising:

> Say Choc, Ring Magazine has me rated 10th & as "Fighter of the month." So I hear. They aren't out yet so its off the record until I hear for sure. Did you see *Sporting News* with the write up? Wasn't bad was it?[7]

On February 9, John and LaVern made the trip to Miami Beach and settled into the Mayflower Hotel in preparation for the Thornton fight. LaVern was surprised at the heat and how different the climate was. That same day, across the Atlantic in Paris, Cerdan, taking the same chance or calculated risk of losing a bout before his matchup with LaVern, scored a four-round knockout over a lesser opponent.

In Miami, the anticipated crowd of twelve thousand with a gate of forty thousand dollars never materialized. Instead a disappointing turnout of twenty-three hundred showed up to watch the match. On the day of the fight, a Miami newspaper write-up read, "With everything to lose and nothing to gain except a $5,000 check, LaVern Roach squares off with Al Thornton tonight in the feature of four ten-rounders."[8]

LaVern, fresh off his upset win over Janiro, was highly favored. Thornton, sporting a 10-3 record, was on the same fighting card as the Janiro-Roach fight, losing to William Poli in a four-round preliminary. The article continued, "Thornton who recently beat Freddie Flores, after losing a close one to Pete Mead, admires Roach's boxing ability, but does not think the Plainview flash can knock him out."

LaVern, while in Miami for the Thornton bout, revealed his self-confidence and future ambition in an interview with a local sportswriter. "Roach is one of the few fighters who exude confidence without being cocky." Asked if he thinks he can lick the European middleweight champion, Roach smiled and replied, "I wouldn't have accepted the fight if I didn't think I could win."

The writer continued, "Roach, who was the hottest number produced in pro pugilism last year, likes fighting but only as a means to an end. When he makes enough money, he'll go into the ranching business." In the same interview, comanager Chris Dundee asked LaVern, "You'd like to win the middleweight championship before you quit, wouldn't you?"

"Certainly," Roach agreed. "But I am not going to fight too long. I sort of think I'd like to become a cattleman. There is money in cattle."[9]

In their initial training sessions in Miami Beach, both fighters put on impressive performances. LaVern was reported being sharp as a tack, doing no wrong. "His timing and footwork were excellent and he continually belted his sparring mates with both hands."

These words came from the opponent's observer: "Thornton was almost as impressive as he works with Chico Pacheco and Oswaldo Silva. The Rochester, Pa., clouter landed some rocking blows in his workout."[10]

LaVern took charge as he won the first two rounds. The third round was a draw, with LaVern coming back and winning the fourth. The fifth round once again was a draw. LaVern, as he was accustomed to doing, came back strong in the sixth round with his left jabs and a solid right to Thornton's heart. The seventh round started with LaVern landing a shower of lefts and rights to Thornton's head and face. By the end of the frame, Thornton's left eye was nearly swollen shut, causing ring doctor Leo Honigsberg, official boxing commission physician, to stop the fight. LaVern was awarded a TKO for his nineteenth consecutive victory and his twenty-fourth victory out of twenty-five professional fights.

With the knockout, LaVern proved Thornton wrong. The AP write-up in Saturday's morning news summed it up: "LaVern Roach, sensational young middleweight from Plainview, Texas, annexed another scalp to his belt here Friday night. Roach hung a technical knockout on Al Thornton in the seventh round in a ten-round fight at Flamingo Park before a disappointing turnout of 2,300 fans."[11]

With the Miami and Paris fights out of the way, there was nothing to prevent the match with the European middleweight champion and number-four contender, Marcel Cerdan, from taking place on March 12 at the Garden. The winner of the Roach-Cerdan fight would be rated as the top contender for Rocky Graziano's suspension-tainted world championship.

The two most famous people to come out of Casablanca, Morocco, during the first half of the twentieth century were Rick Blaine, the fictional American expatriate and owner of the Café Americain, played by Humphrey Bogart in the movie *Casablanca*, and the real-life French Algerian Marcel Cerdan, who was known as Le Bombardier Morocain (the Moroccan Bomber) and the Casablanca Clouter.

Marcellin Cerdan was born on July 22, 1916, in Sidi Abbes, Algeria (French Algeria). When he was fifteen, Sidi Abbes became the location for the training of the French Foreign Legion and the headquarters of its First Foreign Regiment.

All his older brothers boxed, so young Marcel followed the family tradition. Before turning professional in 1934 at age seventeen, Marcel gained a lot of street-fighting experience against the young Arabs, who greatly outnumbered the French youth in Casablanca. Combining this boxing experience with playing league soccer, Marcel developed speed and footwork that would serve him well in the ring.

All of Cerdan's early fighting took place in and around Casablanca and Algeria, where he won his first nineteen bouts. The Parisians finally lured him to France, where he fought his first fight on the mainland on October 7, 1937, beating Louis Jampton. Then on February 21, 1938, Marcel beat Omar Kouidri in Casablanca for the French welterweight title. He ran his unbeaten streak to thirty-five before losing to Harry Craster in London on a disqualification on January 9, 1939. He rebounded from his first loss with six straight victories, culminating with a victory in Milan over the Italian favorite Saverio Turiello on June 3, adding the European welterweight title to go along with his French welterweight title. He fought just one more bout, winning on June 18, 1939, before joining the larger fight against Germany.

Shortly before his twenty-third birthday Marcel joined the French Navy, becoming one of many promising fighters who had their boxing careers either cut short or interrupted by the war. Like Rick Blaine, Marcel found himself leaving Paris and retreating to Casablanca. With the German troops invading France and their subsequent march into Paris on June 15, 1940, Marcel's boxing career was put on hold for eighteen months with a 53-1 record.

With the Germans still occupying France and Paris, Marcel was allowed to return to boxing in his birthplace of Casablanca in January 1941. He quickly picked up where he left off, winning sixteen straight fights before losing in the eighth round to Victor Buttin by a disqualification in Algiers. In an effort to show that life as usual was going on under German rule, Marcel was coaxed into returning to the ring in occupied France. He won fights in Nice and Marseille before returning to Paris. On September 30, 1942, Marcel was set to fight Jose Ferrer (not the movie actor) in Paris for the middleweight championship of Europe.

With both the French boxing fans and occupying German troops concerned about the fight lasting past the nightly curfew, Cerdan promised an early end. He kept his promise by knocking out Ferrer in just eighty-three seconds of round one. In the confusion, reminiscent of the Von Trapp family exit in *The Sound of Music*, Cerdan departed the arena and was able to get out of the country on a forged exit visa and returned to Casablanca. The Nazis, not pleased with the move, quickly awarded the questionable title to Ferrer.

Soon after his return, the Allied Forces invaded North Africa. Cerdan was allowed to join the Free French Navy and began fighting exhibition bouts in the former colonies in order to help raise funds for the underground resistance. He fought his next eleven matches on North African soil against members of the Allied Forces boxing teams, including some Americans, and was victorious against all. During this time period he added the Inter-Allied middleweight championship to his collection of trophies.

As the European stage of the war wound down, Marcel was boxing on the recaptured soil of the Allied Forces. He fought again in Paris as well as Rome. By the end of the war, he had a remarkable record of over seventy wins against only two losses, both by questionable disqualifications. In addition to regaining the French middleweight championship, his international reputation grew.

After the war, Cerdan continued boxing in Paris, with a couple of bouts in Spain and Portugal. He and his camp were ready to begin their invasion of the United States in a quest for the world middleweight title. Observing Cerdan and his conquests of European middleweights was Mike Jacobs, always looking for fighters to showcase in the Garden.

The Roach fight wasn't the first on American soil for Cerdan. The Frenchman's debut in the States was against Georgie Abrams, one of Chris Dundee's original Dandees. The twenty-six-year-old Abrams, a favorite of Chris's, sported an impressive 47-5-3 record. One of his losses was a 1941 Madison Square Garden fight against Tony Zale for the world middleweight title. Abrams started off strong by knocking down Zale in the first round for a nine-count. Zale recovered, and the two battled furiously for the full fifteen rounds. At the end of the fight Zale was the winner by a unanimous decision.

On December 6, 1946, in his fourth headliner bout in the Garden, Abrams fought Cerdan, who was making his first appearance in boxing's ultimate showcase before a crowd of 16,971. Many in attendance came to see how the Frenchman, with a sterling record of 97-2-0, would fare in the Garden against one of Amèrica's best.

The match was a bloody ten-round battle with Cerdan coming out on top with a unanimous decision, although many in attendance thought it a draw. He then returned to Paris just long enough to win the European middleweight title and quickly returned to the United States to continue his quest for the world title.

Next up were two American fighters, Harold Green and Anton Raadik, both expected to be formidable opponents. Marcel answered with a questionable second-round TKO of Green and a hard-fought ten-round unanimous decision over Raadik. Along with a few more European victories, these fights pushed Marcel's world ranking to number four among middleweights.

The Cerdan-Roach fight was the talk of the town. The headlines of the fight were dominating the sports pages all the way from Paris to New York City to Plainview. Marcel Cerdan was the reigning European and French middleweight champion. With a near perfect record of 105 wins against 2 losses, he was a heavy favorite against his much younger and relatively inexperienced American opponent.

Cerdan arrived in New York on February 28, twelve days before the bout. New York City was a backdrop to the circuslike atmosphere that surrounded the fight. You could not pick up a newspaper or magazine without seeing a photo of LaVern and Cerdan along with a four- to eight-column headline covering the upcoming match. Sportswriters were fighting for position to have the next interview with the boxers.

One newsperson with an inside track to LaVern, even though she knew

John Abood, Jane Miller, and LaVern at Stillman's Gym. Courtesy of the LaVern Roach family.

little of the boxing business, was Jane Miller of the Associated Press. Miller was the daughter of Mr. and Mrs. E. B. Miller of Plainview. Who better to interview the upcoming boxer than someone from his home-town? The Roach camp readily granted Miller and her associate, Mitchell Curtis, an interview and photograph session to take place at Stillman's Gym on March 3.

The headline for her interview read, "Interview Shows Roach Is Proud of Texas, Likes to Fight and Confident of Victory." In her article she de-scribed Stillman's Gym as "a Hollywood producer's dream of an intro-duction to the fight game." LaVern tried to apologize for having the in-terview at Stillman's, but Miller would have nothing of it. After all, it was her idea. She was appreciative of the fact that she had been one of the few, if not the first, females to hold an interview in the "center of the boxing universe"—smell, grime, and all.

She continued, "We found LaVern to be all that the sportswriters con-tend he is. Paramount, he is proud of being a Texan—secondly, he loves to fight. When I asked him about his opinion of a recent fight, he sorta grinned and said, 'I don't like to watch fights. I just like them when I'm in the ring.'"

She pressed him to comment on his recent win over Janiro, and the only response she received was, "He's a great little fighter with a hard punch. I enjoyed that fight more than any I ever had."[12]

Johnny Abood introduced Miller to trainer Charley Goldman as he gave LaVern some pointers on bobbing and weaving. As he was giving his instructions, she described the look on Charley's face as saying, "That's my boy."

She quoted Abood, "This is a fine business when you have a top boy; otherwise, it's tough. LaVern isn't afraid of anything—he knows what he can do and if that isn't enough, it just isn't."[13] LaVern showed the most ex-citement when the conversation turned to the Plainview group, who were chartering a plane to watch their local hero in action.

Mitchell Curtis, who accompanied Miller, filed his own AP report as well. The headline of his article, which appeared in print on March 8, read, "New York AP Man Comes Away Exhilarated after Interviewing LaVern Roach in Stillman's Gym." He started off his interview echoing Miller's comments: "Texans can be proud of LaVern Roach, win, lose, or draw with Marcel Cerdan in Madison Square Garden, New York on March 12." Curtis continued with a barrage of questions, quickly an-swered by Roach:

Curtis: "Can you lick Cerdan?"

Roach: "Well, this is the big one. I hope I can make it."

Curtis: "Are you going to spar today?"

Roach: "No. I'm in pretty good shape now. I don't want to fight my fight in the gym."

Curtis: "Are you thinking beyond the fight and victory?"

Roach: "Certainly. I am anxious to get back to Plainview and I'd like to play some golf. That's a great game."[14]

The interview moved to the second floor of the gym so LaVern could go through a routine of shadow boxing, skipping rope, rat-a-tat-tatting the small bag, and punching the large bag. As Curtis continued the ques-tioning, he observed that "LaVern was completely oblivious of the admiring glances from most of the fifty other boxers in the huge room. Even in this brief warming up, he paid attention only to what he was doing and heard only the few words of advice tossed occasionally by Goldman, who was walking around him in large circles."

The interview finished with a lunch, consisting of only potato soup for LaVern, and a rubdown by Abood. Conversation centered on the boxer's greatest pride, "being a Texan." When asked how the coming fight looked to him, Abood answered, "The kid is in good shape. We think we are going to win. We've got our strategy planned. We think it will work."[15]

The fight was set for Madison Square Garden on Friday night, March 12, 1948. LaVern wasn't the only one representing his home state in a sporting event that weekend at the Garden. The next night featured a sold-out basketball game highlighting two future pro all-stars and Hall of Fame basketball players. Slater Martin, five-foot-ten guard of the University of Texas, was leading his team against six-foot-seven Dolph Schayes's New York University in the semifinals of the National Invitation Tournament. The Plainview contingency, not scheduled to depart New York until Sunday morning, were successful in finding tickets to see a Texas team challenge a New York team on the basketball court. (NYU beat UT 45-43 on a shot with six seconds left.)

The local bookies made Cerdan a favorite by a two-to-one margin. Few gave LaVern any chance at all, although there were some notable exceptions. Lester Bromberg, boxing reporter for the *New York World-Telegram*, was the lone New York sportswriter to give the nod to LaVern. "Cerdan's attack—a hurricane of two-handed punching—can be hell in the ring for five rounds. This fight is ten rounds. Roach takes a punch and is styled to claw back and I think he can win."[16] Jack Hand, a New York sportswriter, chipped in, "This corner gives him a solid chance to do it."[17]

Georgie Abrams, familiar with both fighters, believed LaVern had a chance against the Frenchman. Cerdan in his first fight in the Garden on December 6, 1946, pulled out a narrow victory over Abrams. Abrams and LaVern had been sparring partners for a couple of years. "A tough nut to crack, he's so unorthodox and a pretty good belter," Abrams said, summing up Cerdan's boxing technique. "But LaVern is no soft touch. He's a natural infighter and counter fighter and he lets nobody take the play away from him." He went on to say, "Roach will have more stamina than I did. After all, I'm no kid. He's 10 years younger than Cerdan."[18]

Nearly everyone else thought LaVern was too inexperienced to handle Cerdan, but they thought the same when LaVern got into the ring with Janiro. Sportswriter Bill Corum of the *New York Journal-American* gave warning to the Frenchman's camp: "I think most people are under-rating the cocky, leather-throwing Lavern. He reminds me of Tunney in his quiet determination that destiny guides him toward his ultimate fate. He'll be in there punching from first bell till last—if he's around to hear it—and Mercurial Marcel had better be in top form for the encounter."[19]

New York sportswriters were having fun with the names of the boxers and the different backgrounds of the two. Lewis Burton of the *New York Journal-American* headlined his sports column on fight day as "What's in a Name? Marcel and Lavern, Not a Dance Team, But a Pair of Ring Title Seekers." He then wrote the following ode:

> For Joe, Jim, Jack, Bill, Will and Bob
> (He-man names that carry a throb),
> For Mickey, Harry, even Leach,
> Mourn with us, oh! Friends on the beach;
> We're rooting now for Marcel.
> For Tom, Fred, Stan, Butch, Slug and Tex
> (Who can tell what is coming next?)
> Mourn ye, for the terrible change;
> Look what they've sent up from the range:
> We're rooting now for Lavern.

He continued his entertainment in his column. "A couple of fellows named Marcel and LaVern simply had to be fighters. How else could they survive under such a handicap? Tonight, their paths cross. Marcel Cerdan, French Moroccan middleweight is an 11 to 5 favorite over the blue-eyed guy from where the deer and the antelope play, Lavern Roach of Plainview, Texas, in the top ten at Madison Square Garden."

Then he continued a bit more seriously, "Possibly under the mistaken notion that Marcel and Lavern are a dance team, 15,000 clients, grossing about $75,000 will attend. The embattled gentlemen are not only fast on their feet, however, but capable with their fists. The prize at stake is the number one rating for a shot at the middleweight championship owned by Rocky Graziano, the outcast."[20]

LaVern proved that he could take the kidding in stride by revealing

LaVern towing in Cerdan with Forrest Ferguson and John Abood looking on.
NY Daily News via Getty Images, Bob Costello, photographer.

that "when he graduated from high school in Plainview, Tex., he was of-fered a scholarship by a girls' school."[21]

A boxer's personality and character are often revealed at the official weigh-in where they come face-to-face outside the ring for the first time. Roach and Cerdan appeared relaxed and confident, neither showing signs of intimidation. After the weigh-in was completed, both fighters, now fully dressed in their Sunday best with suits and ties, were giving the media a chance at some picture taking. The two were standing facing each other with about a foot's distance separating the two. LaVern was flanked on his left side by his manager, Johnny Abood, and Marcel had two of his handlers behind him. One translated for Cerdan, since the Frenchman spoke no English.

Earlier in the day LaVern had been presented a gold deputy sheriff's badge, making him an honorary deputy sheriff of Hale County (of which

Plainview is the county seat). This was done through the courtesy of Sheriff Ted Andrews, who sent the badge to New York with a local group of twenty-six businessmen who arrived earlier in their chartered DC-3. LaVern pinned the badge on the left lapel of his suit coat. With cameras flashing, LaVern grabbed his badge with his left hand and at the same time grabbed the left lapel of Marcel's suit coat with his right hand as if to tow him in. Whether Cerdan understood the West Texas gesture of "being towed in," he smiled and displayed what may have been real and not fake surprise. The headline photo appeared on the front page of the *New York Daily News* and later in the French sports magazine *Miroir*.[22]

After their initial meeting, Cerdan made the following comment about LaVern: "I was surprised how handsome Roach is; he must have to beat the girls off with a stick."[23] For his part, LaVern shared in a letter to Choc Hutcheson, "He's a rough looking 'hombre,' but that's a sign he gets hit."[24] Marcel did not have the pretty look of a Roach or a Janiro, but featured a ruggedly handsome face accented by a smile with his gold teeth.

Adding to the importance and drama of this bout, on the day of the fight, the following article appeared in the *New York World-Telegram*:

Graziano Status Prompts Tourney for Fill-In Champ

The possibility of an elimination tournament to determine a temporary middleweight boxing champion for New York was seen today following a meeting between Sol Strauss of the Twentieth Century Sporting Club and Eddie Eagan, chairman of the State Boxing Commission. The winner of such an elimination would reign until the status of Rocky Graziano, suspended champion here, was changed. Tonight's bout between Cerdan and Roach would figure in the tournament. Others to be considered would be Steve Belloise, Ray Robinson, and Anton Raadik. If the elimination goes through, it probably would culminate in a big outdoor match this year.[25]

The stakes were high for both men, who coveted a chance at the middleweight crown. There was a high probability that the winner would soon become the next middleweight world champion. There was even a slim possibility that the winner of this bout could be crowned middleweight champion, depending on the outcome of the commissioner's ruling in regard to Graziano. The stakes were higher for Cerdan than for LaVern. "If Roach prevailed, Cerdan believed, he would lose his chance at the world middleweight championship, the crown he coveted."[26] Age was becoming a major factor for him, already past the prime age for most boxers. At only twenty-three years old and with one loss, LaVern could lose the fight and still have plenty of time to challenge again.

LaVern and Marcel both preferred a title bout with Rocky Graziano as their next fight, but the champ's out-of-the-ring problems prevented this from happening. Besides, Sol Strauss, with the advice of the ailing Mike Jacobs, wanted otherwise. They envisioned the newspaper headlines— former Marine boxing champion, LaVern Roach, from Plainview, Texas, sporting a flashy 25-1 boxing record against the French and European champion, Marcel Cerdan, with an even more impressive record of 105-2. Both were considered military heroes even though neither ever saw combat duty. LaVern had just come off of his lopsided victory over Tony Janiro, and Marcel had put away Abrams, Green, and Raadik.

The fight was set with a capacity crowd expected. Among the spectators were the usual show-business celebrities attracted to featured bouts in the Garden. In addition, the audience included two women, each cheering for her own man. "Watching Roach in the ring for the first time will be Evelyn Winkles, of Plainview, Tex. But Cerdan will offset this romantic interest with a special guest of his own, Edith Piaf, French night club singer."[27]

Cerdan wasn't the only French citizen looking for success on American soil. Edith Piaf, his number-one fan and lover, was a famous French singer whose life is well chronicled in the book *No Regrets: The Life of Edith Piaf,* written by Carolyn Burke. Their affair started innocently in Paris in 1946 at the Club des Cinq, a nightclub where Edith was performing. In the audience one night was Marcel and his friend Jo Longman. They asked Edith to join them after the show. She obliged. Cerdan, although a married man with three children, was immediately taken with Edith, charmed by her voice and her presence. At the same time Edith was tiring of her involvement in one of her many love affairs. They both showed a mutual interest, and a romantic relationship soon followed. Before his fight with Georgie Abrams, Edith cabled Marcel, "Know that all of Paris is with you. And that little Piaf sends you a piece of her heart."[28]

It was a toss-up as to who was making the biggest splash in New York

City, Edith in the entertainment world or Marcel in the world of sports. Edith made her American debut at the same time as Marcel the previous fall. On October 9, 1947, Edith and her entourage boarded the *Queen Elizabeth* for their trip to New York City for her engagement at the Playhouse Theater. Opening night was October 30. Those in attendance that evening included Gene Kelly, Noel Coward, Lena Horne, Greta Garbo, John Garfield, and Marlene Dietrich. She was warmly received by the star-studded audience, especially after the performance of her signature song, "La Vie en Rose."

Marcel was in New York City at this time. Because of his marriage, they tried to keep their affair a secret, which proved an impossible task due to their high press profiles. After her New York debut, Edith and Marcel returned to France and continued their romance. Both returned to New York for Marcel's match with LaVern.

Unlike Evelyn's childhood of being the all-American girl, growing up in a respected middle-class family in the innocence of small-town Plainview, Edith spent her childhood years growing up in her mother's brothels in a seedy section of Paris. At a young age, she gave birth to an illegitimate daughter.

Just like Cerdan, Edith's career started in the streets, not of Cerdan's Casablanca, but in Paris. She was discovered early, with a passionate and powerful voice that came out of such a small body. Her success skyrocketed as she appealed to both the élite and the common people of the slums where she came from. After obtaining stardom in France and Europe, she was ready to take on America.

LaVern finished his last prefight workout on Wednesday, March 10. Instead of Stillman's, LaVern had been working out at an obscure, semi-private gym located on the East Side to get away from all of the media and hoopla. In addition to two hard rounds of boxing, he hit the light punching bag for two rounds, followed up with one round of loosening up, receiving instructions from Abood and Goldman. After the training session, Goldman gave a sigh of relief. "I'm glad that's over. You never know when something's going to happen at the very end of training—a cut eye, or other injury. He's in the pink of condition."[29]

Evelyn and her mother, Vera, decided to travel to New York City by train. LaVern's uncle Forrest Ferguson flew to New York on the chartered flight with the Plainview businessmen. LaVern provided tickets to the

Charley Goldman taping LaVern. Courtesy of the LaVern Roach family.

fight for the three of them. After the match they planned on sightseeing New York City for a couple of days, returning to Plainview in a new car that LaVern was going to purchase with his fight money.

Edith Piaf, though not a boxing fan, had been given a couple of tickets by sports journalist Bill Corum. They had met earlier in the week while she was performing at the Versailles.[30]

One of the biggest surprises at ringside was the appearance of Mike Jacobs, president of the Twentieth Century Sports Club, who flew in the previous day from his home in Florida, where he had been recuperating from his cerebral hemorrhage. Jacobs hadn't been to a boxing match in two years.[31] His presence was an indicator of just how big a fight this was. All of the big shots were in attendance. The popular broadcaster Steve Ellis found his way into LaVern's locker room prior to the fight for an introduction to the Texan.

Although the gate failed to reach the $100,000 purse both camps were looking for, a large crowd of 16,905 spectators paid $80,030 to witness

John Abood, unknown, LaVern, Charley Goldman, and broadcaster Steve Ellis introducing himself to LaVern. Courtesy of the LaVern Roach family.

what had been built up as the fight of the season in New York City. "The evening had a distinct French flavor, with the Tricolour hanging over the ring alongside the Stars and Stripes, France's Ambassador to the United States sitting in a ringside seat in formal dress, and a party of sailors up in the gallery from a French liner anchored in New York harbour."[32]

The fight represented a contrast in styles. Cerdan was a brawler, a throwback to the old barroom style of fighting. What he lacked in finesse, he made up for in raw power. He looked for that one knockout punch that could immediately end a fight in his favor. His overall record included fifty-five knockouts. His best weapon was a left hook coming from up high. LaVern adhered to the more classic, orthodox, stand-up style of boxing. He relied on a superior jab, a smart hook, quick reflexes, and the conditioning that allowed him to outlast most opponents.

The plan of attack set for LaVern by his handlers was infighting—moving in and fighting Cerdan close up with bursts of hooks and uppercuts, while using his speed to avoid Cerdan's knockout punch. If successful, he could tire out his older opponent. They figured the longer the fight went on, the better LaVern's chances.

Cerdan and his handlers were also confident of the victory. They didn't seem overly concerned with LaVern's knockout punch. They felt Cerdan could absorb LaVern's best. Their main concern was the fight going the distance. They wanted Cerdan to go for a quick knockout. They knew a longer fight favored the younger fighter due to his stamina and superior conditioning.

Prior to fight time, telegrams came pouring into LaVern's dressing room. Over forty messages were received from fans across the nation. Many were from friends and family back home, including his most faithful fans, Choc and Stark, and from his high school football coach, Finis Vaughn. Newly acquired fan Jane Miller of the Associated Press sent her best wishes and good luck. Friend and former Marine Corps correspondent and reporter Ty Primm and boxing teammate Ray Klingmeyer joined those wishing LaVern success. A very brief telegram, showing great Texas pride, came from Yonkers, New York, with the words, "Whoever heard of a Frenchman whipping a Texan?" signed, "Your Texas friends."

Much to the shock and disappointment of the Cerdan camp, the third man in the ring for the evening's event was Arthur Donovan, who refereed Roach's previous three bouts against Arnold, Janiro, and Kronowitz, all victories for LaVern. Concerned about a possible bias in favor of the American and former Marine, Cerdan's manager Lucien Roupp sought out New York ring chairman Eddie Eagan before the bout. After a brief conversation, Roupp understood Eagan's reply to be, "Don't worry. That man won't be in there tonight."[33]

The fighters received a roaring reception as they entered the arena from their respective locker rooms, with LaVern receiving the louder response. The evening's attire featured Cerdan, weighing in at 156½ pounds, wearing black trunks, and Roach at 156 pounds, donning white trunks. The much anticipated main event at the Garden was about to begin. After the introductory formalities, the bell sounded for the opening round.

LaVern came out, much to the surprise of Cerdan and his corner, as the aggressor. From his ringside seat, Joseph C. Nichols of the *New York Times* reported, "Roach, nine years younger . . . flashed boxing skill that

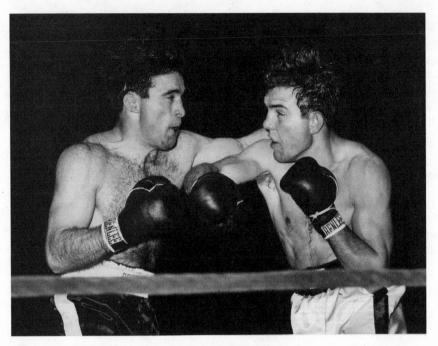

Marcel Cerdan and LaVern. LaVern draws first blood. Courtesy of the LaVern Roach family.

enabled him to take the first round by a clear margin." He clearly outboxed the Frenchman in the initial round. Cerdan threw a few wild punches in an effort to quickly end the fight but failed to connect. LaVern opened up a slight cut on Cerdan's lower lip, drawing the first blood. Even with a bloody lower lip, the first round seemed to confirm to Cerdan what he had been told: "Roach was a capable youngster, but without the power to hurt me."[34]

Round one was a wakeup call for the Frenchman. Between the first and second rounds, Cerdan's corner instructed him to take the youngster seriously and go after him. They didn't want the fight to linger because they knew that LaVern's style was to only get stronger as the fight progressed. Cerdan took the instruction to heart and at the bell charged out of his corner and caught LaVern with a short left, flooring LaVern for the first time in his career.

Roach would later say that he glanced away for a split second when the punch took him down. He took a nine-count and bounced back up, but he wasn't the same the rest of the fight. Cerdan, sensing that LaVern had been hurt, went for the kill with a barrage of punches. What happened next was one for the ages. Every reporter covering the fight described the event in their own words. Jesse Abramson of the *New York Herald Tribune* perhaps summed it up best:

> They wrestled each other down, with Cerdan on top. The Frenchman jumped up. Roach went to one knee. Jack Watson, the knockdown timekeeper, kept yelling that it wasn't a knockdown. Referee Arthur Donovan seemed content to consider it a knockdown. There was a mental tug-of-war between the two officials, while Roach rested on one knee. Finally Watson started counting, and Roach took eight. How long he was down there was no telling. Nat Fleischer timed the rest at 32 seconds from the time they both went down. Anyway it was a marathon count. Cerdan, his hair flying, came in clawing and pounding. He staggered Roach, who snatched at Cerdan, then went down and took a short count of two.[35]

The bell sounded, ending round two. "The Battle of the Long Count" was over. Fleischer, editor and publisher of the *Ring*, at ringside with his stopwatch, recorded this in his annual *The* Ring *Record Book* as the longest count in boxing history. It has remained a topic of heated discussion. For the record, the chief official in the ring is the referee, whose instructions surpass those of the timekeeper.[36]

The consensus of ringside observers was that if not for this mix-up, the fight would have ended right then. The crowd, not aware of the battle going on between Donovan and Watson, didn't care about the perceived oversight and was anxious for the fight to continue. Cerdan's corner, now more confident than ever, didn't seem to object all that much at the time but became more suspicious of Donovan's actions. Regardless, LaVern was given a reprieve, and the fight continued.

Rounds three, four, and five delivered mixed results, depending on which of the dozen or so New York newspapers you read. According to Abramson, "Having missed the second round knockout Cerdan paced himself. He pounded Roach through the third and fourth, throwing combinations to the head, sometimes missing with a right and catching the Texan with a left. Roach rallied briefly in the fifth, raking short rights to the jaw at close quarters."[37]

Describing the same rounds, Gene Ward of the *Daily News* wrote,

"[Roach] made Cerdan miss in the third and then came ripping back in the fourth and fifth, counter-punching effectively and beating the Frenchman to the draw with short, zippy lefts."[38]

Round six saw the advantage swing back to Cerdan as his corner was yelling at him that "he had shot his bolt," meaning he was blowing his opportunity. This seemed to work as Cerdan sent body and head shots to LaVern in rapid succession. After six rounds, Ward had each scoring three rounds each.

Round seven saw the momentum continue with Cerdan, even though LaVern connected with rights to his opponent's head.

LaVern seemed more alert as round eight started. He was able to deliver two lefts to Cerdan's face. At a point where both fighters were exhibiting signs of fatigue, Cerdan delivered a long right that curled around LaVern's neck, the force of which drove LaVern to the mat. LaVern took a two-count and then got back up. Cerdan, sensing an opportunity to finish the fight, delivered a left hook and a right to the jaw that sent LaVern sprawling to the canvas. LaVern was forced to take a full nine-count after this pounding.

From the crowd came the loud voice of the diminutive Edith Piaf, surprising herself by yelling, "Go on, Marcel, kill him!" Until this fight, "She had taken no interest in boxing; in fact she hated it."[39] In another area of the arena near ringside were Evelyn, Vera, and Forrest. Evelyn, witnessing her first fight with the exception of the youth matches that LaVern refereed back home, wondered why anyone would want to be a fighter. Somewhere in the distance were the Plainview contingency, pulling for their local hero.

At the end of the nine-count, LaVern solely on instinct got up on some very shaky legs. Cerdan delivered the same combination of a left hook and a right to the jaw, sending LaVern to the mat for the third time in this round and sixth time for the fight. LaVern once again was able to quickly get up on the count of two. The crowd wondered how much punishment the former Marine could take and soon got their answer. Cerdan delivered a right to the chin that sent LaVern to the canvas for the fourth time in the round.

Referee Donovan, having seen enough, walked over to LaVern, patted him on the back, and waved the end of the fight, not giving him a chance to get up again. The fight was stopped at 2:31 in the eighth.

Cerdan won his 106th fight. After the applauding, cheering, and congratulations that accompany the end of a fight, the boxers headed for their respective dressing rooms. Although there was celebration in the winner's locker room, there was also a feeling of *What's next?* Jo Longman, Cerdan's promoter, said, "It should be a tribute for two years of work. For two years we keep coming here and they keep telling us: 'next you will fight for the championship.' Nothing happens. If they want us to wait for eight years, that is all right too. Only by then Marcel maybe will be too old."

Longman was standing in front of Cerdan, who was being photographed. Standing nearby were his manager Lucien Roupp and Lew Burston, Cerdan's American business representative. Longman continued with an ultimatum: "The next time we come back, it must be for the title. What right do they have to tie up the title? Is it a world title or is it not?"[40]

With the title tied up by Graziano's out-of-the-ring actions, Marcel joined Tony Zale as a victim of Graziano's boxing plight.

It was a subdued mood in LaVern's dressing room. LaVern lost his second professional bout after a string of eighteen straight victories. For the first time in his career, LaVern had not only been knocked down but suffered a TKO. His dream of becoming a world boxing champion had taken a setback. How serious a setback was yet to be determined. This might have been his one and only chance, since few boxers ever get a second chance.

Inside the dressing room LaVern was sitting on his dressing table with that captivating smile, answering questions from the reporters. "It was my equilibrium. After the second round I couldn't get it back. I was strong, but I couldn't get my equilibrium."[41]

"He hits hard?" a reporter asked.

LaVern responded, "Yes he does. He's a fine fighter, but I wasn't hurt. What I mean is the punches weren't actually hurting. I didn't actually feel pain but my equilibrium was like this," as he motioned with his hands. He held his right hand as he would extend it to shake hands and he waved back and forth.

The reporter continued, "Was it a short right he hit you with?"

LaVern: "I didn't see it."

Another reporter said, "It was a long right," as he demonstrated. "From away back here."

LaVern smiled and shrugged his shoulders: "Well, I suppose everybody has to get beat some time. He's a fine fighter but I hope some time to be able to fight him again." (A possible rematch was highly unlikely. As part of the contract, Cerdan was guaranteed a rematch with LaVern in case he lost to him. The Cerdan camp did not agree to a reciprocating clause. By winning, Cerdan secured the right to fight for the championship. Win or lose the championship, Cerdan's age was catching up on him and a return bout with LaVern was very doubtful.) "I wasn't overmatched. I wasn't overmatched, and I don't want John Abood to be blamed." He said this as he put his hand on Abood's shoulder. Abood had been standing next to LaVern throughout the press conference.[42]

Abood joined in the conversation: "Oh, it's my fault. I'll take the blame."

Coming to Johnny's defense, LaVern said, "No, it isn't," while looking straight at Johnny. "No, it isn't." He continued, "I did just what Johnny told me not to do. I dropped my left and got caught with a right. That is exactly what Johnny told me not to do."[43]

LaVern, after his session with the press, was reading the handful of telegrams from his most faithful followers expressing their regrets when he heard a commotion outside his dressing room door. As he got up and opened the door he was greeted by the twenty-plus Plainview business-men who chartered the flight to see him fight. "Hello, gang," LaVern said. "I'm sorry I let you all down."

A middle-aged fellow replied, "No you didn't. You didn't let anybody down, and we want you to know we're still all with you."[44] Those words of encouragement were exactly what LaVern needed to hear.

The write-ups and interviews after the fight would have you think that two different fights occurred in Madison Square Garden that night. The Texan had been whipped by the Frenchman, but Cerdan himself had nothing but praise for LaVern, describing him as "a tough boy whom he had to hurt with more punches than he has needed to knock out any other opponent." When questioned about the "long count," Cerdan said, "One is happier without a world's record like that one. I admire your tall women and beautiful buildings, but not your long timekeepers."[45]

When asked what she thought of the fight, Edith Piaf said, "I've felt all sorts of emotions but these go far beyond them. It's fantastic to see one of our guys, all alone in the ring among thousands of 'Ricains' (Americans), defending our prestige."[46] On the Sunday after the bout Ms. Piaf, "in spite of several flattering offers to continue her current American appearances, notably one from the Clover Club in Los Angeles, flew back to Paris on the same flight with Cerdan."[47]

The French newspapers were full of praises for Cerdan. The headlines of the popular French sports magazine *Miroir* read, "LaVern Roach 108th Victime de Marcel Cerdan."[48] Under the headlines were one large and three small photos of the fight. The interior of the sixteen-page magazine contained three more pages of exclusive articles along with nine more fight and prefight photos. Even the Communists used the outcome as political Cold War propaganda when the following headline appeared in a French newspaper the next day: "Commies Hail Cerdan Victory." The short article read, "Marcel Cerdan's victory over LaVern Roach in Madison Square Garden last night was headlined today in all the French newspapers. Communist newspapers claimed the victory was 'a blow to American capitalism' which had been counting on a Roach victory."[49] At least the French spelled LaVern correctly.

The next evening, LaVern, showing only a slightly swollen eye from the pounding that he received from Cerdan, took Evelyn, Vera, Forrest, and the Nat Hymans to dinner at the Copacabana. Meanwhile, Cerdan, sporting a black eye, was seen in a tuxedo with Ms. Piaf at one of New York's finer nightspots.

Dinner at the Copacabana. Forrest Ferguson, Evelyn, LaVern, the Nat Hymans, and Vera. Courtesy of the LaVern Roach family.

Observation Tower, Empire State Building, New York City. LaVern, Evelyn,
Vera, and Forrest. Courtesy of the LaVern Roach family.

CHAPTER 12

A Fading Star

To see a man beaten not by a better opponent but by himself is a tragedy.
—*Gus D'Amato*

After the Cerdan fight LaVern spent a couple of days showing Evelyn, Vera, and Forrest the sights of New York City. While in the city they stayed with LaVern at 470 Elmwood. There were several vacant bedrooms since Abood's plan to fill them with boxers never materialized. They all headed back to Plainview in LaVern's new 1948 Plymouth sedan, paid for out of the proceeds of the Cerdan fight with the money left over after paying Johnny back the money owed to him. LaVern wanted a sports car, but Abood convinced him that the sedan was more practical. According to Choc, LaVern was a fast but safe driver and possessed the reflexes of a race car driver. Abood did not want to take the chance of his prize boxer being hurt in a car accident. Boxing was dangerous enough.

LaVern did like to drive fast. While driving home through the winding roads of Oklahoma, Evelyn broke the heel off of an expensive shoe while pushing her feet down on her side of the floorboard as he navigated some sharp curves. Upset at breaking the heel off an expensive pair of shoes purchased for the trip, she said, "Don't you think you are driving too fast?" LaVern, even with her mother and his uncle in the backseat, let out a rare display of emotion and answered, "Shut up."[1] (This was the only incident that Evelyn could think of when pressed by the author to reveal something about LaVern's bad side.)

After a wild two-month journey, which included the two Madison Square Garden fights with Janiro and Cerdan and the Al Thornton fight

LaVern daydreaming. Courtesy of the LaVern Roach family.

in Miami sandwiched in between, LaVern was going to get that much-needed rest before he returned to New York to continue his boxing career. At least that was his initial plan.

Soon after returning to Plainview, LaVern and Evelyn decided on the spur of the moment to get married before he returned to New York. On April 7, 1948, they crossed the state line to Clovis, New Mexico, where they were secretly wed, with only her parents knowing of the marriage. The reason for the secrecy was to keep the news from Johnny Abood. LaVern wanted to tell Johnny in person and at the right time about the nuptials, not wanting the news to leak out and have John pick up a New York newspaper two thousand miles away and discover that his star performer had tied the knot.

Johnny Abood, like most managers, didn't particularly want any of his boxers to marry. He felt that once fighters married, their priorities shifted, and he would lose a certain amount of control. He was correct on both accounts. The newlyweds somehow were successful in keeping their nuptials a secret for the next few weeks.

As a youth, church had always been a big part of Evelyn's life. Now, especially since the birth of Ronnie, Evelyn felt the need to give her child the same spiritual foundation that she received as a child. LaVern attended church sporadically before marriage and led a Christian-like life, but had never been baptized. Now that he had taken on the responsibilities of a husband and father, he decided to join an established religion. On April 25, 1948, LaVern was baptized into the fellowship of the First Baptist Church of Plainview, where Evelyn was already a member. LaVern continued to work out and keep in condition. He also used this time to referee a couple of professional fights in Amarillo.[2]

Well rested from the Cerdan fight, it was now time for LaVern to return to New York and resume his career. He decided it would be best to arrive alone. This gave him a chance to break his news to Johnny Abood without Evelyn there to absorb any aftershocks.

He also kept his marriage a secret from Choc. LaVern, having been born on George Washington's birthday, always tried to emulate the first president by not telling a lie. He let his guard slip upon his return to New York in a letter to Choc:

> I wish I could be with Evelyn every day. Right now I am so lonesome I can hardly sit still. Boy when the day comes for Evelyn and me to get married, and I know I want [sic] have to leave her again, I'll certainly be a happy man. It's really funny how a woman can come into a man's life, and change everything. Right now she is the most important thing in the world to me, so I have to get busy and make a lot of money so I can give her all the things she deserves. I don't know why I'm pouring my heart out like this, but I guess it's because I'm lonesome. Take care now and write soon.[3]

At the time of this letter, he was already married.

Boxing once again had been replaced as the most important thing in LaVern's life. The first time it was the war. This time it was love.

Soon after returning to New York, LaVern informed Johnny. Not exactly enthused about the situation, Johnny nevertheless helped LaVern make housing arrangements for the newlyweds. LaVern returned to Plainview to tell his family and friends, including Choc, of the marriage. After a brief visit, they packed up what few belongings they had and LaVern, Evelyn, and Ronnie headed to New Jersey.

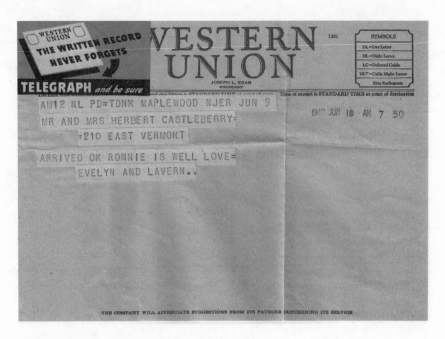

Telegram from LaVern to Herbert and Vera Castleberry on safe arrival. Courtesy of the Roach family.

They arrived at their destination on June 9. The first thing LaVern did was send the above Western Union telegram to Herb and Vera.

They took up residence in a rental house at 16 Edge Terrace, Maplewood, New Jersey, and began settling in. For LaVern this was a totally new experience. After eighteen years living at home with his parents and brother and sister, three years living in Marine barracks, and two years sharing a house with sparring mate Harold Anspach, he now had become the man of his own household. Not only did he have a new bride, but also a beautiful blonde-haired daughter who was about to celebrate her third birthday. He enjoyed every minute of being a husband and a father.

He introduced Evelyn and Ronnie to the New Jersey beaches and the Atlantic Ocean, where Ronnie loved the beach, especially playing in the sand.

After setting up their new home, one of the first things LaVern did was invite his good friends Choc and O. R. Stark to visit them at the end of the summer. Both accepted and scheduled their trip in late August.

Evelyn's Texas hospitality soon began to have an effect upon John

LaVern and Ronnie at the beach. Photo taken by Evelyn Roach. Courtesy of the LaVern Roach family.

Abood. Shortly after their arrival, John, along with Charley Goldman, came over. In a letter to Vera and Herbert, Evelyn wrote,

> Charlie [*sic*] Goldman, the little short man that is LaVern's trainer brought me a cute little thing for the wall. It is a cup and saucer with a flower in it. The cup sticks to the inside of the saucer. [She drew a sketch of it.] I had never seen him [before]. He got it at Utica and gave it to me. Johnny gave Ronnie $5 to get a birthday present. He had a fit over her.[4]

LaVern loved being a dad. Along with that came a bit of overprotection. Evelyn wrote to her mother,

> LaVern was on the warpath this morning. Ronnie came home from Lynn's house crying. Lynn is a brat, she teases Ronnie. LaVern told her right out in the yard where her mother could hear, "If you can't play right little lady you stay home and don't ever come back up here."

He really loves Ronnie. When people say something about him being so good to Ronnie, he resents it. He doesn't want people to ever say that she is anything but his. He says of course she is my girl. When he comes home every day he has to go out and find her so he can cuddle her a little. He really sticks out his chest because people think she is cute. LaVern is playing ball with Ronnie. She is saying "catch it Daddy."[5]

After a three-month break from boxing, it was time for LaVern to get back to business. His first target was Rocky Castellani, of Luzerne, Pennsylvania, a young middleweight with an impressive 17-1 record. The Castellani camp wouldn't take the fight. A rematch with Billy Arnold was proposed but also turned down. Boxers were leery to fight LaVern, figuring he had something to prove after his loss to Cerdan. Finally the Roach camp found a comer in Aaron Perry on his own turf in Washington, DC, on July 12, 1948.

With the fight only a month away, LaVern started his rigorous training routine at Stillman's. His daily regimented routine still included waking at six, running from four to eight miles, eating two meals a day, working out in the gym in the afternoon for several hours, and getting ten hours of sleep each night. On July 9, LaVern broke training and headed to Washington. He stayed at the Ambassador Hotel on Fourteenth and K. In a letter dated July 11 to Vera and Herbert, he wrote,

Well I guess you're in church this morning and I imagine Evelyn is also. Bless their hearts, I sure miss them and I can't wait to get home again. Ronnie is so sweet and I really miss having her around, for she is always asking me questions. She asked me the other day if I fight in the gym. Boy she is as smart as can be and nothing slips her ears.[6]

Although it had been four months since his last fight, John Abood and Chris Dundee felt LaVern was in great shape and ready to work his way back to Madison Square Garden, where he had given Tony Janiro a good walloping and put up a whale of a fight against Marcel Cerdan. Nat Fleischer, who watched LaVern train earlier in the week, told Dundee, "I will stick to my statement of two years ago, that Roach is destined to win the middleweight title." LaVern was made a five-to-eight favorite over the hometown boy. Perry, the same age as Roach, was also trying to make a comeback after recent poor performances darkened his once bright future.

The fight was held at Griffith Baseball Stadium, known for starting the tradition of presidents throwing out the first ceremonial pitch to start the baseball season. William Howard Taft was the first president to do so in 1911. It was also home of the Washington Redskins football team. LaVern, even after losing to Cerdan and with a four-month absence from the ring, proved that he was still a good draw at the gate as four thousand fans showed up at the old baseball stadium to watch the fight. The purse for the evening was twelve thousand dollars. The prefight headline news read, "Roach May Meet Graziano If He Defeats Perry." "If Roach wins, plans are to book him against Rocky Graziano, recently disposed middleweight title holder, in New York's Madison Square Garden next September."[7]

Much to Abood's satisfaction, LaVern's marriage didn't seem to hinder his ring readiness. Despite the longest layoff in his professional career, he scored a solid ten-round unanimous decision. From the tone in LaVern's locker room afterward, one would have thought that he lost the fight. "I am glad this one is over with," he said to Johnny Abood. "I looked terrible and didn't have any snap to my punches at all."[8]

From the looks of their fighter, the men in Aaron Perry's locker room might have disagreed with this assessment. Perry was sitting there with cuts over both eyes and had blood running from his mouth and nose.

LaVern had improved his record to 25-2. The Associated Press scored it seven rounds for LaVern, one for Perry, and two even. At the end of the tenth, LaVern got a standing ovation from the crowd. Although Perry had many local supporters cheering for him, the Marines showed up en masse to support their World War II boxing hero. LaVern started his comeback victoriously.

Up next was an August date with Anton Raadik to be held in Chicago. Raadik had been a victim of Cerdan there the previous year. In case the Windy City deal fell through, a fight with Rocky Castellani was back on in the Garden in September. The Raadik deal indeed fell through, and the Roach camp scurried to find a replacement for the month of August in their plan to schedule at least one fight a month. Charley Zivic proved to be a capable replacement. The fight was to be held on Zivic's home turf at Forbes Field in Pittsburgh on August 3.

LaVern returned to New Jersey to resume his new duties as husband and father to Evelyn and Ronnie. In a letter to Choc he wrote,

> Ronnie and Evelyn are well and said to tell you hello. She likes it out here and we sure are happy. This married life is O.K. so you had better try it sometime. . . . Ronnie is having the time of her life out here with these kids.

In the same letter he told Choc that he and Evelyn were looking forward to Choc and O.R. coming out to visit them next month, hoping he could take some time off to show them the city and all it had to offer. Still not used to being married, several times in the letter he had to cross out the word "I" and replace it with "we."[9]

Forbes Field, built two years earlier than Griffith Stadium, opened in 1909. It was the third home of the Pittsburgh Pirates and the first home of the Steelers. The fight would be the first held in the old ball park since the summer of 1946. More importantly it gave home-field advantage to Zivic, a name used by a former Pittsburgh fighter that went over well with the Steel City crowd. Zivic, alias Charley Affif, was an up-and-coming fighter the same age as LaVern.

> Choc, the Perry fight wasn't too bad, but it wasn't too easy either. He was in good shape and everybody said he fought one of his best fights, of course. I was a little sluggish after 4 months, but still felt pretty good. I should feel better Aug. 3rd against Charlie Zivic in Pittsburgh, or at least I hope so. John said today that he was trying to get Sonny Horne for Aug. 28th in the Garden. That is if I can beat this Charlie Zivic. He's tough and will make a rough fight, so I can't take any chances. Keep your fingers crossed and wish me luck. John also said I may fight Rocky Castellani in the Garden in Sept. if everything goes right, and I hope it does.[10]

Everything didn't go right for LaVern against Zivic. As LaVern described the fight,

> Dear Choc, Just a fast line to let you know I dropped a close one to Charlie Affif. I just couldn't get off fast enough and he had an awkward style. Should have banged him anyway, but it was just one of those nights. That little clip I use on my bottom teeth came off and went through my lip in the 6th round. It's made out of plastic so it

really went through it. The blood helped sway the judges plus the fact that he's from Pittsburgh. Hope I can get a rematch next month and if I do, I'll punch his rear off. Say, O.R. is ready to come out so I will be expecting you next month. I am not fighting for a month or so, so maybe you can see one of them. Hope so. Tell your folks hello for all of us. Wish all of them could come out with you. Be good now and don't work too hard.[11]

LaVern suffered only his third defeat. The fight went the full ten rounds, and he lost on points. The loss to Zivic resulted in LaVern losing the Castellani and Sonny Horne fights. He would not fight again until October 4, against Johnny Hansbury at Turner's Arena, Washington, DC.

In the meantime Choc and O.R. made their trip to New York and stayed with LaVern, Evelyn, and Ronnie. LaVern seemed to be able to relax and enjoy the company, taking his mind off of boxing, except for the upcoming fight between Cerdan and Tony Zale for the middleweight championship to be held on September 21. During Choc and O.R.'s stay, in a letter to Vera and Herb, LaVern wrote and expressed disappointment in not being the one to fight Zale for the championship:

> I've got a lot of work ahead of me in the next 3 months, so keep your fingers crossed and wish me luck. I'm going to be O.K. so don't worry about anything. I've got to get on the ball and punch some of these guys around, for there's lots of money floating around. Tony Zale is getting 120 thousand for this Cerdan fight so that's not hay. Maybe next summer I'll get the chance at some of that big money and I hope I do.[12]

LaVern and Evelyn showed Choc and O.R. the sights of New York City and New Jersey. They all had a good time at the beach, enjoyed a little golf, went to the ice show and the racetrack, and even accompanied LaVern to Stillman's Gym to watch him work out. At Stillman's they were introduced to Charley Goldman, John Abood, Angelo Dundee, and a host of others in the boxing business. On another day they went to see Tony Zale train for his upcoming fight against Cerdan.

Joining LaVern, Evelyn, Choc, and O.R. at the racetrack was Suzanne Knox, a nearby neighbor, home from college for the summer. At the track one of the jockeys recognized LaVern and came over to chat with him. LaVern asked, "Can you give me a tip on the races?" "Sure," replied the

At the racetrack. Choc Hutcheson, Suzanne Knox, Evelyn, and LaVern. Photo taken by O. R. Stark. Courtesy of the LaVern Roach family.

jockey. "Don't bet!"[13] Ignoring the advice, LaVern and party donated a few bucks to the racetrack, while having a good time.

Although LaVern felt he was calming down and improving, Evelyn and Johnny Abood felt differently. Both were concerned about LaVern and his state of mind since the Cerdan fight. LaVern, from the beginning, tried to shield Evelyn and Ronnie from the boxing world. Since the Cerdan fight was the only fight she had ever seen in person, he did take her to Stillman's Gym once, an experience she didn't intend to repeat. Even though LaVern tried to leave his work at the office, it was becoming more and more apparent to Evelyn that the missed opportunity of not winning the Cerdan fight was always in the back of his mind, as she wrote back home:

> Dear Ones, Well, LaVern is getting dressed. He is really going to have to settle down. John said he has looked worse than he ever did. He said it is his frame of mind and he is going to wait for him to come around before he matches him again. DON'T MENTION THIS to anyone, LaVern doesn't know it. More than likely it is the letdown after the Cerdan fight.[14]

Evelyn shared her concern with Choc and asked him to observe La-Vern's behavior while he was there visiting. In another letter she wrote,

> LaVern is fighting Friday night up in Utica, N.Y., not very far from
> here. He doesn't know who but it will probably be an unknown. John
> won't match him with just anyone now. Who do you think will win
> the title? This guy that talked to Choc in the gym said, "Lavern could
> beat him [Cerdan] every way in the world in a year's time." He didn't
> know Choc knew him [LaVern]. He also said "Cerdan was underrat-
> ed by Americans in general." Choc has been evaluating LaVern every
> day and he says he will be okay. This man said "Roach had one thing
> that none of the other fighters had, 'Brains.'" He said "that boy learns
> something every time he boxes in the gym and in a little while he will
> have the killer in him." Anything I tell you regarding fights you keep
> to yourself and don't tell anyone because you can't talk about those
> things.[15]

The man telling Choc this was Charley Goldman, LaVern's trainer, who
at the same time continued training Rocky Marciano across town.

The Cerdan-Zale fight took place on September 21 at Roosevelt Stadium, in Jersey City. Edith Piaf was at ringside, just like she had been in
his fight against LaVern. By now Marcel and Edith had become France's
best-known celebrities. They paraded in public as friends who had a common goal of conquering America, he with his boxing and she with her
singing. In private, a torrid love affair continued. The few journalists who
knew held on to the information to honor Marcel's request to keep it private so that his wife, Marinette, and his three children wouldn't find out.

Zale was an eight-to-five favorite to retain his crown. After they
touched gloves and Cerdan performed the ritual of crossing himself,
the match began. Both fighters fought viciously for most of the fight, exchanging blow for blow. Finally in round twelve, Cerdan landed a right
uppercut that took its toll on the Man of Steel. Edith burst into tears and
shouted, "You won, Marcel. You're the world champion!"[16] For someone
who didn't know the first thing about boxing a year earlier, she had come
a long way. After a few more sold-out performances for Edith at the Versailles, the couple returned to Paris and continued their so-called secret
love affair. After losing his title to Cerdan, Tony Zale, the Man of Steel,
hung up his gloves at the age of thirty-four.

The outcome of the bout deeply depressed LaVern, who felt that if he had beaten Cerdan, he would have been the one in the ring against Zale fighting for the championship. On several occasions after sparring with Zale at Stillman's he would come home and tell Evelyn that Zale wouldn't accept his challenge. This was a known trademark of Zale, who often avoided risky fights that he thought he might lose.

Meanwhile, apparently unaware of Johnny's plan, LaVern sent the following letter to Vera and Herb, the day after the Cerdan/Zale title fight:

> Guess you heard the fight last night and know how I feel. Zale got only a hundred and twenty thousand dollars so I guess he'll have to go on relief. Sure wish I could have been in his shoes, and I would have been if I had beaten Cerdan. Boy next time if I ever get the chance, I won't be caught looking off. The next year is going to be a busy one for me because I am going to stay busy. If I do good Friday the 24th, I'll probably fight the 30th in New York. It doesn't matter as long as I keep feeling good for I want to have 15 or 20 fights in the next year. I'm beginning to get relaxed and am doing good so the more experience I get the better off I will be. This guy I'm fighting is named Jimmy Taylor and he is a pretty rough boy so I'll have to be on the ball. I'll be okay though so don't worry about me.

LaVern switched gears in the letter and talked about Ronnie. He then finished the letter with these words:

> Well Choc is leaving today at 3 so I'm driving in to take his suit cases. He sure enjoyed the fight last night and he and John came home together. John sure likes him and Choc likes John. Well I'll run along now. Evelyn is about to start her ironing. Hope all of you are well.[17]

With company gone, LaVern turned his full attention back to his craft. As promised, John set up LaVern against Johnny Hansbury, an unknown from Washington, DC. The previous loss to Zivic, especially in his own backyard, wasn't a huge negative on LaVern's record. Jake LaMotta, who fought him three times, described Zivic as "one of the toughest little customers whoever pulled on gloves."[18]

A loss to his next opponent would be a staggering blow. Hansbury came into the fight with a record of seven wins, four losses, and one draw. On October 4, LaVern suffered the most humiliating defeat in his boxing career. Unknown Johnny Hansbury dealt LaVern a blow in a unanimous eight-round match held in the Turner Arena. Hansbury would win his next fight and then lose the following two, giving up the sport in March 1950, having never fought outside of the Washington area. His career record was 9-6-1, with the win over LaVern by far his biggest victory. According to Choc, it was a slow, dull bout with LaVern badly off form.[19]

Johnny Abood had seen enough. After a heart-to-heart talk with his fighter, they agreed that it would be best for LaVern to take a break, perhaps even retire. At the age of twenty-three, the young Texan had beaten twenty-five other professionals, including a decisive victory over Tony Janiro. He nearly went the distance with the current world champion Marcel Cerdan, whose hands delivered LaVern's only knockdowns. With only four losses, the pride of the Marine Corps and Plainview, Texas, was coming home—with no parade, no gift of a car, not even a hero's welcome.

Autograph signing at the Lubbock Boys Club. Left to right: Dean Fawcett, LaVern, Jackie Chancy, Hugh Carlen, and Bobby Owens. Courtesy of the LaVern Roach family.

CHAPTER 13

Lubbock, Texas

You can't go home again.
— *Thomas Wolfe*

After LaVern finished up his business in New York, he and Evelyn said their good-byes, packed up their belongings, and with three-year-old Ronnie, headed home to a new and different lifestyle. LaVern left Plainview as an eighteen-year-old boy, served in the Marines for three years, became a world-class boxer, and now was returning with wife and child to an uncharted future.

They initially settled in Plainview, staying with Herb and Vera. LaVern took over the operation of the O.K. Tire and Welding shop for a while but soon sold out. Becoming disenchanted with some of the fair-weather friends who jumped ship since he was no longer considered a celebrity, they moved forty-three miles down the road to Lubbock, which offered more job opportunities and a warmer reception from his Lubbock friends and fans.

He continued his financial support of his mother, dad, and sister with the proceeds from the sale of the business and some money left over from the Cerdan fight. He made the down payment for a house for his parents, paid their monthly house payments, and provided for their needs as well as for his own new family.

LaVern went to work selling insurance for Southland Life, one of the larger insurance companies in the area. With his winning smile and personality, he was a natural salesman. Being well known and having a good reputation and self-discipline—the traits that served him well in the

2613 36th Street, Lubbock, Texas, LaVern and Evelyn's Lubbock residence.
Photo taken by the author.

Marines and in the boxing profession—served him well in the insurance
business. They took up residence at 2613 Thirty-Sixth Street, a small
two-bedroom, one-bath house in central Lubbock.

Lubbock wasn't New York City, but it was much bigger and had more
to offer than Plainview. Except for always losing to the Lubbock High
School football team, LaVern held pleasant memories of Lubbock, from
the times he boxed there on their Golden Gloves team to his visits with
Choc and his family.

Lubbock, formed in the late 1890s, had a population of over seventy
thousand, thanks to the growth of Texas Tech College with its enrollment
of over seventy-five hundred and Reese Air Force Base, used during the
war as a pilot training base. Even with the increasing number of students
and airmen, cotton was still king and agriculture the primary source of
employment.

Braniff Airlines served the Lubbock community, commencing commercial flights in and out of the city as early as 1945. LaVern, during his

LaVern and Evelyn.
Snowy day in Lubbock.
Courtesy of the LaVern
Roach family.

boxing days, used the airline to travel back and forth from the East Coast. For culture, Lubbock even had its own symphony orchestra.

Although he excelled in the insurance business, as he had in every other phase of his life, LaVern wasn't happy selling insurance. He felt he was taking advantage of his customers by using his name and reputation to get in the door and getting them to buy his company's product.

He missed boxing. He stayed in shape by regularly working out and occasionally sparring with a regular group of guys at the Lubbock Boys Club. He enjoyed working with youngsters, giving pointers and encouragement, even officiating some of the bouts. As a teenage pugilist from Amarillo, Earl Chism remembers that LaVern, unlike the other officials who left the ring and building after a fight, always stayed and took time to critique the boys after officiating.[1] His boxing instructor training in the Marines came in handy as he used these skills to help promote the sport.

"Headlines, June 17, 1949, LaMotta Wins Title by Knockout as Cerdan Is Unable to Answer Bell for 10th."² Cerdan returned to the United States to defend his championship against challenger Jake LaMotta on June 16, 1949, in Detroit's Briggs Stadium. Although Edith was not able to make the trip due to a three-week engagement at the Paris Copacabana, her heart was with him as she wrote, "I'll be in your gloves, your breath, everywhere. I'd like to bite LaMotta's ass, that bastard. He mustn't touch you or he'll answer to me. *Au revoir, mon petit*, my boy, my life, my love."³

LaMotta failed to get the message. The Raging Bull won the first round as Cerdan suffered a shoulder separation when shoved to the mat. He was still able to continue and even won the second round. Round three was even, but for the remainder of the fight Cerdan was put in a position of just having to defend himself, hardly throwing a punch. He fought bravely until the start of the tenth round, when Jo Longman, his manager, threw in the towel to stop the fight, against the wishes of his defenseless fighter. Jake LaMotta was the new middleweight champion. Marcel Cerdan held the coveted middleweight crown for less than a year.

Back in Texas, preparations were finalized for an exhibition match to be held in Plainview, featuring LaVern as the star attraction. Local promoters had been trying to get LaVern to showcase his boxing skills before his hometown audience ever since he turned pro. Prior to moving to Lubbock, his prolonged communications were ongoing with Johnny Abood, who was no supporter of exhibitions. Each time it appeared that such a showing might take place, something always happened to derail it. A poll of the student body at Texas Tech favored an exhibition fight in Jones Stadium over a rodeo, but it never materialized. Back home and in control of his time, LaVern chose to ignore the advice of Abood and successfully negotiated an exhibition match.

The Plainview Jaycee organization finalized arrangements for a five-bout outdoor boxing exhibit to take place in Plainview at the Bar None Rodeo grounds. It had been ten years since the residents of the South Plains witnessed a professional match. On September 18, 1939, former heavyweight champion Max Baer demonstrated his boxing ability for the local crowd by scoring a second-round knockout of Babe Ritchie at the Fair Park Stadium.⁴

LaVern's opponent for the evening was Howell Steen of Dallas. They were scheduled for six rounds. The card also featured professional bouts, including a local favorite from nearby Levelland, Bill Henderson, who was trying for his eighteenth victory in twenty bouts. His opponent was Freddie Maes of Denver. Other local favorites included Hale Center's Leonard Duncan, in his first pro bout, against Jimmy Boggs in a four-round light heavyweight match; heavyweight J. D. Kirkpatrick of nearby Petersburg battling Gene James; and welterweights Hubert Gray and Jerry Sargent squaring off in a four-rounder.

Over twenty-five hundred local fans were present for the evening festivities. Tickets for the event were priced at $1.75, $2.75, and $3.75. The referee for the night was Lubbock's O. J. "Bo" Sexton.

In the opening bout, Gene James scored a surprisingly easy victory over Kirkpatrick. In his defense, Kirkpatrick had accepted the fight only three days earlier and seemed out of shape.

In the next fight, Hubert Gray, whom LaVern listed as his toughest amateur and whom he had lost to in a state semifinal match back in 1941, started off fast against Jerry Sargent. Gray's southpaw style baffled Sargent, just as it had LaVern years earlier. After being floored three times in the sixth and final round, Sargent asked Sexton to stop the fight, and Gray was awarded a TKO victory at 1:48.

In the third fight Duncan finished strong in the fourth round to score a narrow decision over Jimmy Boggs. Neither fighter scored a knockdown. Up next was LaVern's chance to showcase his talent before hometown fans. Except for the plane full of men who made the trip to New York City, this was the first time for the home crowd to watch LaVern in a pro fight.

LaVern, as always, was in good condition. His opponent, Howell Steen, a seasoned fighter from Dallas, came into the fight with a pro record of 22-15-2. Hubert Gray, who had beaten Steen eight months earlier in a Dallas bout, told reporters before the fight that "Roach shouldn't even work up a sweat."[5]

Gray proved to be right. LaVern turned in a good boxing performance, winning every round on the *Lubbock Avalanche Journal*'s unofficial card. The crowd, perhaps not understanding the format of an exhibition match, was looking for a knockout from LaVern. The local residents, not pleased with what they were watching, gave little applause during and after the match. A few jeers were even heard. LaVern's goal was to give the crowd their money's worth by going the full six rounds and not trying for a knockout, which he could have easily accomplished.

According to Choc's ringside account, "Steen's style of close-in slug-ging must have seemed like a slow waltz from the mid to back rows of the arena. LaVern was able to dish out most of the punishment while blocking Steen's charges. Making it worse was Lavern's apologetic ges-ture to Steen after delivering a straight right which shook his opponent in second-round action."[6] This experience added fuel to LaVern's disen-chantment with his hometown fans. He wrote Abood, telling him the ex-hibition match was successful and that he had made some money from it, never mentioning the crowd's negative reaction. In hindsight he discov-ered why John was so opposed to exhibition fighting.

In the finale, Bill Henderson mollified the crowd as he knocked down Freddie Maes in every round. In the first round he scored two knock-downs. In the third round Maes once again took to the canvas but was saved by the bell. Henderson then ended the fight in the fourth round with a knockout. The appreciation of this fight was recorded by the crowd's loud applause. Henderson had won 147 out of 150 amateur fights before turning pro in 1948. He boxed professionally for a short period of time, making enough money to return to Lubbock to continue his education at Texas Tech College.

The crowd's apparent displeasure with his performance didn't prevent LaVern from coming away with a good feeling about the match, consider-ing his nine-month layoff. It intensified his desire to return to the action. He began to think seriously about a comeback. In the meantime he con-tinued selling insurance and found time in his schedule to play a little golf.

Since moving back home, LaVern had more family life. Time was spent with Evelyn and Ronnie doing the things that normal families do. About nine months after returning to Lubbock, Evelyn gave birth to a seven-pound, ten-ounce boy, Richard James Roach, on August 8, 1949. As proud as he was of Ronnie, he was equally proud of little Rickie. He sent telegrams to all of his Marine and boxing buddies, including Johnny Abood, announcing his son's arrival.

As a result John Abood, not known for his correspondence, wrote Choc,

> It has been a very hot summer up here. I had my family up in Maine
> and commuted every weekend. I received LaVern's wire and certainly
> was happy, for his sake, that it was a boy. He wrote me and told me
> his show was a success, and made some money also, he did not have

much trouble with his opponent. If that is so I am glad, because I was very much opposed to his giving an exhibition. Only champions and outstanding challengers give exhibitions. But since he quit boxing and was licked in his last few fights, even his home folks would not be interested in his exhibition and it would make him enemies. But he would not listen to me.

Ty Primm was in New York a few weeks ago. He tells me that they received a wire at his office about Roach's exhibition and that Roach lost the decision. Choc, when I heard that, it was like sticking a knife in my heart. I was inclined to believe him, since Roach never sent me any clippings about the show and said as little as possible about how he felt.

P.S. Robinson looked great beating Belloise. I still do believe the Roach of the Sal Ritchie fight would be the only one to beat Robinson.

After dominating the welterweight division for the past ten years with an occasional fight against a middleweight, Sugar Ray Robinson was ready to set his sights on the middleweight crown. This win, against a good fighter named Steve Belloise, increased his record to 97-1-2.

Even though LaVern seemed to be doing well in insurance, he also knew how to do the math. He was making peanuts compared to what he could be making in the ring. It was painful for him to pick up a newspaper and read what the boxers back east were making. He could make more in one average fight than he could in a whole year selling insurance. Evelyn always knew that LaVern's heart was still in boxing and that it would be just a matter of time before he would want to go back for one last shot at that elusive title. She was determined not to be the kind of wife to hold her husband back from his lifelong dream.

LaVern contacted Johnny and told him that he was in good shape, had his head on straight, and was ready to make a comeback. Johnny welcomed him back and agreed to set him up again.

The Knox residence, 475 Elmwood, Maplewood, New Jersey. Courtesy of the
LaVern Roach family.

CHAPTER 14

The Comeback

Make your mark in New York and you are a made man.
—*Mark Twain*

On November 20, 1949, after being back in Lubbock for only a year, LaVern and Evelyn packed up their belongings along with four-year-old Ronnie and three-month-old Ricky and headed back east. They arrived in Maplewood, New Jersey, at noon on November 23, the day before Thanksgiving. Although he had been far away from New York City for over a year, LaVern's name and photo were still present in *Madison Square Garden's 1948–1949 Boxing Magazine and Program*. Marcel Cerdan was listed as middleweight champion while LaVern was mentioned as a title contender along with Anton Raadik, Tony Zale, Rocky Graziano, Rocky Castellani, Steve Belloise, Jake LaMotta, and Charlie Zivic.[1]

John made arrangements with the Knox family for LaVern, Evelyn, and the kids to move in with them until permanent accommodations could be found. William (Bud) Melborne and Constance (Con) Knox, along with their daughter, Suzanne, lived at 475 Elmwood in Maplewood, New Jersey, across the street from where LaVern and Anspach resided after their discharge from the Marines. The Knox family treated LaVern and Anspach like family and readily welcomed LaVern and his family into their home. Their house had extra living space, which they offered to LaVern, Evelyn, and the kids. Suzanne, even though a college student and away at school most of the time, became a good friend with Evelyn and LaVern. She and Evelyn, approximately the same age, became like sisters. Suzanne, like everyone else, adored Ronnie and Ricky.[2]

LaVern wrote the first letter back home to Vera and Herb on Thanksgiving Day:

> Guess you figured we weren't going to write but, I've finally found
> time. We arrived at 12 PM yesterday so we made pretty good time.
> Didn't have any trouble & the kids are both feeling fine. Ronnie is re-
> ally having a good time and Rickie feels good.
>
> John was glad to see me & thinks everything will be O.K. I've got
> to buckle down & do good for this is my last fling. I think that I will do
> good, for I feel O.K. & want to do good.
>
> Evelyn is down in the cellar washing now is why she wanted me to
> write. Mr. Knox is fixing the turkey & Mrs. Knox is fixing pies. They
> really are nice & we're lucky to have them to be with. We're going to
> try to find us a place to live as soon as we can for I don't want to im-
> pose on them. . . . Hope you have a good Thanksgiving.[3]

Johnny missed LaVern and was glad to have him back in the fold. After quickly adapting to their new housing arrangement, it was time for
LaVern to get back to work. LaVern wrote to Choc,

> We're about to get settled and I'll start training tomorrow. I sure feel
> good and am going to get back in the money Choc. John was glad to
> see me back out here and he thinks I can make a lot of money. I guess
> I'll fight around Christmas if everything goes right. He says there are
> fights for me in the Garden in February if I show good and I'm going
> to. We are using a private gym on Second Avenue instead of Still-
> man's. We can train like we want to and work when we get ready. . . .
> Hope all of you are well. Keep your fingers crossed and wish me luck.[4]

The living arrangements with the Knox family worked out fine. La-
Vern paid for groceries, but Mrs. Knox insisted on doing the cooking,
since Evelyn spent most of her time washing, ironing, and taking care of
Ronnie and Ricky. They refused to take any rent money. In return, Bud,
who didn't own a car, used the Roaches' car whenever necessary. Bud, an
executive with Bulkey Dunton Paper Company, like so many New Jersey
residents, took the train into the city each day for work.

The two families blended well. This living arrangement was meant to
be only temporary until LaVern earned some money. LaVern and Evelyn
planned on getting their own residence so as not to take advantage of the
Knox family's hospitality.

On December 9 LaVern went into the city to watch Jake LaMotta fight Robert Villemain in a ten-round nontitle bout at Madison Square Garden. It was a unanimous decision for Villemain. Both judges scored it 7-3, and the referee had it 5-3-2 in favor of Villemain. After watching the fight, Lavern came home and told Evelyn, "I can beat either of them. LaMotta [the current world middleweight champion] isn't nearly as good as I had him figured. He looked awful."[5] The fight bolstered LaVern's resolve even more.

LaVern was a different person since returning to the East Coast. In a letter dated December 10 to Herbert and Vera, Evelyn wrote about LaVern,

> He really has a business attitude. He trains so well and John says he looks better than he ever has. He is settled and not flighty like he once was. He also wanted to study the fight and that is new too. He keeps saying, "make me a little money and get out." He doesn't plan on staying in long but he is really cheery after seeing that [LaMotta] fight.[6]

The middleweight division was less crowded and muddled than a year before. After the Cerdan fight, Tony Zale removed himself from any future title consideration by retiring. At thirty-four he was considered an old man. Cerdan and his manager put a rematch clause in the contract with LaMotta, just in the event that they were to lose the fight. Cerdan returned to France to train for his rematch and to be with Edith. The fight was scheduled to take place in September, and Edith wanted to make sure she would be there to take a chunk out of LaMotta.

As Cerdan boarded a ship for the United States to continue his training, Edith found a way to avoid the press and joined Marcel on board. Once in New York, Marcel trained while Edith performed at the Versailles nightclub. In *No Regrets*, Carolyn Burke gives the following account: "[Edith] planned to sing *Hymne a l'amour* for the first time in public on September 15, opening night at the Versailles: it was about Marcel and herself, she told her entourage. The crowded nightclub audience, full of such celebrities as Cary Grant, Gary Cooper, Rex Harrison, Barbara Stanwyck, and Claudette Colbert, greeted her as the 'queen of song.'"[7]

The bout, set for September 28, was postponed until December 2 due to a shoulder injury sustained by LaMotta. Edith was overjoyed, figuring this would give them more time in New York. Marcel, much to her objections and disappointment, returned to Casablanca to see his family. After the visit and a training match outside of Paris, Marcel broke training camp and was set to sail to New York for his fight. He phoned Edith to inform her of his plans.

Edith insisted that he catch the next flight out so that they would be able to spend more time together. Marcel agreed. He gave the following statement to the French press: "I have to beat LaMotta, I will beat LaMotta. I'll be perfect on December 2. You can be sure I'll come back to France with the middleweight crown placed securely on my head." He bought a ticket for the night flight of October 27. Prior to boarding the plane he gave the following statement to a nationwide audience listening on their radios: "I'm so eager to get back to New York and Madison Square Garden that if I could have left sooner I'd done so."[8]

The plane with Marcel, manager Jo Longman, thirty-five other passengers, and eleven crew members took off but never reached its destination, disappearing in the early morning hours of October 28. The Lockheed L-749 Constellation crashed into the Azores, killing all on board.

One of the great middleweights of all time was suddenly gone. Marcel's boxing record was an amazing 111 wins, including 65 knockouts, against only 4 losses. Three of his four defeats were by questionable disqualifications. Angelo Dundee, who first met Cerdan in Paris during the war, called him "one of the greatest and most underrated middleweight fighters ever."[9] LaVern would never get the rematch with Cerdan that he wanted.

Cerdan's death and Zale's retirement left the reigning champ Jake LaMotta, Rocky Graziano, and the newcomer to the middleweight division, Sugar Ray Robinson, as Roach's major roadblocks to the championship.

Word quickly spread that LaVern was back in town, ready to resume his career. When promoters Harry Markson and Al Weill found out, they immediately approached Abood and Chris Dundee and offered LaVern a chance to fight Rocky Graziano. The fight would be held in the Garden with LaVern guaranteed to make at least ten thousand dollars.

Abood and Dundee discussed the offer, both feeling the timing was not right. LaVern needed several tune-up fights before taking this kind of chance. LaVern, although anxious to fight Graziano, agreed. Dundee reported to the press, "If LaVern shows he has his old stuff, the Graziano shot will be there for him whenever we want to take it, and if he doesn't stand up, there's no use getting his brains knocked out even for $10,000."[10] Instead they settled for a fight in New Bedford, Massachusetts, against Johnny Crosby, where LaVern was expected to make seven hundred dollars.

In a letter to his parents, LaVern made the mistake of mentioning a possible Graziano fight after the first of the year. Stanley, not one to keep things to himself, contacted the *Plainview Herald* and told them that La-Vern was expected to fight on December 20 but didn't know who his opponent was going to be. He then told the *Herald* that LaVern was going to fight Graziano early next year.

When LaVern received the news clippings from the Plainview paper, he was furious. He wrote letters to Choc and to Vera about his displeasure with his mother and dad:

> Mother and daddy are like kids. Boy that burns me up. I told them I "might" fight in a couple of weeks and that I "might" get a chance to fight Graziano. So, they built a story out of it. I wrote and told them that I didn't want them to say anything about my business anymore. If the paper wants any news they can get it from somebody else. There are a bunch of characters in Plainview who know you when you are on top but won't speak when you aren't getting your name in the paper. I don't care if they don't ever get any information for it doesn't matter to me.[11]

LaVern started both letters with these same words and then finished the letter to Vera and Herbert by telling them about Ronnie and Ricky. He finished the letter to Choc talking about his medical condition:

> Choc, I've found out what was the matter with me before. Those 3 vertebras between my shoulders went out of joint. I remember after my last fight that the Doc said they were out of place. The last couple of weeks I've felt real good then a couple of days ago I boxed and couldn't do anything. I was nervous and couldn't rest and felt weak so when I got home I went to an osteopath & he said I had three vertebras out between my shoulders. He put them back & my arms & legs relaxed, my head cleared up & I felt like a new man. The next day I could do anything I wanted to do & it really felt good. John is taking me to a specialist today to see why they keep coming out. I remember when I was going to Washington for my last fight that I felt the same way I did the other day. I hope I keep feeling good for I want to fight in a week or so.[12]

Christmas Day, 1949. Ronnie with doll, Ricky, and LaVern. Photo taken by Evelyn Roach. Courtesy of the LaVern Roach family.

The Roach and Knox families spent Christmas Day together, exchanging presents and enjoying the holiday festivities.

After Christmas, LaVern was anxious to get back to his regular training routine. In a letter to Choc, he wrote,

> Choc, just a line to let you know I'm fighting in Fall River, Mass. next Tuesday, Jan. 2nd against Johnny Crosby. I don't know him but he's boxed a lot of good boys. If things go right I'll fight every week for a month or so. Keep your fingers crossed & wish me luck. I've been feeling real good lately & am boxing 7 and 8 rounds every day in the gym. I went 11 one day but they weren't hard.[13]

In a letter the same day to Vera and Herb, LaVern added,

> I told mother and daddy about [the fight] in their letter and told them not to mention it to the press. I told Choc about it so it will probably be in the newspapers [in Lubbock].[14]

LaVern's first fight in his comeback effort was held at Page Arena in New Bedford. LaVern came in weighing 159. Crosby, with an unimpres-

sive record of 2-15-1, weighed in at 155. It wasn't much of a fight. LaVern
floored Crosby twice for nine-counts before the fight was halted at 1:25
of the first round. His win was his twenty-sixth in thirty fights. It wasn't
the fight that LaVern really wanted or needed. Although it built up his
confidence, he hardly worked up a sweat.

LaVern was feeling better and better every day, as he explained to
Choc:

> I feel good for a change & I think I am on my way up, Choc. The Doc
> that is working on me says I'll be okay. He's found several nerves that
> were knotted & says that has been my trouble. Hope he can fix me
> up or at least keep me feeling the way I am. I feel better now than at
> any time since I fought Sal Richie & that was a long time ago, before
> Janiro. I am boxing in Phil., Pa next Thursday against some good boy.
> He's fought everybody & is a wise old boy. If I can do good with him
> I'll know I'm on the right track so keep your fingers crossed.[15]

There were indications that the rocky relationship between Evelyn and
Johnny Abood was improving. They had gotten off to a shaky start when
LaVern informed Johnny of their marriage well after the fact. Johnny felt
a little betrayed and disappointed that LaVern had kept the nuptials a secret. Most boxing managers are used to being in charge of their fighters
and don't welcome such surprises. Abood's control over his boxer didn't
even compare to some of the other boxing managers. Word on the street
was that Al Weill, Rocky Marciano's manager, told Rocky that "when it's
right for you to marry, I'll tell you." It is believed that Rocky and Barbara
Marciano waited three years for him to approve their marriage.

Evelyn wrote in a letter to Vera and Herb,

> LaVern feels good and John is well pleased. He had a heart to heart
> talk with LaVern and told him he was glad he married and I am out
> here. That everything has turned out for the best and that he was hap-
> py about everything. You know LaVern is going to do good. I feel sure
> of that. He is so conscious of it and entirely different from before. He
> has lost that big shot attitude and came down to earth. We both have
> a different attitude. He says "I am going to make a little money and
> quit." We are going to keep it if we are lucky enough.[16]

George LaRover of Philadelphia was everything that Johnny Crosby wasn't. LaVern had his hands full. LaRover, a seasoned fighter, came into the bout with an impressive record of 66-25-6. Except for Cerdan, La-Vern had never fought a boxer with that many wins. The fight was held in Philly at the Metropolitan Opera House on January 12. Bold headlines in the *Philadelphia Daily News* read, "Roach Headlines Met Card with LaRover." In the article Chris Dundee was quoted as saying, "We have been offered as opponents for LaVern in the Garden, Paddy Young, Harold Green, or Morris Reif, but I feel that LaVern needs several fights before accepting those fights."[17]

As LaVern and Bud Knox got into LaVern's car and left for Philadelphia, Evelyn sat down and wrote to Vera and Herb,

> LaVern and Mr. Knox left early for Philadelphia and I am holding my breath. He looks wonderful and is very determined. Boy does he train and no monkey business. He is really serious this time. John lectures all the time about his being a grown man now and has a family. John is really so much better. [John and Eleanor] gave Ronnie the cutest little purse. Knox's are wonderful. Their life circulates around LaVern's training. They have certainly been a help to us. LaVern comes in and studies insurance every day. You've never seen him so full of business. Mrs. Knox says he has aged so much the last year that he looks like a man and not a boy.[18]

A small crowd of 2,143 fans paid a total of $4,969 to see the fight. LaVern weighed in at 160, a nine-pound advantage over LaRover. Roach beat the local favorite in a unanimous eight-round decision. There was only one knockdown in the fight, and it occurred in the first round when LaVern connected with a short straight right to the midsection, sending LaRover to the mat for a nine-count. As reported in the Plainview newspaper, "LaVern failed to land many heavy punches. LaVern failed to take advantage of many openings in the clinches. He staggered LaRover with three in the second round but LaRover was able to hang on until the bell. LaRover's best round was the seventh when he landed a hard right followed by three left hooks that baffled Roach."[19]

Referee Charlie Daggart and Judge Lou Tress each awarded LaVern six out of eight rounds. Judge Joe Sweeney scored it five rounds in favor of LaVern, two for LaRover, and one draw. Things were not going to get any easier for LaRover, because next up for him was Sugar Ray Robinson. LaVern's twenty-seventh win earned him $993.80.

LaVern, after having read how the Plainview paper reported that this had been a difficult fight, countered in a letter the next day to Vera and Herb:

> Just a line to let you know that I'm okay. Won the fight pretty easy, but had to work hard. He didn't hit me 3 punches & all he wanted to do was hold on after the first round. I knocked him down in the first round, and then couldn't get him to open up after that, so I could punch. I needed the work & the 8 rounds were good for me, but I wish it had been 10. They scheduled it for 8 but I don't know why. We sure got a lot of publicity, & I laughed because I had the headlines in the third largest town in the US & still can't get a write up in P.V. Doesn't matter for I don't care whether they ever write anything or not.[20]

Evelyn echoed what LaVern was saying in her own letter written the same day:

> You can ignore that write-up mother because he got wonderful ones in the Philadelphia papers and that certainly carries more weight. Besides Mr. Knox saw the fight and he lost one round for a low blow that hit the guy and bounced off and hit his hip.[21]

LaVern started a letter to Vera and Herb that Evelyn had to finish because he had to go and train. She did so as follows:

> I feel like a dog that I haven't written you in two days. . . . I hope you will forgive me. Mr. Knox went with LaVern to Philadelphia for this fight. He told me he had never seen anyone make such a change. That LaVern acquired such a dignified air was nice to those people but would have no part of them. I don't know what has happened but LaVern is so independent with John anymore. The year he laid off was wonderful for him. He talks about insurance all the time. John told the papers [LaVern] would settle in N.Y. and LaVern laughed and said (to me) no. Keep all of this to yourself. Chris Dundee got LaVern in front of John and told him what a nice wife he had—tickled me even if it isn't true—and keep that to yourself—don't I get confidential.[22]

The next day, LaVern, in a letter to Vera and Herb, started off by joking with Herb:

> Well another day is here & I'm going to get to work soon. I wish I was a farmer & then I wouldn't have to do anything. [Herb was a farmer.]

> Have a good one coming on January 25th with Sonny Horne in St.
> Nicks but it won't be broadcast. It should be a good fight but I can beat
> him. We were offered a bout in the Garden Jan. 27th but John wants
> me to wait a while. I'll probably fight there next month if everything
> comes out okay. Keep your fingers crossed. Evelyn is looking better
> all the time & getting prettier. Bless her heart. I sure have a mighty
> sweet wife.[23]

He spent the better part of the day writing letters to his parents, Choc,
Johnny Mason, Vera and Herb, and a few others. Much of the content in
the various letters was the same. He shared the news that Sonny Horne
turned down his fight. He was disappointed, but they were trying to
schedule another. He then criticized the fair-weather friends back home:

> I want to box in the Garden next month. A lot of people will open
> their eyes & start being friendly when I get in the Garden again. Boy I
> have no use for about half the people back home. I can look back and
> see how they change as soon as they thought I had quit fighting. It
> doesn't matter what they think or do, for I know who my friends are.
> They can all kiss my rear if they want to.

In his letter to Choc, he added,

> I'm having Angelo Dundee send you some publicity on each fight or
> at least he said he would. He asks about you & said he used to hear
> from you all the time.[24]

He expressed his disappointment to Vera and Herb of being turned
down for his next fight:

> We should have something lined up in a day or so & I hope we do. I
> want to get a couple more under my belt then take on Graziano. Don't
> frown, Vera, for I can beat that guy. It would be nice if I could have a
> big outdoor fight when you come out next summer.[25]

LaVern, for a couple of years now, just short of an obsession, had his
sights on getting into the ring with Rocky Graziano. In December 1947,
after the Kronowitz bout and prior to his bout with Janiro, LaVern gave
an interview to the *Plainview Herald* stating such: "Confident that I can
beat Graziano any time. I have studied motion pictures of him watching

every move that he makes. His style is very similar to that of Herbie Kro-nowitz. I am convinced more than ever that I could beat him."[26]

LaVern's next fight was scheduled for January 30 against Armondo Amanini at Eastern Parkway Arena in Brooklyn. That fight was can-celled, and then a bad cold laid LaVern up for several days, forcing him to cancel a Garden appearance against Jimmy Flood. He displayed his disap-pointment over his cancelled fight in a letter to Choc:

> If I hadn't had the cold I would have fought Jimmy Flood Feb. 10th. I'd like to have him for he draws good & if I beat him I could get Gra-ziano. That's what I want, for a win over him would put me in line for a title shot. I need a couple of more fights Choc & then I'll fight anybody. I hope I can get a Garden bout before long. I'm hoping I can get back on top so I can make a lot of those big shots out there eat their words.[27]

His wish was granted as his next two fights were lined up. In a letter to Choc a few days later he wrote,

> Well I'll fight Tues. 14th in New Bedford, Mass. against Jimmy Taylor, if I don't take more of a cold. I get so mad when I start feeling bad from a cold. Right now I'm okay but I can feel a cold coming on. I'm going to a Doc in a minute & see if he can't check it. I also have a bout lined up in St. Nicks Feb. 22nd against Georgie Small so I hope things come off as planned. I need two more & if I can do good against Tay-lor and Small I'll be ready for anybody.[28]

Over a month after the LaRover fight, Roach was finally going to fight again. His plan of fighting once a week was first derailed by cancellations and then by the cold bug. The bout was set to take place at Page Arena in New Bedford, the same site where he fought Johnny Crosby six weeks earlier in his first fight back after his layoff.

LaVern was taking the same calculated risk that he took before the Cerdan fight, as he had already signed to face Small at St. Nick's and had agreed to fight his Cherry Point teammate, Joe Rindone, in the Rhode Is-land Auditorium in Providence on March 6. A loss to Taylor could cancel these. The Small bout was to be televised nationwide, and a good showing there would all but assure LaVern of a crack at Graziano in the Garden.

LaVern left for New Bedford, where he was a guest of the Chema fam-

Jimmy "Cannonball"
Taylor gets off to a flying
start. Courtesy of the
LaVern Roach family.

ily, owners of Chema's Health Farm at Acushnet. LaVern served in the
Marines with Pete Chema, one of the Chema boys. Headlines in the lo-
cal paper read, "Roach Endangers St. Nick Bout Against Rugged Foe."[29]
Matchmaker Manny Arruda announced that Roach should be made the
favorite, but some felt that Roach's limited activity since fighting the late
Marcel Cerdan would cause him to lose this fight.

Taylor came into the fight weighing 158½ to LaVern's 159. A head
shorter than LaVern, earning him the nickname "Cannonball," Taylor
had a record of 16-45-5. A small target, he had only been knocked out
twice, going the distance in all of the other fights.

The Valentine's Day fight went the full ten rounds, which pleased
both LaVern and the same crowd that a month earlier witnessed the first-
round knockout against Crosby before many had even taken their seats.
The headline the morning after the fight read, "LaVern Roach Decisions
Taylor." The article continued,

> The leading challenger for Jake LaMotta's 160-pound crown was giv-
> en a terrific fight all the way by the rough and tumble puncher from
> Manhattan, with defeat staring him in the face as late as the latter part
> of the seventh round, he had to pull out all of the stops in the late go-

ing. It was a bruising brawl all the way and the gathering of 774 customers, who braved the snowstorm and rain, were well rewarded by
the slashing battle of close range fighting.[30]

LaVern never fought an opponent as short as Taylor, which made him
a small target. After the fight LaVern stated that he knew what he was
getting into with the elusive, squatty Taylor, but wanted someone who
would give him a battle, which he got. It was a unanimous decision, but
the judges had it very close. Judges Dick Monroe and Jim Leddy, both of
New Bedford, scored it 97-94 in favor of LaVern, while Referee Ed Mc-
Donald scored it even closer, 96-95.

The win over Taylor moved him one step closer to a fight with Graziano, Robinson, or LaMotta, whoever owned the crown at that time. First
he had to get by Georgie Small the following Wednesday, February 22, at
St. Nick's Arena.

Georgie Small at punching bag. Courtesy of boxingrec.com.

CHAPTER 15

Georgie Small, the Mighty Atom, and Rita

Once that bell rings you're on your own. It's just you and the other guy.
—Joe Louis

LaVern's next fight was against Georgie Small. Georgie, the same age as LaVern, was born in Brooklyn, New York, on June 30, 1925. Small, like LaVern and most fighters, grew up in poverty and learned how to fight at a young age.

As a Jewish kid, Small had to be tough to survive the neighborhood gangs that roamed his streets. A lot of tough guys in those days ended up getting in trouble with the law, and young Georgie was headed in the same direction. If it had not been for a professional strongman who lived nearby and took him under his wing, Georgie could have ended up in gangs or even worse. This neighborhood strongman went by the name of "The Mighty Atom."

In real life, the Mighty Atom was Joseph Greenstein. In some ways, young Georgie reminded the Mighty Atom of himself. He, too, was Jewish and learned the hard way how to defend himself in the anti-Semitic atmosphere that prevailed at that time in Eastern Europe.

As soon as he could, Joseph Greenstein took his young family and moved from Poland to Galveston, Texas, where he became a dockworker. The story goes that sometime in 1914 Joseph was shot in the head by another man obsessed with having Greenstein's wife, Leah. The bullet hit him right between the eyes. Not only did it not kill him, the impact flattened the bullet. Joseph thought that he possessed some sort of "mental powers" and soon turned his attention to discovering and developing them. He began traveling the country, showing off his newfound abilities as a performing strongman and making good money. Small in stature, weighing only 140 pounds with a height of five-foot-five, Joseph took on the name "The Mighty Atom." He became one of the twentieth century's most notable strongmen and was labeled the world's strongest man.[1]

Some of the feats that he performed included

- Driving 20 penny nails through a two-and-one-half-inch board with his bare hands.
- Bending horseshoes, spikes, and steel bars with his hands.
- Biting chains, nails, or quarters in half with his teeth.
- Breaking as many as three chains by just expanding his chest.
- Swinging by his hair from an airplane.

Georgie quit high school at the age of eighteen and went on the road with the Mighty Atom as he traveled around the country performing his acts at county fairs, carnivals, and wherever there was an audience to watch and pay him to perform his amazing feats. The Mighty Atom taught Georgie how to maximize his strength. After a couple of years on tour, they returned to Brooklyn, and Small began his professional boxing career at age twenty.

The routine for young boxers was to start out with a four-rounder, move up to a six-rounder, then an eight-rounder, and then hope to be good enough for the ten-rounder or main event. He fought his first professional fight on August 7, 1945, in the MacArthur Stadium in Brooklyn against Lee Bryant. Georgie won with a first-round knockout. Small then fought four of his next five fights either in MacArthur Stadium or the Broadway Arena, both situated in the friendly confines of Brooklyn. He quickly became a local favorite.

His seventh professional fight was on November 2 against Charlie Hilton. It was a preliminary four-rounder and the first time he fought in St. Nicholas Arena. The fight went the distance, and Georgie won on points. On the same night, 365 miles down the eastern seaboard in Norfolk, Virginia, LaVern Roach knocked out Baudelio Valencia in a four-round preliminary. Valencia was the first common foe for both men. Georgie fought Baudelio twice—the first bout on December 28, in a four-rounder held in Madison Square Garden. The fight went the distance, with Small winning the decision. Their rematch was held on Georgie's home turf at the Broadway Arena in Brooklyn on February 19, 1946. This match was a six-rounder with the same results.

The only other common opponent for both boxers was a journeyman named Charley McPherson. LaVern fought him first on October 14, 1946, in St. Nick's Arena in a preliminary six-rounder. The fight went the distance, with LaVern winning on points. Georgie had his turn with McPherson three months later on January 25, 1947, in Ridgewood Grove Arena located in Queens. Georgie won on points in this eight-round bout.

The toughest fight for Small to date was against Lee Sala, held a little less than a year before on March 28, 1949, in Cleveland, Ohio. Coming into the fight Sala was sporting a record of fifty wins (twenty-six knockouts) against only one loss. It was a main event that went all ten rounds, with Sala winning unanimously.

Georgie had last fought on November 11 of the previous year, a preliminary eight-rounder in the Garden against Vinnie Cidone. He won that fight with a knockout in the seventh round. Cidone came into that tilt with a very respectable record of 32-4. Up to this point, Georgie had never fought a top contender.

Georgie Small was living the life that he dreamed of . . . nice clothes, a fancy car, and beautiful women. He paid his dues and was now a big shot in his neighborhood. Everyone, even his old adversaries, claimed to be his friend. Fighters like Georgie never had to carry their own bags on the way to the gym. There were always the young neighborhood kids who would fight over the right to carry his bag. That was just part of being a prizefighter.

Everyone knew Small. It was always, "Hi Georgie, good fight, Georgie. Hey Georgie, do you think you could give me a small loan until payday for an emergency?" Being kindhearted, Georgie often gave in, never expecting to be paid back. His photos soon made the papers and made it difficult to go anywhere without being noticed.

He learned one of life's hard lessons: nothing comes without a price tag. A career in boxing is no exception. Boxing is a profession, more than any other, that takes a toll on the body each and every time you get into the ring. You get hit in the head, in the jaw, in the eye, in the nose, on the ear, in the chest, under the heart, in the kidneys, and often a few misplaced punches land below the belt. Temporary and permanent scars show up, not to mention the bruises, black eyes, broken teeth, cauliflower ears, and broken bones. It is all in a day's work. It is what boxing is all about. To Georgie, it was all worth it. One only had to look at his flashy new convertible, expensive wardrobe, gold jewelry, and pick of the girls to realize he had made it.

In 1949 a friend introduced Georgie to Rita. She, of Irish descent and from a poor Brooklyn neighborhood, was different from those "other" girls who flocked around Small. After their first date, Georgie gave his usual command that he gave to all of his girls: "Telephone me."

Rita laughed and didn't call.

The mutual friend got them back together again for a game of miniature golf. Georgie and Rita hit it off better his time. He realized that Rita was different from the glamour girls he had been dating. "There was something about her that spelled wife-and-mother." A summer romance followed, with the two of them falling in love. Georgie was ready to settle down and start a family. He soon asked Rita to marry him, but not until after his match with LaVern.[2]

Rita would have been very content if Georgie never fought again. Nothing could have pleased her more if he were to quit boxing and take a regular job with a guaranteed weekly paycheck, even if it were much less than what he was making in the ring. Georgie was not ready to quit, however. Life in the ring was all that he knew. He wanted to continue working his way toward that elusive big fight, the one that would bring the big money and a possible shot at the middleweight championship. They compromised. Georgie agreed that after a few more fights, if the golden belt that he had been chasing was not there, then he would quit and find another way to support Rita. Win, lose, or draw, the wedding bells were in the near future for the young couple after the fight with LaVern.

Georgie, known as the Brownsville Banger, fought just seven times in 1949, which was not much for that era's fighters. The match with LaVern was Small's first fight of 1950.

February 20, 1950—Forty-Eight Hours before Fight Time

At the Hotel Edison located in Midtown Manhattan, just steps away from Times Square, LaVern's handlers—John Abood, Charley Goldman, and Chris and Angelo Dundee—along with everybody else who was important in boxing were attending the Fourth Annual Dinner of the New York

Boxing Managers' Guild. Among the items discussed was the effect that television was having on the industry.

The argument was made that television was keeping fans away from arenas, which was causing reduced income for pugilists. As a result of the meeting, the Boxing Guild decided to strike in an effort to get the television media to split profits with the boxers. They would be successful in obtaining their goal before year's end, but this was not going to have any effect on the Small/Roach fight. They would receive only a percentage of the gate and no television revenue for their upcoming fight.[3]

While the festivities were going on at the Hotel Edison, LaVern and Evelyn were putting Ronnie and Ricky down for the night. Before going to bed, LaVern decided to write one last letter that evening.

> Dear Choc, Finally got around to answering your last letter. Guess the first thing is to give you a brief idea of what happened in my last fight. I thought I won every round but you know how some people like those wild swings. Any way it was a fair fight and I didn't get hit 3 times. I caught most of his punches on my arms. Enough of that & back to this one on my <u>24th</u> birthday. <u>Ha.</u> Small is a pretty good boy & plenty smart, but doesn't fight too often. It will be a good win for me if I can look good. I'm in top shape & should win, but keep your fingers crossed. My nose is a little sore & we thought we'd call it off, but I think I'll be O.K. Hope so anyway. Sure hope you can all come out next summer. We'll be settled by then & it will be nice to have you visit us even if we can't get you to stay with us. I'll finish later. Have to hit the sack.[4]

Earlier that morning Evelyn wrote to Vera and Herb:

> Dear Mother and Herb, it is a windy day. Reminds me of West Texas. They have so few windy days here. LaVern hurt his nose in the gym. He had it x-rayed to see if it is broken. If it is he won't fight Wed. That is a fine birthday present for him. If he wins though it will be swell. If his nose is broken I will write on the outside that the fight is off. It was so good to have Suzanne home yesterday. She wants LaVern and me to come to the President's Ball when she graduates in June. It will be formal and LaVern would have to wear a tux. After this fight we are going to see "South Pacific." You know Mary Martin is in it. You are

really going to have fun out here when you come. Everyone is going to the fight but Mrs. Knox and me. John says LaVern did the right thing to marry. But he is still a stinker, just between you and us. I have to iron and a million other things.[5]

Evelyn finished and mailed her letter the following day. LaVern decided to finish his letter to Choc after his bout with Small and mail it the next day.

CHAPTER 16

Back at St. Nick's

The sport, like life, is "sudden death." A fighter can lose at any time; yet no matter how
far behind he can maintain hope of winning until the very end.
—*Thomas Hauser*

February 22, 1950

This was no ordinary day for New York City, as its residents prepared
to celebrate George Washington's birthday along with Ash Wednesday,
the beginning of Lent for the Christian community. As he woke up at six
o'clock, these events, as well as it being his twenty-fifth birthday, were not
the most important things on his mind. It was fight day, which took pre-
cedence over everything else for a boxer. As far as a birthday celebration,
there is always tomorrow.

He went through his normal fight-day routine. After breakfast, Evelyn
drove him to the train station. The plan was for Bud to later drive the car
to St. Nick's, watch the fight, and for he and LaVern to return home. As
they made their way to the station, the weather conditions deteriorated,
causing the roads to ice up over the snow that was already on the ground.
Cold, snow, and ice were the forecast for the day, keeping many residents
from celebrating the patriotic and religious holiday events scheduled for
the day.

LaVern caught the train into the city and went about his preparations
with the physicals and official weigh-in. After lunch he had time to catch
a matinee at one of the nearby movie theaters. At approximately 6 p.m. he
called Evelyn and visited for a few minutes. He told her about the movie
he saw and then asked her if she was going to watch the fight on televi-

St. Nick's billboard sign.
Reprinted by permission of
boxrec.com.

Back of Roach/Small admission ticket, purchased by author from Anita Kivell. Photo by author. Author's private collection.

sion. She said she wasn't going to. "I am glad you're not," LaVern said. "It is going to be a tough fight. Everything will be all right, but I am glad you are not going to watch it on television."[1]

After saying good-bye to Evelyn, LaVern headed for St. Nick's, where he had another prefight observation from Dr. Schiff, who pronounced him fit.

After dropping LaVern off at the train station, Bud returned home. Later in the afternoon, due to the road conditions, he decided to leave early for St. Nick's. On the way Bud picked up Eddie and Bridie, LaVern's friends, who attended the fight with him. They found their way into St. Nick's and found their seats. Soon the fight began. They watched and cheered LaVern on as the first seven rounds belonged to him.

Back in Maplewood, Evelyn was invited to the home of Mr. and Mrs. Ernest W. Strubbe, who lived two houses down the block at 471 Elmwood Avenue, to watch the bout. Evelyn, not sure why she changed her mind, agreed to come down after she put the kids down for the night. "Maybe," she said, "it was because I believed what LaVern didn't know wouldn't hurt him. He had never told me, but I sensed that if he knew I was watching, it wouldn't be good for him." Besides, Mrs. Knox offered to watch the kids.

After Evelyn tucked the kids into bed she carefully made her way to the Strubbes'. The Cerdan match was the only fight she had witnessed. "I wasn't worried through the first seven rounds. He was winning the way he thought he would. LaVern was less nervous for this fight than I have ever seen him. Before the fight he told me, 'I am in the best shape ever and I feel pretty sure of this one.'" Up to this point LaVern had been correct in his prediction.[2]

Back at St. Nick's Arena

By the start of the eighth round, the unpleasant odor of cheap cigars and cheap perfume permeated the air. Even though the arena was less than half full, the noise level was still deafening to the ears of those in attendance while television viewers watched from the pleasant confines of their living rooms.

Round eight: Halfway through the round, Small, with a desperation punch, caught LaVern square in the mouth with a solid right, causing a deep gash to open up inside of LaVern's upper lip. Although LaVern's knees buckled from the blow, he was able to shake it off and finish the round. Only six minutes left in the fight.

Round nine started with LaVern receiving instructions from his corner to be cautious and keep up his guard. He had the fight won and just needed to stay away from Small's punches. At the same time Small was receiving his instructions from his corner to keep the pressure on LaVern and look for the knockout opening. Round nine ended with LaVern somehow avoiding going down from Small's flurry of punches. Both boxers were showing signs of tiring. Georgie was giving LaVern everything he had, but the Texan was still standing. Small thought to himself, *LaVern looks fresher than I am.* Three minutes to go as the bell rang for the tenth and final round. "Scorecards of both judges and Referee Frank Fullam had the Texan out front in the first nine rounds."[3]

Round ten: LaVern and Georgie met at the center of the ring and touched gloves again at Fullam's instruction as the customary boxers' handshake to start the tenth and last round. LaVern returned to his corner and shuffled out toward Small. Three minutes separated LaVern from an almost assured victory, while only a knockout could save Small.

At the sound of the bell for the tenth, Georgie came out of his corner and landed the first punch to LaVern's mouth, where the blood started flowing from the cut that he had received in the eighth. Blood spurted on Small's white trunks. Roach moved in, and they traded punches. Small landed a straight right to LaVern's chin, knocking him to the canvas. LaVern lay on his back as Fullam picked up the count from the timekeeper at the count of four. The count reached seven when LaVern sprang to his feet. Fullam wiped off LaVern's gloves to make sure they had not picked up any ring resin from the canvas and then backed off to let the bout continue. Less than two minutes from the final bell.

LaVern appeared groggy but determined to continue and finish. Some fans began to yell, "Stop the fight, stop the fight."[4] LaVern tried to continue throwing punches, but Small was all over him, connecting from all directions. A left hook struck LaVern on the chin and knocked him back on his heels. Before he could recover, a straight right caught him on his bloody chin and sent him down to the canvas for the last time. With sixty-three seconds left in the fight, Fullam waved his hands from side to side to indicate the end.[5] Georgie Small had recorded an upset knockout over LaVern, only the second time in his career that he had been knocked out.

Dr. Alexander Schiff, one of the boxing commission's staff physicians, immediately climbed into the ring to remove LaVern's mouthpiece and help his handlers revive the stricken pugilist. He quickly regained consciousness and was helped to his corner, expressing disappointment at having lost. As he was placed on his stool in his corner, LaVern told Dr. Schiff, "I'm okay, but my luck seems to be running out."[6]

As the television cameras continued to roll, Fullam approached LaVern's corner.

"LaVern, are you alright?"

"Sure!"

"Do you know where you are?"

"Sure!" said LaVern. "I'm in St. Nick's."[7]

Evelyn, thirty miles away in New Jersey, had seen enough.

In the eighth round I felt sick. I knew that Small was hurting him.

After the 10th round knockout, I saw LaVern escorted to his corner, where he stood up and put on his robe. As soon as I saw him tie a knot in the sash around his robe, a ritual that he performed after every fight, I felt he was okay. I thanked the Strubbes and left to come home.[8]

Once she reached the confines of the Knoxes', she checked on Ronnie and Ricky, making sure they were all settled in, and then decided to wait up for her husband. Knowing that it could be a couple of hours before he and Bud could get home due to the treacherous weather conditions, she changed into her robe and decided to do some ironing.[9]

Back in St. Nick's the television cameraman, not receiving any instructions to stop filming, continued to focus on LaVern's corner, where he appeared to be talking to his handlers and apparently fully conscious. He made several unsuccessful attempts to stand up on his own strength, but each time he slumped back on his stool. Dr. Schiff left the ring and was replaced by Dr. Vincent Nardiello, also of the commission's staff. By this time the 1,832 fans who had paid $5,343 to watch the fight had cleared out and the cameras finally stopped rolling—ten minutes after the fight's conclusion, well longer than normal—leaving the nationwide television audience in a state of dismay and confusion.[10]

Dr. Nardiello gave LaVern an injection of caffeine sodium benzoate, a respiratory and cardiac stimulant. He immediately dropped, became limp, and nearly fell off his stool, having to be held up by Johnny Abood and his seconds. LaVern then lapsed into unconsciousness. Dr. Nardiello, with the help of three other doctors, worked on LaVern for several more minutes as he was held up on his stool.

The doctors were not able to bring LaVern out of his unconsciousness. A stretcher was brought into the ring, and he was placed on it and carried into the dressing room. Here the medical team continued to work for another fifteen minutes with no luck, after which an ambulance was called to transport LaVern to St. Clare's Hospital, the closest medical facility. He was accompanied by Johnny Abood, Bud, Dr. Nardiello, and Dr. Schiff. The doctors' consensus was that the fighter had suffered a concussion. His last heartbeat and blood pressure taken before he was placed in the ambulance showed slight improvement, causing Abood to put out the word that LaVern would recover. John sent his handlers home.

At the hospital, after removing fluid on his spinal cord and taking X-rays, LaVern was placed in an oxygen tent and fed intravenously. Two other doctors, H. Easton McMahon and Frank Ferlaino, helped attend. The tests of his spinal fluid confirmed a brain contusion and a probable subdural hemorrhage. Dr. Nardiello reported that LaVern was in very bad condition. A call was placed to a brain specialist, who lived in Bayside, Long Island, but the roads were impassable and he wasn't able to come in. A neurosurgeon, J. A. McLean, was called in to examine the brain injury.[11]

The hospital reported to the press that "LaVern's condition was serious and said he still was unconscious at midnight." Dr. Nardiello added that it would be forty-eight hours before a decision could be made on his chances of survival.[12]

Bud Knox, not being able to help at the hospital, decided to drive LaVern's car back to his home in Maplewood. Before he left the hospital, Johnny Abood pulled him aside and instructed him not to tell Evelyn the extent of LaVern's injuries, only to tell her that they were keeping him overnight for observation and there was no need for her to come to the hospital.

Due to the icy road conditions, Bud finally arrived home at around 2 a.m. The drive took him twice as long as it normally would. As he entered the house alone, Evelyn asked, "Where is LaVern?' He replied, "They took him to the hospital so they could observe him overnight. There is no need for you to worry." The answer seemed to satisfy Evelyn, and she prepared to go to bed.

Bud then told Constance LaVern's real condition. Constance convinced Bud that he had to tell Evelyn the truth, which he did. Evelyn, now somewhat in a state of shock, got dressed, and she and Bud drove to the train station where they caught the next train into the city. It was safer than driving.

As they were making their way into the city, she looked out the train window and observed her warm breath fogging up the glass. As Evelyn drew her head away and the fog started to disappear, she noticed a strange pattern that formed on the window. After closer examination, it resembled a human skull, an image that totally alarmed her.

Her memory drifted back to a time when they lived in Lubbock when she woke up crying from a bad dream. It woke LaVern, and he asked her what she was upset about. She told him that in her dream she saw him lying in a coffin. This memory haunted her now even more.

Once they arrived at the train station, a cab carefully drove the icy streets of New York and delivered them to the hospital. She was taken to the room where her husband was being attended to. As she and Bud opened the door, a complete silence fell over the room as John Abood made a very awkward greeting; he wasn't expecting to see either one of them. No one knew what to say. Evelyn went over to LaVern's bedside. There he lay in an oxygen tent, looking as if he was in a peaceful sleep. The vigil continued through the morning hours with very little said by anyone.

As dawn arrived, a phone call came for Evelyn. The only phone available was one in a phone booth in the hospital lobby. A nurse led her to the lobby, which was crowded with reporters from the various New York newspapers, each trying to get the latest update on LaVern's condition. Evelyn could barely make her way to the phone booth, trying her best to ignore the reporters' insensitive interview requests. At the other end of the line were LaVern's parents, who had already been contacted by the local Plainview press.

Evelyn, not really knowing what to say to Stanley and Rosa Inez, wasn't able to tell them anything that they didn't already know. She politely ended the conversation as quickly as she could. She then placed a call to Vera, asking her mother to come at once. After the phone calls, she fought her way through the reporters with the nurse running interference for her.

As word got out that LaVern was in critical condition, the pastor of their church, Reverend Bateman, showed up at his bedside to help console Evelyn and keep her company.[13]

During the night and early morning hours the word of LaVern's injuries spread beyond the New York press. Newspapers across the nation reported that the popular, good-looking, former Marine boxer from Plainview, Texas, was in critical condition from injuries suffered in the ring the night before. The news was in all of the morning newspapers. Front page of the *New York Times*: "Roach in Hospital after Fight Here," "Texan, Knocked Out by Small at St. Nicks, Suffers a Concussion of the Brain."[14] As word got out, more reporters showed up at St. Clare's, hoping to get a story.

Back in Plainview, Vera contacted her brother James Churchwell, who offered to fly to New York with her. Claude Hutcherson, owner of the

Hutcherson Flying Service in Plainview, offered to fly Vera and James to Dallas, where they could connect to a commercial flight to New York City. They were to leave Plainview at around 1:00 p.m. and fly to Dallas to catch a 4:30 p.m. American Airways flight that would arrive in New York at 10:30 p.m.[15]

Shortly after the noon hour at St. Clare's Hospital, with Evelyn, John Abood, Bud, and Pastor Bateman in the room, LaVern's condition took a turn for the worse. At 12:50 p.m., February 23, 1950, one day after his twenty-fifth birthday, with Evelyn at his bedside, Raymond LaVern Roach passed away.[16]

CHAPTER 17

Pointing Fingers

The answer is always in the entire story, not a piece of it.
—Jim Harrison

The hospital issued the following statement concerning LaVern's passing: "The patient was in deep coma, and there was respiratory failure with final cessation of heart action at 12:50 p.m. due to the after effects of a cerebral hemorrhage and brain damage."[1] Shock waves resonated across the nation. Among the first to be informed of the news were Vera and her brother James as they were boarding the private aircraft to depart for Dallas. Vera and James were flown to Dallas, where they caught the next plane to New York City.

Evelyn faced some big decisions, and she had to make some alone and quickly. After LaVern died and before she left the hospital, Reverend Bateman pulled Evelyn aside and asked her if there could be a local funeral service in New Jersey before LaVern's body was shipped back to Plainview for burial. She listened as he told her that due to his popularity a lot of people in the area would want to pay their last respects to the popular young boxer. Although not cherishing the idea of having to go through two funerals as well as a graveside service, she reluctantly agreed, knowing that LaVern would have wanted it.

All of the details had to be carried out quickly. John helped her make the initial arrangements at the hospital for moving the body. Due to the nature of the death, an autopsy was required before LaVern's body could leave the hospital. After these arrangements were made, Evelyn was eager to get home to Ronnie and Ricky. By this time, the word was out about

LaVern's death, and the hospital lobby was packed with reporters. Evelyn and Bud were allowed to exit through the back entrance, going through the morgue so that they could avoid the newsmen.

They took a cab to the train station and returned to Maplewood, where the car was quickly retrieved. Bud carefully drove back to his house on the icy and slippery roads. A few blocks away as they approached the house, they could see a large gathering of vehicles lining both sides of the street in front of the house. As they approached they could tell it was reporters, some still in their cars, while others filled the lawn and the wraparound porch. One was seen knocking on the front door and the most brazen trying to peek in the windows, not realizing Evelyn wasn't even there. Bud drove past, pulled into his driveway and into the garage, where they would be able to enter the house through the back entrance and avoid direct contact with the reporters.

Once inside they found Constance trying to keep Ronnie, awakened by the outside noise and commotion on the porch, in the back room and out of sight of the activity outside. On a table nearby were dozens of unopened birthday cards for LaVern. Evelyn and Bud proceeded to go from room to room, pulling down the window shades to block the reporters who were attempting to peek in. She then held Ronnie tightly in her arms, resolved not to show tears. When asked by Ronnie where her daddy was, Evelyn simply answered, "Daddy has gone to heaven."[2]

Newspapers and radio and television stations nationwide were reporting the tragic death of the popular young boxer from Texas, who had won the hearts of a nation during his brief boxing career. Bill Henderson, the up-and-coming pugilist and friend of LaVern's, was driving back from one of his pro fights in Arizona when he heard the news from his automobile radio. "I decided right then to quit boxing."[3] One of the first to broadcast the stunning news was Joe Cummiskey, sports director for WPAT, North Jersey Broadcasting Company in nearby Paterson. At 6:45 p.m., on Thursday, February 23, 1950, only six hours after LaVern passed away, Cummiskey went on the air. His emotional diatribe lasted six minutes, starting with,

> **The BIG NEWS tonight is SAD news . . . BAD news.**
> It's the story of LaVern Roach, a clean-cut, upright kid of 24 [sic], who is dead tonight from injuries suffered in the ring.

Investigation Ordered In Ring Death of Texan

By JACK HAND

NEW YORK, Feb 23 — (AP) — A two-pronged investigation was ordered Thursday into the death of Middleweight Boxer Lavern Roach of Plainview, Texas, who was fatally injured Wednesday night in a St Nicholas Arena bout with Georgie Small of Brooklyn.

The district attorney's office scheduled a full investigation Friday of boxing's first fatality of 1950.

DETECTIVE LIEUTENANT Henry Delvin of the New York City police said all persons concerned with the bout would be questioned. He said he saw the match and "there does not appear to be any negligence at this time."

Chairman Eddie Eagan of the

LAVERN ROACH
Meets Death in Ring

PLAINVIEW, Feb 23—(UP) His parents were stricken down by grief and shock as Plainview went into mourning Thursday for Lavern Roach, its foremost fighting son, who died in New York from a prizefight ring injury.

Mr and Mrs Stanley Roach were not accessible to the hundreds of persons who wanted to offer condolences. Close friends said both were in a state of shock and under a doctor's care.

New York State Athletic Commission called an open hearing for Friday morning, Eagan said a preliminary examination indicated no infraction of the commission rules.

ROACH, A HANDSOME ex-

Referee Frank Fullman had the Texan out front in the first nine rounds of his last fight. Early in the battle he outpunched Small with a solid left hook although he appeared to be off in his timing.

A TERRIFIC RIGHT hand punch to the jaw, just as Roach was starting a left hook, smashed the Texan to the canvas for a count of nine in the last round. Roach, acting on instinct alone, followed through with his hook, spun weakly and flopped flat on his back. Out cold for seven counts, he bounced up jerkily like a mechanical doll to beat Fullman's count.

Seconds later, Small battered Roach to the canvas again and he collapsed flat on his back. Referee Fullman quickly stopped the fight without a count, reaching down to remove the boy's mouthpiece. Dr. Alexander Schiff, a commission doctor, was in the ring immediately.

After Roach was half-dragged to his corner he came to and opened his eyes. Talking to his trainer he said, "Damn it, this would happen."

THE STRICKEN boxer was taken to the same hospital where Carmine Vingo was carried after his knockout loss to Rocky Marciano at Madison Square Garden, Dec 30. Vingo left the hospital Feb 10. Both suffered similar injuries.

Roach was placed under an oxygen tent and fed through the veins. He was unconscious from the time he left the ring on a stretcher.

GEORGIE SMALL
Hears of Roach's Death

Newspaper headline, February 23, 1950. Article by Jack Hand, Associated Press.

After placing blame with the greedy side of boxing, including the rushing of LaVern back into boxing by Gene Tunney, Nat Fleischer, and Johnny Abood, Cummiskey continued,

> This afternoon Abood stood at the bedside in Saint Clare's Hospital.
>
> What was he thinking? What were his feelings? What he did say this afternoon was THIS: "What <u>can</u> I SAY??? / He was the <u>nicest</u>, / the <u>cleanest-cut</u> kid I ever knew."

Cummiskey finished with these words:

> Tonight, there are the usual postmortems. A few politicians are demanding investigations. . . . They're getting their names in the paper. . . . They're being talked about in the bars and grills. . . . It's a big sensation.
>
> But The Kid—he's gone. Chairman Eddie Eagan says "an unfortunate accident."
>
> Doctors say: "cerebral hemorrhage." . . . His widow says— nothing. His two kids? Veronica [*sic*], four, and Richard, six months . . . What can they say? They can hardly talk.
>
> It's over—it's done. . . . And 1950 has its Number One Ring Death of the Year.
>
> Come on, Engineer Chick Gulino—you must have some feelings about this. Play a record. Play the Marine Hymn. You're a Marine; play that Marine Hymn for the Fighting Marine from Texas, LaVern Roach—The Kid who couldn't miss. The Fighter of the Year in '47!
>
> PLAY THE MARINE HYMN. . . .[4]

Cummiskey, angry and upset, wrote out this script immediately upon hearing the news of LaVern's death. Having closely followed the boxing career of the kid from Texas and taking a shining for him, Joe was furious. Even though he did not have all the facts straight, he openly expressed what many listeners felt.

LaVern's death made front-page news across the country. The *Washington Post* devoted three-fourths of its front-page sports section to La-Vern. On February 28, a headline out of Austin, Texas, stated, "House

Expresses Regret at Death of LaVern Roach." The article read, "The House unanimously passed a resolution Monday expressing regret over the death of boxer LaVern Roach of Plainview. The resolution, by Reps. Harold M. LaFont of Plainview and Preston Smith of Lubbock, described Roach as a fine young man who was a symbol of clean living, courteousness, quick with a smile and was considered one of the outstanding athletes his town ever produced."[5]

The boxing and legal authorities, sensing the public outcry over his death, began their investigations immediately. The following day, Friday, February 24, two separate investigating bodies, the New York State Athletic Commission and the District Attorney's office, began proceedings.

As the investigations started, it didn't take long for the unconfirmed reports and accusations to come in from numerous outside sources, including many viewers who had witnessed the fight on their five-inch black-and-white televisions from their living rooms, most complaining that the fight should have been stopped earlier.

Some unsubstantiated reports stated that LaVern had been unfit for the bout because of old head injuries from the Cerdan fight. Another report stated the cause was the recurrence of a broken nose. From Paterson, New Jersey, came an unofficial report that both LaVern and Johnny Abood had been advised not to go through with the fight because of his painful and dangerous nose condition.

Heinie Miller, executive secretary of the National Boxing Association, issued a report from his office in Washington, DC: "I advised LaVern in 1948 to quit boxing because his reflexes had slowed considerably."[6]

Most of the accusatory statements were aimed at the prefight physicians who examined LaVern and at referee Frank Fullam; they were at the top of the list of both investigating bodies.

Prior to the hearings, an autopsy had been performed Thursday afternoon by the chief medical examiner, Dr. Thomas A. Gonzales. His examination revealed that LaVern had died from a subdural hemorrhage and ruptured pial emissary vein in the brain. He concluded that it was an "accidental death." An additional footnote to the autopsy report disclosed "an old chronic heart condition which could have been a rheumatic heart; but had been cured and had no part in his death."

The first hearing convened was that of the State Athletic Commission under the direction of its commissioner, Colonel Eddie Eagan, who announced that the results of the inquiry would probably be made public the next week. It would be an open hearing with ten witnesses called: Georgie Small; Dan Dowd, executive secretary of the commission; Dr. Jacob Silverstein of Milburn, New Jersey; Dr. Nathan Zvaifler of Newark, New Jersey; Drs. Alexander Schiff and Vincent Nardiello, both commission physicians; Dr. Frank Ferlaino, chairman of the commission's Medical Advisory Board; referee Frank Fullam; John Abood; and Oscar Goldman, commission inspector.

The witnesses were called. The first line of questioning concerned the prefight medical exams. The greater part of the testimony dealt with LaVern's reported sore nose. LaVern had complained to Abood of having pains in his nose at the end of Saturday's workout at Tommy Marra's Gymnasium. John said he and LaVern had considered calling off the fight because of this pain, but that they would have a physician examine him first.

On Sunday, February 19, an appointment was made with Dr. Silverstein. At the end of the examination, Dr. Silverstein referred them to a nose specialist, Dr. Nathan Zvaifler of Newark, and advised them to call the fight off if Dr. Zvaifler found anything wrong with the nose.[7]

Dr. Zvaifler testified that he saw LaVern on Monday and found nothing wrong with his nose. The X-rays were negative, showing no evidence of a fracture. LaVern told the doctor that the pains had ceased, and Dr. Zvaifler told him to use his own judgment as to whether his nose would prevent him from fighting Wednesday night. John, as his duty required as LaVern's manager, had already reported the sore nose to the Athletic Commission and the International Boxing Club, which was functioning as the promoter of St. Nicholas Arena.

John told the commission that he took LaVern to the gym Monday afternoon for a workout to see if his nose was all right. He brought in Cocoa Kid, one of LaVern's sparring partners, to spar and to give the nose a good workout. According to Abood, LaVern said he felt no pain, so he advised matchmaker Ted Brenner to go ahead with the bout.

On Monday afternoon, upon receiving notification from Abood, Dr. Nardiello examined LaVern thoroughly and found nothing wrong. That same evening, in the letter that was never finished or mailed, LaVern wrote Choc, mentioning the soreness in his nose.

There were no examinations on Tuesday.

On Wednesday, the day of the fight, LaVern was examined three more times. Dr. Nardiello met with him at 11 a.m. prior to his regular prefight weigh-in exam and again found nothing wrong. Commission staff doctor Alexander Schiff performed the noon prefight weigh-in exam, finding nothing wrong with LaVern. Schiff said he really mashed LaVern's nose and found him to have no pain and that he was in overall excellent condition. An hour later at the noon weigh-in, Dr. Nardiello was told by LaVern, "I have never felt better in my life."

As a precautionary measure, Dr. Schiff gave LaVern an oral examination in his dressing room just prior to LaVern entering the ring for the fight and found nothing wrong. Doctors Zvaifler, Nardiello, and Schiff all testified that LaVern appeared in excellent condition. Dr. Schiff concluded that "nothing happened to LaVern's nose during the fight that might have caused his death."

The testimony of referee Frank Fullam was next. Fullam had come under a barrage of criticism, especially from those not associated with boxing. When asked by the United Press the day before why he didn't stop the fight earlier, he gave two reasons: "(1) Roach appeared to be in 'good shape' and (2) If Roach could have remained on his feet for '63 seconds longer' he would have won the fight."[8] Fullam continued by giving his qualifications as a referee: he was a boxing instructor at the New York Athletic Club and had refereed thousands of fights since his retirement from the ring fifteen years earlier. As a professional middleweight he had fought in twenty-five boxing matches. Before that he had been a national amateur middleweight boxing champion. He added,

> Because of my long experience as a referee, and because of my experiences as a fighter I do not become excited by the sight of blood or by the cries of spectators. I know that the cries for a fight to be stopped may be coming from gamblers.
>
> When Roach came out of his corner for the tenth round, he appeared to be in good shape. He forced the fight until nailed by a right to the chin. That dumped him on his back. He jumped up at the count of seven. I watched him closely as I wiped off his gloves. Although he was bleeding from the mouth—as he had been since the eighth round—he still appeared to be in good shape.
>
> Because of the beating he had given Small in the earlier rounds,

I knew he had the fight wrapped up if he could stay on his feet for a little more than a minute. They started exchanging. Suddenly Small nailed Roach with another right that dropped him. I knew Roach had enough, so I stopped the fight at 1:57 of the 10th. He was conscious when I talked to him in his corner. Then he suddenly passed out.[9]

Fullam, the next day, gave a more condensed version when he testified before the commission, but added, "[LaVern] became aggressive each time he was hurt or knocked down."[10]

Dan Dowd, executive secretary of the commission, gave testimony supporting Fullam's, as he reported to the commission that the only way LaVern could have lost the fight going into the tenth round was by a knockout since he was way ahead on all three scorecards.

Georgie Small, accompanied by his manager, Sol Gold, appeared before the commission. The tearful fighter seemed to be traumatized. He stated, "I was so surprised and upset by Roach's death that everything seems to be turning around in my stomach. I was so tired in the tenth round, I felt worse than LaVern looked." When questioned if Roach seemed groggy after the first knockdown, Small replied, "No. Up to the knockout, he was forcing the fight."[11]

Johnny Abood, the last to appear before the commission, corroborated Fullam's response: "Roach said he felt all right after a rather slow ninth round, and insisted that he would take charge in the tenth." Abood finished up his testimony by saying, "Roach was happy, confident, and in perfect shape before the fight. He was determined to make good."[12]

On Thursday, the previous day, the district attorney's office dispatched a lieutenant of detectives to the International Boxing Club headquarters to issue summonses for a hearing. The hearing would take place after the commission's hearing, since most likely the same witnesses would appear at both.

The district attorney's office began its inquiry later on Friday. As expected, the same witnesses left the commission inquiry and journeyed to the district attorney's office to repeat their testimonies. Unlike the commission hearing, the DA's office would conduct a closed hearing. The DA's office issued a statement that their results would be issued at the conclusion of the probe unless some grounds for an indictment became evident. If such evidence surfaced it would be kept secret and presented to a grand jury. Starting late on Friday, most likely the inquiry would be adjourned and finished Monday.

The questioning was done by Assistant District Attorney George Monaghan, who was in charge of the Homicide Bureau. He was assisted by staff members Harold Birns and Andrew Seidler. New York City Police Detective Lieutenant Henry Devlin stated that he attended the fight, and "there does not appear to be any negligence at this time."

In addition to the same ten witnesses who had testified at the commission hearing were the ring judges, inspectors, deputy commissioners, the seconds and trainers of each fighter, and a few others, totaling about twenty in all.

Sitting in on the hearing was New York City Police Captain Peter Brennan. After testifying at this hearing, Georgie Small, who had been on what amounted to house arrest, was cleared of any criminal wrongdoing and was free to depart.

As the investigations moved forward, funeral services were held the next day—Saturday, February 25—at Knapp's Colonial Parlor in East Orange, New Jersey, at 3:30 p.m. Marine Corps personnel from the Dover, New Jersey, Marine Barracks served as honor guard. With floral arrangements lining and filling up every inch of vacant space in the parlor, Reverend Romaine F. Bateman, pastor of the First Baptist Church, Millburn, New Jersey, officiated. Many of the three hundred or more who gathered in the funeral home to pay their last respects didn't even know LaVern. They came to say farewell to a fallen hero who had won the hearts of everyone he came in contact with, either in person or through the news media. Two Marines, Privates First Class Lloyd Summers and Fred Thomas, stood at parade rest flanking the flag-covered coffin throughout the ceremony.

Among those in attendance with Evelyn were Vera and her brother James Churchwell. LaVern's parents, still in shock, weren't able to make the trip and waited back in Plainview for the return of his body.

Also present was LaVern's mentor, manager, and friend, John Abood, along with many of his Cherry Point boxing teammates. Curtis Moore, a professional fighter who was on the receiving end of one of LaVern's knockouts during the national Golden Gloves Tournament, came to pay his respects. Alongside Georgie Small were International Boxing Club promoters of St. Nick's, Harry Markson and Ted Brenner. Harry Don-

(NY1)EAST ORANGE,N.J., Feb. 26—MARINE HONORS FOR FIGHTER—Two Marines form an honor guard as a bugler sounds taps over the flag-draped casket of middleweight fighter LaVern Roach, an ex-Marine from Plainview, Texas, at services here yesterday. Roach died Thursday as a result of injuries received in a bout Wednesday night at New York's St. Nicholas arena. His body was sent to Texas for burial.Left to right:Pfc. Lloyd Summers, Sgt. Joseph A. Marino and Pfc. Fred C. Thomas, Marines from the Dover, N.J. ammunition depot.(AP Wirephoto) (Okh/pr1140Ostf-jr)1950

Marine bugler Sergeant Joseph Marino sounds Taps as the honor guard of Privates First Class Lloyd Summers and Fred Thomas stand at attention. Colonial Funeral Home service, February 25, 1950, in East Orange, New Jersey. Courtesy of the LaVern Roach family.

ovan (brother of referee Art Donovan), who had lost two Marine sons, was present to pay respects. Also in attendance was a seventy-year-old Marine bugler by the name of Herbert Baldwin, a veteran from the Spanish-American War. He and others came to show their respects to a fine young man who lived among them and was a beacon of light to the sport of boxing and their community.

Reverend Bateman, speaking off the cuff, spent the better part of the hourlong service describing how LaVern was different from most boxers by the type of life he lived, and this difference could be credited to his faith:

> Two doctors in the hospital, seeing me in LaVern's room, asked me what a boxer and a Minister had in common? I said that this was an uncommon situation for our boxer had a deep channel where feeling ran with a surprising surge of a spiritual experience. LaVern had an experience of heart that gave him that "difference" that everyone

recognized. He had knowledge of Jesus Christ as his personal Saviour. This knowledge and respect made him different from the next fellow. It could well be inscribed on his tombstone: "HE WAS DIFFERENT."

Reverend Bateman concluded his eulogy, "I prayed that LaVern might quit the ring and become a minister of the gospel, but God had a different set of plans."[13] Common with Baptist preachers, Reverend Bateman gave an altar call at the end of the service. Twice during the service, Georgie Small visibly broke down. The service ended with the words, "Farewell, Marine," and then the organist played the Marine Hymn. Taps was played by Marine bugler Sergeant Joseph Marino. The Marine Honor Guard took their places as pallbearers. There wasn't a dry eye in the room.

After the service, Georgie Small, still showing the bruises and cuts on his face from the beating he had taken, trembled as he stood for a brief moment in front of LaVern's coffin before embracing Johnny Abood. With Markson and Brenner on both sides of him, he approached Evelyn. He had been dreading this since the moment he first heard of LaVern's death. What can you say to a widow when it was your punch that killed him? Sobbing, he got out the words, "I'm so sorry."[14] That was all he could say as he walked away.

After the funeral, William (Dixie) Walker of Florence, Massachusetts, friend and boxing teammate at Cherry Point, made this statement to reporters, who had gathered like vultures outside the funeral home trying to interview anyone who would talk to them. "He always wanted to go to the top," Walker said, "and every Marine who knew him was in his corner. If I tried to tell you what a nice guy he was, you wouldn't believe me. He was a good boy—an all-around good boy. Everybody liked him." Howie Brodt added, "Who would have believed it that less than two years after their fight in the Garden both LaVern and Marcel Cerdan would be dead?"[15]

Evelyn finally broke her silence.

Now that it is over I am free to say that no matter how much money a man makes in that business, it isn't worth the chance he takes. LaVern felt differently. If anyone asked him whether the game was dangerous, he would toss it off with, "Sure, but you can get killed driving a car, too." I felt I had no right to ask LaVern to give up the ring. After all, he was a boxer when I married him.[16]

LaVern's flag-draped casket was transported to Penn Station, where it was placed on a train as a Marine guard played Taps. At 6:59 p.m., February 25, LaVern was going home again, but this time for good. Evelyn, Ronnie, Rickie, Vera, and Evelyn's uncle James flew to Texas the next day, Sunday, February 26.

Reverend Bateman, in a letter to Stanley and Rosa Inez, LaVern's grieving parents, wrote,

> This letter is written by one whom LaVern called, "My northern Pastor." It was a disappointment to me and to many in the New York area that you both could not be with us at the service in East Orange, when 300 friends from every walk of life gathered to pay respects to your boy, and many hundreds more were bowed with grief as they read the fitting tributes published in all the papers. Few men in New York have ever had so many friends. Once you knew LaVern you always felt you gained a friend. His clean-cut life and beaming and open countenance were a distinguishing factor in gathering such a mass of admirers.[17]

LaVern's body arrived in Amarillo on Monday evening, February 27, at 11 p.m. Funeral arrangements were provided by Lemon's Funeral Home of Plainview, which took the necessary measures to see that LaVern's body was transported from Amarillo to Plainview.

LaVern's second funeral service took place at 3 p.m. the next day at the First Baptist Church in Plainview, Texas, with his "southern" pastor, Dr. A. Hope Owen, officiating, assisted by Reverend Bill Ware. The Marine League of Amarillo provided the honor guard. As many as twelve hundred people filled the lower and upper levels of the church building. Massive floral arrangements, a testimony to the young boxer's popularity, were in abundance throughout the sanctuary. The Exordium was given by Dr. Owen followed by a prayer from a Chaplain Lively.

In his sermon, Dr. Owen talked about LaVern's interest in life and clean living. He proposed that there were three possibilities before every life: "There is a possibility of making a mess of life; a possibility of making a mixture of good and bad in life; a possibility of making a masterpiece in life." He continued, "Our endeavors should be in the third possibility and that is where LaVern lived his life. Not any boy in Plainview that ever talked to LaVern but what he talked to him about clean living and a clean life. It was true that even when he was back in the other part of the country, the boys liked to be around him, and he challenged them to a higher life, a cleaner life."[18]

Interment followed in the Plainview Cemetery. Pallbearers included Mick and Johnny Mason, Plainview High School football coach Finis Vaughn, O. R. Stark of Quitaque, J. R. Callahan, Bob Lake, and Choc Hutcheson of Lubbock.

The graveside service was surrounded by floral arrangements, one shaped in the figure of boxing gloves. Buried with full military honors, a squad of Marines fired the three-volley salute over the grave after his body was lowered to its last resting place in the snow-covered cemetery on the southern outskirts of Plainview.

Back in New York

After hearing the testimony of all of the witnesses, District Attorney Frank S. Hogan issued the following statement: "From review of the evidence, it appears to be that there has been no criminal negligence. Since a death occurred as a result of this contest, however, I deem it to be in the public interest to present all of the facts to a grand jury for its determination."[19] The evidence was then turned over to a New York grand jury. On Friday, March 3, after a three-day inquiry, District Attorney Hogan announced that the grand jury found no criminal negligence in the death of LaVern and closed the inquiry with a vote of "no indictment."[20]

One witness to the fight, who wasn't called to testify before either committee, later added more drama to an already muddled set of circumstances surrounding the prefight events that fateful evening. A few weeks after the fight, J. J. "Jack" Duberstein, New York's deputy commissioner to the state athletic commission, was having a conversation with a couple of reporters when he dropped a bombshell by saying that the fight came within a few minutes of being called off. As a representative of the SAC he was assigned to St. Nick's that evening.

According to his account, the opening bout on the card was ready to get into the ring for their 8:30 start. Duberstein wasn't going to let the preliminary go on unless both main event fighters were present. Small was already there, but LaVern was a no-show. The evening matchmakers,

Marines firing three-volley salute, February 28, 1950, at Plainview Cemetery.
Courtesy of the LaVern Roach family.

having visions of being forced to give the money back to the fans, argued with Duberstein with no success. Duberstein held his ground. No Roach, no show.

At 8:25, five minutes before the preliminary bout was scheduled to start, LaVern finally appeared. As Duberstein started to give him a call down, LaVern just smiled and answered, "Gee, Commissioner, the roads are awfully slippery tonight. I took my time since I wanted to get here in one piece. I promise you, Commissioner, it will never happen again." Duberstein was taken in by the Texan's jovial and yet sincere apology. After the fight he held LaVern's arm as he was moved to the dressing room where the doctors continued to check him.

The deputy commissioner recalled that other fighters had died in the ring, and many others had been injured. "But, I'll tell you, few of them were like that Roach kid. He was a wonderful guy, always laughing and pleasant. He wasn't like a lot of those other kids, hoodlums and ruffians. He was a good clean-cut boy."[21]

As a result of their own investigation, the New York State Athletic Commission concluded that no rules or regulations had been violated in the handling of the case.

Grave marker of LaVern Roach, Plainview, Texas, cemetery.
Photo by the author.

CHAPTER 18

Boxing Changed Because of LaVern Roach

*When you die, there's a little excitement in the house for a few days,
and the years roll over you and you are forgotten.*
—*Damon Runyon*

Boxing has been and always will be a dangerous sport. But according to author Joyce Carol Oates, "Boxing is not our most dangerous sport. It ranks approximately in seventh place, after football, Thoroughbred racing, sports car racing, mountain climbing, et al."[1] Death, the fourth man in the ring, hovers above the squared circle every time two fighters enter its domain, always ready to claim a victim. This comes with the territory. The *Ring* reported eighteen pro and amateur worldwide ring deaths in 1949, with nine occurring in the United States. There had been a total of fifty-nine ring-related deaths since 1945, none of which had the same effect as LaVern's death.

One difference, according to Bill Cunningham, sportswriter for the *Boston Post*, was "If that fight hadn't been televised, only a comparatively small number of people ever would have known what actually did happen and none of them had the training necessary to understand what they just saw." But it was televised with an audience of perhaps as many as a million or more observing what was the first nationally televised match in which a boxer died from injuries received in the ring. Many, knowing that the Texan was hurt, went to bed not realizing the severity of LaVern's injuries until the next morning. As one television viewer later stated, "Thank God, the fight had been televised in black-and-white. The amount of blood that flowed was beyond description."[2] It was the first ring fatality of the year. Death from a sporting event entered American living rooms for the first time.

Other than being nationally televised, another difference causing the uproar was that LaVern was unlike all other boxers. As Reverend Bateman suggested, LaVern was different. Although anger may have been the driving force for some boxers, including Jake LaMotta and Rocky Graziano, that wasn't the case for LaVern. LaMotta and Graziano grew up in impoverished neighborhoods where fighting for survival was the norm. Both were angry young men who took their pent-up rage into the ring with them. They were angry at family members, at authority figures, and at society in general. Joyce Carol Oates quoted Jake LaMotta, in his autobiography, *Raging Bull*, in which he openly admitted, "I didn't care if I killed an opponent or if I was killed in the ring." She went on:

> He fought for nearly a dozen years under the belief that he had killed a man in a failed robbery as a teenager and had gotten away with it. As a result when he entered the ring, his life or his adversary's life didn't mean a thing. The fact that he just didn't care made him a monster in the ring, allowing him to win many fights on his pent-up anger. Later on after he discovered that the victim of the robbery didn't die and actually showed up at a victory party for Jake (never knowing that Jake was the robber) his aggression in the ring and in life subsided along with his performance. He never was the same boxer again and his career declined rapidly.[3]

From the very first time he put on boxing gloves as a young boy, LaVern was an anomaly to the sport of boxing. He never felt or exhibited anger in or out of the ring. He never wanted to hurt anyone or be hurt. To him boxing was a sport, the ultimate competition. Each time he entered the ring, victory was his ultimate goal—to be better than his opponent by scoring more points or being the last man standing at the final bell. He never had any intention to injure or inflict permanent damage to his opponent. He didn't even like to watch boxing; he just liked to box. LaVern spent his youth boxing; playing football, basketball, and baseball; running track; and working, while LaMotta and Graziano served time together in reform school as teenagers. LaVern was different.

Having served in the Marines, he was a hero and an inspiration to thousands of other service men and women at home and abroad during the war. Many followed his career after the war ended. His fan base included all ages and wasn't limited to just men and boys. After the Cerdan fight he received a letter from sixteen-year-old Louise O'Brien of Marlborough, Massachusetts:

> Could you please tell me if you have any publicity pictures that you give out to your fans? If so, would you please mail me one as I follow all your fights with interest. I have heard many of your fights on the radio, and I have a brother in the Marines and am naturally interested in your career. I am very interested in sports and I am a junior in high school and have just received my basketball letter.[4]

His career was closely followed by fans all the way in the Honolulu Territory of Hawaii.

Ben Winser's letter to the editor of the *Plainview Herald* read, in part, as follows:

> As a fellow Texan from Cuero, I write this on behalf of the number of fight fans in the territory, extending our highest sympathy for the loss of a great citizen and boxer from your city, the late LaVern Roach. He was my favorite fighter, who will live in my memory forever.[5]

Boxing lost one of its brightest stars. A nation lost a role model for its youth. More important, a wife lost a husband, and two small children lost a father. According to Evelyn,

> After we married, our life pretty much revolved around his boxing career. I was very happy being his wife. He was a good and loving husband and father. He was in all ways a gentlemen, never loud, rough or prone to use foul language. He was fun to be around. He loved Ronnie and Rick. Shortly after LaVern was killed, Ronnie (age 5) was looking out the windows in the sunroom at my mother's home in Plainview and the wind was blowing a gale outside. She said, "Mother, I wish this wind would blow me right up to heaven where my daddy is." All I could say was, "Honey, me too."[6]

Things like this weren't supposed to happen. He was a nice guy, whom everyone liked and looked up to. Any character flaws that he may have had were well-hidden. Good guys like LaVern were not supposed to die this young, not even in the ring.

Twice, both before and after the Cerdan fight, Nat Fleischer, known as Mr. Boxing, had predicted that LaVern would go all the way to the middleweight championship. His was a brilliant career cut short. According to Angelo Dundee, a boxer's peak years are from the ages of twenty-five to twenty-nine. LaVern was just starting to reach his full potential. With the death of Cerdan, the retirement of Zale, and the aging of LaMotta and Graziano, LaVern could have looked forward to having several battles resulting in big paydays with Sugar Ray Robinson.

As a result of LaVern's death, the sport of boxing, always with its critics, came under closer scrutiny by its detractors and the general public as never before. A headline out of Albany read, "State May Outlaw Pro Boxing If Fighters Aren't Protected." The article went on to say, "State Legislators warned yesterday that professional boxing might be outlawed in New York unless steps were taken to protect fighters from death and injury. Sharp criticism of the ring profession developed in the assembly over the death last Thursday of middleweight LaVern Roach in New York City."[7]

Assemblyman Max M. Turshen, a Brooklyn Democrat, served notice that he would introduce a bill to outlaw boxing unless steps were taken. During assembly debate, Turshen quoted an editorial in the *New York Daily News* referring to Roach's death as "murder" and blamed it on the "fault of society." The bipartisan attack on boxing included Republican Assemblyman Richard H. Knauf of Binghamton urging the Ways and Means Committee to support his bill calling for fifty thousand dollars to probe boxing.[8]

The battle lines were drawn. On one side were those who wanted to see boxing banned altogether. On the other side were those who wanted to see the sport made safer. The following statement was issued by the American Medical Association's Committee on the Medical Aspects of Sports, in an article that appeared in the July 1950 issue of the *Journal of the American Medical Association*:

> A recommendation that boxing be banned at all times and places where optimum protection cannot be provided. Recent fatalities and serious injuries have dramatized the dangers of boxing. After a thorough review of the arguments of both proponents and opponents of boxing and careful consideration of scientific studies, we feel that the advisability of boxing is a debatable and unsettled issue unlikely of early resolution.

Individually, physicians, like the rest of the populace, were split on whether boxing should be banned. They all agreed that optimum safety procedures were needed.

The boxing authorities had to act and act fast. The very survival of boxing was in jeopardy. If boxing was outlawed in New York, other states would likely follow. Within a week, the New York State Athletic Commission put new rules into effect, calling for stricter medical examination of boxers before and after fights. Under the new rules, boxers had to go through several tests before they ever entered the ring. Licensed boxers were required to go through prelicense examinations by July 1. Each year a fighter had to undergo a thorough exam before being sanctioned for the upcoming year. Boxers received examinations five days before a fight, at the noon weigh-in the day of the match, and before entering the ring.

In addition, the commission opened up a medical room in its downtown offices where boxers underwent stringent testing under the supervision of doctors associated with the commission's Medical Advisory Board. Another rule soon put into place required the referee to stop a bout if a boxer was knocked down three times in any round. LaVern's fight with Cerdan would have ended much sooner if this rule had been in place at that time. Some of these new requirements had been in the works for a couple of years, but not yet implemented. LaVern's death hastened these changes.

The results of the new safety measures put in place were felt almost immediately. It took only a little over a month for them to have a significant effect upon boxing and boxing history. National Boxing Association heavyweight champion Ezzard Charles was scheduled to fight Freddie Beshore on March 29, 1950. The fight was originally to take place on February 28 but was postponed due to a rib injury that Charles suffered in a training session. During a medical checkup prior to the fight, it was discovered that Charles had a bruised heart muscle. The doctors advised not only a postponement but a total cancellation. "The discovery of the heart injury was credited by a commission official to one of the new 'safety' tests that have recently been inaugurated for New York fighters following the death in New York City of Middleweight LaVern Roach after a knockout."[9]

The Charles camp sadly returned the thirty-thousand-dollar advance ticket sale, saying, "We don't know whether he'll be able to fight again." Charles did return to the ring after a four-and-a-half-month layoff and barely defeated Beshore on a TKO in the fourteenth round. Six weeks later he handed Joe Louis only his second loss of his career and became universally recognized as the world heavyweight champion. Fourteen years and thirty-five fights had passed since Louis lost his first fight to Max Schmeling. No one will ever know what would have happened if Charles had been allowed to fight Beshore in March.

Other changes that soon occurred due directly or indirectly to La-Vern's death included a closer look at the physical makeup of the ring itself and an awareness of the material used for corner posts, ropes, turnbuckles, and the canvas flooring. Inspite of the changes put in place by the Boxing Commission, which helped in reducing injuries and saving lives in the ring, the public outcry to ban the sport continued.

After LaVern's death, the following safety measures were recommended:

- At least one physician present at all bouts with absolute authority to terminate the contest for medical reasons.
- The universal adoption of the new, improved shock-absorbing ring padding under the canvas and on the post of the ring to aid in prevention of injuries by striking the head against unpadded surfaces.
- The required use of headgears to minimize lacerations and contusions, and properly fitted mouthpieces to protect the teeth and supporting tissues.
- Experimentation with less padding in the gloves so that the threat of damage to the hand will inhibit the power of the blows.
- Prohibition of the practice of wrapping the hands under the gloves, again with the objective of cutting down the force of blows delivered to the opponent.
- Revision of point systems and scoring procedures to place greater emphasis on skillful offensive and defensive maneuvering and less on the knockout blow.

Although many of these recommendations were given only lip service, some were implemented then and others later, including having a medical person at all Golden Gloves matches.

Proponents of boxing were quick to point out that most of the action took place in the gyms and not in front of the paying public. It would be impossible to have a doctor present at all sparring sessions. Although headgear was used in sparring sessions, its use in a paid fight would reduce the attendance and eventually kill the sport, since most fans watched hoping for a knockout.

In the May 1950 publication of the *Ring*, editor Nat Fleischer wrote a three-page editorial pointing out the obvious. The death of LaVern was indeed tragic. He followed LaVern's career from the first time he refereed his bout in Albuquerque when LaVern was a fifteen-year-old-kid to his last bout against Small. He liked LaVern and went to bat for him several times in his boxing and military careers.

He made several points concerning boxing's medical staff, LaVern's management team, ring officiating, and accidental deaths in particular:

> New York's medical staff for boxing is second to none in the country. Six competent medical men examined him within the week of his fight with Small. Every precaution was taken by his manager to guard him against injury. His own nose and throat specialist, a physician nationally recognized in his specialty, informed LaVern that he could fulfill his contract because there was nothing wrong with him. . . . Was it negligence on the part of his able manager, John Abood, to whom the boy was like a son? It was not. Was it poor officiating? Not that I could see or that anyone in the St. Nicholas Club could ascertain.

Fleischer then lambasted a New York morning paper with a wide circulation for carrying a lengthy editorial calling for abolishing boxing, "the sport of murder," and barely mentioning the recent death of a Notre Dame football player who died from a broken neck from a gym accident and not calling for abolishing that gym course. He then continued his defense of boxing:

> Even one death in boxing is too much, if it can be prevented, but we must realize that officials in charge of boxing throughout the world are doing everything humanly possible to prevent what happened to LaVern Roach. . . . These deaths and accidents just happen as do accidents and fatalities in everyday life.
>
> For every person killed in boxing annually, there are thousands of boys and girls, teenagers, killed by autos and trucks. Yet we don't find

a campaign to eliminate these from our highways.[10]

Although boxing in New York was already at a crossroad, LaVern's death seemed to accelerate the inevitable decline. The sport, already in trouble from bad publicity associated with the underworld, came under attack from those who wanted to see boxing end for humane purposes. Fans were content staying home and watching the bouts free on live television rather than having to pay to attend. Angelo's take was as follows:

> The grass roots of boxing, the small-town and neighborhood boxing clubs where boxers as well as trainers had a chance to earn their spurs and learn the trade, were drying up. First it was the Sunnyside Garden; then they began closing down one by one. By 1952 there was only one small club left for every ten that had existed in the postwar boom year of 1946.[11]

Championship fights left New York, finding new homes in places like Detroit, Chicago, Atlantic City, and eventually Las Vegas. Even Madison Square Garden, the mecca of boxing for decades, suffered from lack of attendance. Big-time boxing in New York was quickly disappearing.

Chris Dundee was one of the first to see the writing on the wall. Shortly after LaVern's death he dissolved his business relationship with John Abood, cut his ties to New York, and moved his operation to the sunny beaches of Florida. His move to Miami Beach was completed before the year was over. Angelo was quick to follow his older brother, relocating to Miami the following year.

How effective were the safety measures that were put in effect? Ring deaths declined by 50 percent. Including LaVern's there were nine ring deaths in 1950 compared to eighteen the previous year, with only three of the nine taking place in the United States. Ironically the last ring death of 1950 occurred on December 21, when Sonny Boy West died from injuries suffered the previous evening in a match held in St. Nick's Arena. After the fight he was transported to St. Clare's Hospital, where he died the next day. The official cause of death was an intercerebral hemorrhage resulting from a cerebral concussion. His death was hardly mentioned in the news.[12]

St. Nick's survived for twelve more years, finally closing its doors in 1962. LaVern and West weren't the first ring deaths to occur at St. Nick's.

Former lightweight world boxing champion Benny Leonard died there in 1947 while refereeing a fight. Two more boxers, Tommy Pacheco in 1960 and Jose Regores in 1961, made up the five who died at St. Nick's during its fifty-four-year history.

As tragic as it was, the death of LaVern Roach facilitated the changes that would help prevent numerous injuries and save the lives of many of those boxers who came after him, sparing the suffering and sorrow experienced by the family and friends of boxing's unsung hero from Plainview, Texas.

What Happened To?

The Boxers

Rocky Graziano—Rocky, after LaVern's death, won sixteen of his next seventeen fights, along with a draw against Tony Janiro. He also recorded a controversial win against Janiro. Rocky tried to regain his championship on April 16, 1952, against Sugar Ray Robinson but was knocked out in round three. He retired from the ring after his very next fight, against Chuck Davey on September 17, 1952, at the age of thirty-three.

> Rocky then turned to appearances on television as a comedian, in movies, and in commercials. He even opened up a pizza restaurant. In 1955 Rocky teamed with author Rowland Barber to write his autobiography *Somebody Up There Likes Me*, which was made into an Oscar-winning movie in 1956 with Paul Newman playing the role of Rocky. Graziano died from heart failure on May 22, 1990, at the age of seventy-one.

Tony Janiro—On March 31, 1950, a little over a month after LaVern died, Janiro fought Rocky Graziano in the first of their three fights. It was a split-decision draw. He fought twelve more fights—winning four and losing seven with the one draw. He never fought for the title. He lost his second fight against Graziano in ten rounds. The third fight was stopped in Graziano's favor with two minutes and forty-five seconds left in the tenth round with Tony leading on the scorecard 6-3 at the displeasure and booing of the crowd. He retired from the ring on June 30, 1952. His loss to LaVern Roach was one of his most lopsided defeats.

> Having proved his critics wrong after his loss to LaVern, winning over eighty of his one-hundred-plus fights, Tony retired at the age of twenty-six. After retirement he worked as a bartender at the Neutral Corner, a popular sports bar located in close proximity to Stillman's Gym. In 1984 he was

inducted into the Youngstown Curbstone Coaches Hall of Fame. Tony Janiro died on February 21, 1985, at the age of fifty-nine of a heart attack.

Jake LaMotta—After LaVern's death, Jake fought four more fights as a middleweight, losing the last and the title to Sugar Ray Robinson on February 14, 1951. From then on he fought as a light heavyweight and a heavyweight until his retirement on April 14, 1954, at age thirty-three. Though contemporaries and childhood friends, he and his buddy Rocky Graziano never met in the ring. Upon his retirement from the ring, Jake followed in the footsteps of Graziano by becoming a standup comic and an actor in movies, as well as owning and managing bars.

In 1970, with the help of Joseph Carter and Peter Savage, Jake wrote his life story, *Raging Bull*, popularized by the Martin Scorsese movie of the same name for which Robert DeNiro won an Academy Award for portraying LaMotta. By 1997 Jake had been married six times. At the time of this writing, at the age of ninety-four he was still living in New York City.

Tony Zale—Tony retired after his last fight on September 21, 1948 (the loss to Cerdan), at the age of thirty-five. Zale was originally cast to play himself in the film *Somebody Up There Likes Me*, but during the filming with Paul Newman playing Graziano, Newman got rough with a few punches and Zale knocked him out. As a result, Zale was replaced for the final fight scene. During his retirement, Zale was labeled as a model family man. Zale died March 20, 1997, at the age of eighty-three.

Georgie Small—After LaVern's death, he cancelled his next fight and he and Rita got married. He fought again on May 26, losing to Kid Gavilán. That was his last fight in 1950. Rita pleaded with him to quit the ring and get a regular job. But Georgie didn't want to quit. Boxing was all he had ever known. It was his way of life, and there was that elusive championship, the same one that LaVern chased.

He fought only twelve more times: five fights in 1951, five in 1952, one in 1954, and one in 1955. His record after the LaVern fight was 5-7-1. Small suffered a long and slow demise, never getting over LaVern's death. He carried it into every fight he had. He was quoted as saying, "Maybe I wouldn't have felt so bad, but I knew the guy. We used to train together at Beecher's Gym, and we'd been friends for years. It ate me up inside." After fighting his last match on April 16, 1955, he became a construction worker.

Soon after, he and Rita were in a bad car accident. Although Georgie soon recovered from his broken ribs, Rita remained in the hospital for six months, eating up all of his boxing earnings.

Opportunity knocked once more on Georgie's door. Sugar Ray Robinson needed someone to fill a boxing card, and his agents called on Small to fight him in a nonchampionship bout. A good showing from Small might jump-start his boxing career or at least make him some badly needed quick cash. He readily accepted, and the fight was set for Boston. A couple of hours before the fight, Robinson claimed that he was ill and cancelled. It was later rumored that Robinson discovered that Small had killed a man in the ring and this contributed to the cancellation, even though Robinson himself had previously dealt a death blow in a fight in 1947.

Georgie went back to his construction job and soon started having physical problems, including blackouts, headaches, and stomach pains, most likely attributed to ulcers from the guilt after the Roach fight. His health continued to fail until he had to quit work altogether and was no longer able to provide for Rita and their three children. Unemployed and with a wife handicapped by the car accident, the once strong and proud boxer became a welfare recipient.

Ten years after that fateful night in St. Nick's, Georgie was interviewed by journalist and author Jimmy Breslin. Small ended the interview with these words: "I wanted to be a fighter. All of my life I wanted to be a fighter. . . . And see what happened. I'm broke and sick. I got my wife broke. I ruined everything. I guess the only thing I ever did in my whole life was kill a friend."

After leading a life riddled with guilt, suffering, and financial woes, Georgie Small died on October 31, 1999, at the age of seventy-four.

LaVern's Handlers

John Abood—John, heartbroken over the ring death of LaVern, quit the boxing business and devoted the rest of his life to his successful textile business and raising a family. He died on September 11, 1986, at the age of seventy-six in Stamford, Connecticut.

Charley Goldman—Charley, without LaVern to train, spent most of his time training the future unbeaten heavyweight boxing champion of the world, Rocky Marciano. Charley died on November 11, 1968, at the age of eighty.

Chris and Angelo Dundee—Chris and Angelo soon moved to Miami and opened their famous Fifth Street Miami Beach Gym, known as Stillman's South. Chris died on November 16, 1998, at the age of ninety-one in Miami after spending six decades promoting boxing. He and Angelo put Miami Beach on the boxing map. Angelo went on to become the best manager and trainer in boxing history, with the likes of Ali, Foreman, Pastrano, Basilio, Dupas, Nunn, and others. Angelo lived in the Tampa Bay/Clearwater, Florida, area and kept involved in boxing until his death at the age of ninety. Angelo died on February 1, 2012, two weeks after attending Ali's seventieth birthday party in Louisville, Kentucky, on January 17, 2012.

All mentioned below are inductees in the International Boxing Hall of Fame located in Canastota, New York. All are directly or indirectly connected with the LaVern Roach story.

Boxers—Marcel Cerdan, Rocky Graziano, Jake LaMotta, Henry Armstrong, Gene Tunney, Tony Zale, Lew Jenkins, Billy Conn, Sugar Ray Robinson, Bob Fitzsimmons, Cocoa Kid, Jersey Joe Wolcott, Rocky Marciano, Carmen Basilio, and Ezzard Charles.

Nonparticipants—Angelo Dundee, Chris Dundee, Art Donovan, Don Dunphy, Charley Goldman, Nat Fleischer, and Mike Jacobs.

Observers—Lester Bromberg, Jersey Jones, Damon Runyon, and Sylvester Stallone.

Family and Friends

Stanley Roach—Stanley lived the rest of his life largely in resentment and bitterness over the untimely death of LaVern. Stanley died in Plainview on December 25, 1968, at the age of sixty-seven.

Rosa Inez (Momma Rosa) Roach—Rosa died in Plainview on October 12, 1993, at the age of eighty-seven. Stanley and Rosa are both buried adjacent to LaVern's gravesite.

Bill Roach—Bill served as principal of Bowie Elementary School in Lubbock from 1962 until his retirement in 1985. Tragedy struck the Roach family once more as Bill and his wife, Betty, a Lubbock Independent School District teacher, were passengers in a small private plane that crashed, shortly after takeoff, into a downtown Branson, Missouri, area on March 20, 2006. The Roaches, along with the pilot Dr. Paul Johnson and wife, Marcia, all close friends, died as they were attempting to return home to Lubbock, Texas, after a Branson vacation.

Beth Roach—Beth, LaVern's sister, married, raised a family, and lives in the San Marcos, Texas, area, close to her children.

Evelyn Roach Trice—Evelyn, a couple of years after LaVern died, met and married a widower who had a young son. Together they had another son and raised a his, hers, and ours family. Her husband of over fifty years, Weldon (Birddog) Trice, died in 2010. Evelyn, the ever beautiful, vivacious, down-to-earth girl who swept LaVern off his feet, lives in relatively good health in the panhandle town of Canyon, Texas, with son Rick.

Ronnie Roach Birdsong—Ronnie lives in Portales, New Mexico, where she is vice president of university relations and enrollment for Eastern New Mexico University.

Rick Roach—Rick served in the army stationed in Korea and upon his discharge used the GI Bill to attend Texas Tech and received a Doctor of Jurisprudence degree. He is the father of James and twins, Kyle and Kris.

Choc Hutcheson—Choc left his career in the press and took his talents into the radio and television business, becoming the first news director at KCBD Television in Lubbock. He later went into the oil and gas business as a self-taught independent oil royalty broker and investor. He and his wife, Virginia, are longtime supporters of the Texas Tech University School of Mass Communications, where he was inducted into its hall of fame in 1990. He was recognized as a Distinguished Alumnus by the Texas Tech Alumni Association in 1996. Choc spends most of his time as a caregiver to his wife of thirty-seven years.

Evelyn's quick departure back to Plainview to bury her husband made it easier for Damon Runyon's prophetic statement ("When you die, there's a little excitement in the house for a few days, and the years roll over you and you are forgotten") to come true. New York and the boxing world soon forgot LaVern Roach, except for an occasional mention by Nat Fleischer in one of his editorials for the *Ring* and an even more infrequent article in some sports magazines; it was as if LaVern never existed. Stories with bad endings are often swept under the carpet and forgotten. Evelyn and the kids would not be there as a constant reminder of the fallen star. Eighteen hundred miles from Broadway provided an easy out for boxing, removing any need to give her a benefit or farewell. Except for a scholarship fund set up by Christ Church in Short Hills, New Jersey, for Ronnie and Ricky, there was no organized assistance to help the young widow and her two children. The Sunday school class's one-hundred-dollar donation in government bonds hoped to spark a flow of contributions for the two children to start them toward a college education.

Just as Damon Runyon's good friend Walter Winchell, radio commentator and renowned journalist, kept Runyon's memory from fading away by establishing the Damon Runyon Cancer Foundation, Evelyn took it upon herself to make sure LaVern was never forgotten in his hometown of Plainview, Texas.

On April 10, 1950, just forty-one days after LaVern was buried, she wrote a letter to the Plainview High School Student Council requesting an appropriate memorial award in LaVern's name. She outlined the criteria for the award:

> In order to qualify for the LaVern Roach Memorial, this senior boy must not make a practice of smoking, drinking, or any other habit harmful to him physically or mentally. Good sportsmanship and clean living will be the determining factors in making this award. He does not have to be an athlete; any senior boy is eligible.

Evelyn felt LaVern would be proud of having such an annual award presented in his name, giving him the hometown recognition that he so badly wanted. An individual plaque was to be given to the recipient of the award, and a large plaque with the honoree's name and graduating year would be displayed in the school's trophy case. That May, Bill Gillespie of the PHS class of 1950 was awarded the first LaVern Roach Memorial Award. On April 24, 2015, Warren Flye became the sixty-sixth recipient of the highest award that a student at Plainview High can receive.

The family since has turned the award over to the local Lions Club to administer. Some of the recipients of this award have gone on to be professional athletes, educators, doctors, dentists, business leaders, military heroes, and good family men.

LaVern's legacy has not only lived on through the lives of these sixty-six individuals but also influenced the lives of the more than ten thousand students who have graduated from Plainview High School since 1950. Most of these students probably have never heard of Tony Zale, Rocky Graziano, Marcel Cerdan, or even Jake LaMotta, but they have heard of LaVern Roach.

Largely forgotten outside of the Plainview/Lubbock area by the boxing and sports world, LaVern Roach will always be remembered and his memory always carried on in the community in which he grew up.

The local media in Lubbock recognized LaVern's athletic achievements by naming him one of the South Plains Top 100 Athletes of the Twentieth Century. On August 29, 1999, the *Lubbock Avalanche Journal* placed him on the select list, which included football's Sammy Baugh, Donnie Anderson, E. J. Holub, Don Maynard, and Clyde "Bulldog" Turner; baseball's Norm Cash; golf's Nancy Lopez and Judy Rankin; track's

THE AWARD AND THE MAN--Boxer LaVern Roach, for whom the highest PHS award is named, is shown in his boxing stance harking back to his days in the ring. Roach was a Plainview boxer who rose to national prominence, and was widely known also for his clean-cut character and high standards. His mother, Mrs. S.J. Roach, still resides in

LaVern Roach, the award and the man. Courtesy of the LaVern Roach family.

Fred Wolcott; and boxing's Lew Jenkins, all great athletes who have been inducted into the Texas Sports Hall of Fame, national sports Halls of Fame, or both.

A national Golden Gloves champion, arguably the best amateur middleweight ever, and among the best boxers ever to come out of Texas, a state he was so proud to be from, his name is nowhere to be found in the Texas Sports Hall of Fame in Waco or in any boxing hall of fame.

Hailed as a hero in his hometown of Plainview, a LaVern Roach exhibit (in close proximity to Jimmy Dean's) is on display in the Llano Estacado Museum located on the campus of Wayland Baptist University. In conjunction, a Walk of Fame is being added to the downtown area to honor LaVern, Jimmy Dean, and a few other celebrities who called Plainview home.

LaVern Roach never fulfilled his lifelong ambition to be a world-champion boxer, but more importantly, he was a champion of his life: a champion husband, father, son, brother, friend, and human being. His memory lives on as an inspiration to future generations. He demonstrated that, through self-discipline, dedication, honesty, and hard work, a person can become a champion of life regardless of one's background and circumstances. LaVern Roach was a true champion in and out of the ring.

LaVern Roach Exhibit, Llano Estacado Museum. Located on Wayland Baptist University Campus, Plainview, Texas. Photo by author.

THE STORY BEHIND THE STORY

Now that you have read the story, read how it developed.

I never met LaVern Roach. On the day he was buried, I was celebrating my fifth birthday across town only a few miles from the cemetery. Three of my older siblings attended school with LaVern and Evelyn. Although members of the same church, I don't know if any of my family members attended his funeral.

Like every young boy growing up in Plainview, Texas, I had heard of LaVern. My very limited knowledge of him consisted of knowing that he was a good boxer from Plainview who died from boxing ring injuries. By the time we got to high school we knew about the LaVern Roach Award, presented to a senior boy who displayed qualities of citizenship, sportsmanship, and high character. We were told that LaVern, a former student at PHS, exhibited these traits. Beyond that, little was known of him—less and less as the years went by.

At the start of my junior year in high school, more was learned about LaVern as a new student enrolled in Plainview High by the name of Ronnie Roach, LaVern's daughter. The good-looking blue-eyed blonde was heartily welcomed, especially by the boys. She moved in with her grandmother, Vera Castleberry, to finish the last two years of her high school education. Now we knew that LaVern, besides being a boxer, had a daughter.

In May 1962, my senior year at Plainview High, Don Ford, my best friend since the fourth grade, was named the LaVern Roach Award recipient. Don, like so many recipients, continued exhibiting the high standards of sportsmanship and clean living by becoming a coach, educator, and family man, influencing many young lives along the way. After my high school graduation, my parents moved away from Plainview, and I enrolled at Texas Tech College in Lubbock, rarely returning to my hometown.

Twenty-one years passed by without my thinking about LaVern. Then in 1983, the name of LaVern Roach popped up again as I attended the funeral of Ed Brown, my brother-in-law. He was buried in the Plainview Cemetery. Upon leaving his graveside service, I noticed a nearby grave marker, different from the others. On the very unassuming marker was the name LaVern Roach. Not a common name; this had to be the boxer for whom the high school award was given. On the bottom of the marker was an emblem about the size of a silver dollar. Closer examination revealed that it was a US Marine Corps emblem. In addition to being a boxer and a father, LaVern had been a Marine.

Eight years later, in 1991, my father passed away, buried in close proximity to LaVern's gravesite. I once again wandered over to look at LaVern's cemetery marker. This process was repeated again in 1998 when my mother died.

Every time I visited the gravesite of my parents over the next several years I found myself being drawn, like a magnet, to LaVern's gravesite. I began wondering more and more about him. *What other facts or perhaps even secrets were buried with him? What were the circumstances of his death?* As these questions never seemed to go away, I set out to find the answers.

I enlisted the help of a high school classmate, Sandy Cantrell Lindeman. Upon graduation, she went to work for the local newspaper, the *Plainview Herald*. Although leaving the employment of the newspaper years ago, she still had contacts. Agreeing to assist me in this project, Sandy called the editor of the paper, who handed over to us their file on LaVern Roach, started by a previous editor back in the mid-1940s.

The file consisted of a large legal-sized manila envelope that had apparently been gathering dust on a back shelf for over half a century. Much of the material was brittle, and the pages had turned yellow over the years. Upon browsing through the fragile contents, the amazing life of LaVern Roach began unfolding for me.

There were hundreds of letters, photos, newspaper clippings, and magazine articles. In the articles his name was being mentioned along with the champion boxers of his time—some names I was familiar with, such as Rocky Marciano, Rocky Graziano, Jake LaMotta, and Sugar Ray Robinson, and some were new to me—Marcel Cerdan and Tony Zale. There were newspaper headlines from all of the major New York papers chronicling LaVern's career, including fights in Madison Square Garden. The one name that captured my attention the most was Angelo Dundee. Having grown up in the Cassius Clay–Muhammad Ali era, I was well aware of who Angelo Dundee was. When I saw letters from Angelo to local newspapermen in Plainview and Lubbock telling about young Roach, I figured that maybe, just maybe, I had stumbled onto a story worth telling.

From the time I first read Harper Lee's *To Kill a Mockingbird* in the early 1960s, I dreamed of someday being a writer. At the age of sixty-five, time was slipping away from me, and I hadn't even come close to fulfilling the dream. Was this my chance? If so, was there enough information available to fill the pages of a book? The answers soon came in rapid succession. A local newsperson at the *Plainview Herald*, Nicki Logan, suggested that I might want to contact LaVern's widow, Evelyn, whom she believed resided in Canyon, Texas, approximately thirty miles north of Plainview.

I found Evelyn's address, wrote, and then contacted her by phone. After all of these years, she seemed surprised at any interest in LaVern, but nevertheless willing to help in any way she could. She suggested that I contact Choc Hutcheson in Lubbock. Soon, it seemed, whichever way I turned, I was being provided with volumes of material—more than enough to write LaVern's story.

Upon discovering that Angelo Dundee lived in the Tampa Bay area, I was able to secure his address and phone number. I wrote, emailed, and called him. To my pleasure he seemed very accommodating and willing to help. After visiting with him on the phone several times, he agreed to meet me for a personal interview. During the interview he wrote a blurb included on page xvi and said he would be honored to help me in any way he could. Angie died less than six months after the interview.

"Some are bound to die young. By dying young a person stays young in people's memory. If he burns brightly before he dies, his brightness shines for all time" (Anonymous).

Author's epitaph to LaVern: You burned brightly before your untimely death, and your brightness still shines.

APPENDIX A

Ring Record

The following records and notes are taken from LaVern's letters to Choc Hutcheson and placed in a journal by Choc. To see the official record, go to BoxRec.com.

First amateur fight in Memphis, Texas, in 1938 at 70 pounds (against Gib). *Overall amateur record (approximate)—100 victories, 5 defeats*

1941: Flyweight. Semifinals in Texas Golden Gloves (TGG). Lost to Jesse Gonzales (close decision).

Flyweight. Finals in New Mexico Golden Gloves (NMGG; eight-state event). Lost to John Patrick O'Leary.

1942: Bantamweight. Quarterfinals in TGG. Lost to Hector Marquez.

Bantamweight: Semifinals in Texas Amateur Athletic Foundation (TAAF). Lost to Hubert Grey.

1944: Welterweight. Semifinals in North and South Carolina Golden Gloves. Lost to Billy Tiger of Oklahoma.

1945: Welterweight. National Golden Gloves champ, winner over Chicago titlist Gilbert Garcia.

Toughest amateur fight: Hubert Grey in Austin TAAF tourney.

Hardest amateur hitter faced: Jesse Gonzales.

Professional Record

KO (knockout); TKO (technical knockout); Dec (decision).

In his career, no LaVern Roach fight ever ended in a draw, and LaVern never fought a rematch.

1. Don Ellis. Won. KO. 5 rounds at Washington, DC. Ellis floored.
2. Jack Alexander. Won. KO. 2 rounds.

3. Hugh Stell. Won. KO. 2 rounds.

4. Jimmy Grimes. Won. KO. 1 round.

5. Baudelio Valencia. Won. KO. 4 rounds.

6. Artie Towne (Henry Johnson). Lost. Dec. 6 rounds, January 28, 1946, in New York City.

7. Buddy Newby. Won. KO. 6 rounds (only account of fight found in Choc's notes).

8. Billy Hearold. Won. KO. 6 rounds.

9. Charlie McPherson. Won. Dec. 6 rounds in NYC. McPherson floored.

10. Manuel Roca. Won. KO. 3 rounds.

11. Arthur Bethea. Won. 3 rounds in Washington, DC.

12. Joe Tate. Won. Dec. 8 rounds.

13. Joe Agosta. Won. Dec. 8 rounds.

14. Leroy McQueen. Won. KO. 6 rounds.

15. Danny Rosati. Won. KO. 6 rounds.

16. Billy Cooper. Won. Dec. 10 rounds in Atlantic City.

17. Indian Gomez. Won. KO. 6 rounds.

18. Vic Amata. Won. Dec. 10 rounds.

19. Sal Richie. Won. KO. 4 rounds.

20. Norman Rubio. Won. Dec. 8 rounds. Semifinal on Lesnevich/Mauriello card at Ebbets Field. Roach gave all of purse—$1,200—to Damon Runyon relief fund. Roach was ill going into bout, but won handily.

21. Billy Arnold of Philadelphia. Won. Dec. 10 rounds. Headliner at St. Nicholas Arena on September 26, 1947. Broadcast on Gillette national hookup, ABC. Decision by 9-1, 9-1, and 8-2 on officials' cards.

22. Jack Kenny. Won. Dec. 8 rounds. Headliner at Broadway Arena in October 1947. Roach won handily.

23. Herbie Kronowitz of Coney Island. Won. Dec. 10 rounds. Headliner before 3,602 ($11,000) at St. Nick's on November 28, 1947. Roach rallied to win close verdict (Unanimous. 5-5 [14-13 on points]; 5-4-1; 6-4). Broadcast by ABC.

As of December 1, 1947, Roach was never on the canvas as a professional. Named in January 1948 as Rookie of the Year by the *Ring* magazine.

24. Tony Janiro of Youngstown, Ohio. Won. Dec. 10 rounds. January 16, 1948, at Madison Square Garden, Roach's first Garden headliner. Crowd: 11,924. Gate: Over $49,000. Roach's share: 17.5 percent (approx. $9,300). No knockdowns. Unanimous decision: 7-3, 7-3, 9-1. Donovan, referee. Broadcast by ABC. Janiro, number-three welterweight, entered ring 6-5 favorite.

25. Al Thornton of Rochester, Pennsylvania. Won. TKO, end of 7th at Miami Beach, Florida. February 19, 1948. Roach won five rounds, two even.
26. Marcel Cerdan of Casablanca. Lost. TKO in 8th round at Madison Square Garden before more than 17,000 (gate: $80,000-plus), March 12, 1948. Roach won first round, was floored by overhand right in opening seconds of round two, and never fully recovered from effects of punch. Down three times in second, three times in eighth before referee Donovan halted fight. Writers gave Roach three (some made it four) of seven completed rounds.
27. Aaron Perry of Washington, DC, at Washington's Griffith Stadium. Won. Dec. June 10, 1948. Roach suffered slight cut in early rounds, but finished strong to win unanimous verdict.
28. Charley (Zivic) Affif of Pittsburgh. Lost. Dec. in 10 on August 3, 1948, at Forbes Field, Pittsburgh. Roach suffered badly cut upper lip from faulty tooth clip. Decision close, but unanimous.
29. John Hanbury of Washington, DC, in October 1948. Lost. Dec. Slow, dull bout. Roach badly off form.

Roach temporarily retires from ring. Enters insurance business at Lubbock. Roach returns to East in late November 1949. Begins training December 1, 1949.

30. Johnny Crosby, Bronx. Won. TKO in first at New Bedford, Massachusetts.
31. Georgie LaRover, Philadelphia. Won. Dec. January. 8 rounds at Met Arena, Philadelphia.
32. Jimmy Taylor, Brooklyn. Won. Dec. January. 8 rounds at New Bedford, Massachusetts.
33. George Small, Brooklyn. Lost. TKO. 10 rounds at St. Nicholas Arena, New York.

Totals.

32/33 professional fights (excluding amateur and exhibition fights) .

27/28 wins (of these, 15 were KOs)

5 losses

It is estimated that LaVern fought over 130 fights during his lifetime.

APPENDIX B:
LAVERN ROACH
AWARD RECIPIENTS

1950: Bill Gillespie	1972: Lee Roy Buckner	1994: Steven Riddley
1951: Weldon Hayes	1973: Scott Hallman	1995: Kip Hardin
1952: Jimmy Hunter	1974: Steve Horn	1996: Jamie Riggins
1953: Lester Ramsey	1975: Rickey Hart	1997: Matt Robertson
1954: Doyle May	1976: Sam Cravey	1998: Jason Gatica
1955: Karl Craig	1977: Stacey Foster	1999: Cody Abercrombie
1956: Tommy Atkins	1978: Ralph Hayes	2000: Josh Carter
1957: Bobby Jack Frye	1979: Royce Coleman	2001: Zack Morris
1958: Jesse McGuire	1980: Kevin Igo	2002: Henry Amador
1959: Elgin Conner	1981: Benito Herrera	2003: Adam Hernandez
1960: Dale Webb	1982: Randy Dorcey	2004: Shun Lacy
1961: Stan Jones	1983: Kenneth Hallman	2005: Dean Kellum
1962: Don Ford	1984: Randy Williams	2006: Jamar Wall
1963: Ronnie Phillips	1985: David McAdoo	2007: Zal Smiley
1964: Donnie Hollis	1986: Jerry Perez	2008: Shafig Richardson
1965: Ricky Etheredge	1987: Paul Vera	2009: Billy Dulakis
1966: Stan Rigler	1988: Willie Ansley	2010: Peyton Bradshaw
1967: David Etheredge	1989: Max Peralta	2011: Prince Dawkins
1968: Joe Don Martin	1990: Steve Thompson	2012: Josh Smiley
1969: Jerry Sisemore	1991: Gilbert Sanchez	2013: Shaimar Jennings
1970: Atancio Gonzales	1992: Brandon Buchanan	2014: Ishmael Soto
1971: Charles Bassett	1993: Caleb Holt	2015: Warren Flye

NOTES

Chapter 1

1. Jack Cuddy, United Press, February 23, 1950.
2. *New York Times*, February 22, 1950.
3. Dundee, *My View from the Corner*, 42.
4. LaVern's letter to Choc, February 21, 1950.
5. *Lubbock Avalanche Journal*, February 24, 1950.

Chapter 2

1. *New York Times*, February 22, 1925.
2. 1930 US Census Bureau.
3. *The Handbook of Texas* (Austin: Texas State Historical Association, 2013), https://tshaonline.org.
4. Ibid.
5. Wofford, *Hale County Facts and Folklore*.
6. Rick Roach, interview by the author.

Chapter 3

1. Lester Bromberg, *Sporting News*, January 29, 1948.
2. *Baytown* (TX) *Sun,* February 24, 1950.
3. *Sporting News*, January 29, 1948.
4. Dan McGill, *Atlanta Journal,* March 10, 1948. McGill, a legend in Georgia sports history, stated that Roach had kinfolks scattered all over Georgia.
5. *Sporting News*, January 28, 1948.
6. Barr, *Remembering Bulldog Turner,* 116.
7. Ibid.
8. Ibid., 117.

9. Red Smith, *New York Times*, November 4, 1981.

10. *New York Sun*, March 10, 1948.

11. *Sporting News*, January 28, 1948.

12. Ibid.

13. *Baytown Sun*, February 24, 1950.

14. *Fort Worth Star-Telegram*, June 28, 1945.

15. Ibid.

16. *Plainview Evening Herald,* January 9, 1948.

17. Ibid.

18. Ibid.

19. *Plainview Herald,* November 7, 1942.

20. Ibid.

21. Cloyce Terrell, interview by author.

22. Johnny Mason, interview by author.

Chapter 4

1. Alvarez, *Parris Island*, 13.

2. *Sporting News*, January 29, 1948.

3. *Plainview Herald*, June 21, 1943.

4. Ibid.

5. LaVern's military records, in author's possession.

6. http://marine4ever.com/Quotes_About_Marines.html.

7. Ibid.

8. *Plainview Herald*, July 10, 1943.

Chapter 5

1. Leatherneck.com.

2. *Indiana Gazette*, June 27, 1992.

3. *Marine Corps News*, June 20, 2008.

4. Dan McGill, *Atlanta Journal*, February 24, 1950.

5. *Sporting News*, January 28, 1948.

6. LaVern's letter to relatives back home, September 4, 1944.

7. *Plainview Daily Herald*, August 29, 1944.

8. *Atlanta Journal*, February 24, 1950.

9. Choc's notebook.

10. *Washington Times Herald*, January 12, 1945.

11. *Plainview Herald*, January 4, 1945.

12. Dundee, *My View from the Corner*, 53.

13. United Press, March 15, 1945.

14. LaVern's poems, possession of Evelyn.

15. *Chicago Tribune*, March 28, 1945.

Chapter 6

1. LaVern's military records.
2. *Fort Worth Star-Telegram*, June 28, 1945.
3. Ibid.
4. Ibid.
5. LaVern's military records.
6. Ibid.
7. Ibid.
8. Ibid.
9. *Atlanta Journal*, February 24, 1950.
10. LaVern's military records.
11. Ray Klingmeyer, phone interview with the author.
12. *The Evening Observer*, January 22, 1946.
13. *Plainview Sunday Herald*, March 3, 1946.
14. Randy Roberts, *Joe Louis, Hard Times Man*.
15. Ibid.

Chapter 7

1. Sugar, *Boxing's Greatest Fighters*. 237.
2. Dundee, *My View from the Corner*, 26.
3. Ibid.
4. *Philadelphia Enquirer*, January 13, 1950.

Chapter 8

1. Evelyn, interview by the author.
2. Ibid.
3. Ibid.
4. Mavis McLean, interview by the author.
5. Choc's notebook, 3.
6. *Atlantic City Press*, November 14, 1946.

Chapter 9

1. *Boxing News,* April 26, 1947.
2. John Abood's letter to Choc, August 1949. Abood, not known for his letter-writing skills, did not date the letter.
3. *Plainview Herald*, August 28, 1947.
4. Choc's notebook, 5.
5. *Plainview Herald*, August 28, 1947.
6. Ibid.
7. LaVern's letter to Choc, September 15, 1947.
8. Chris Dundee's letter to Mr. Hilburn, September 17, 1947.

9. *New York Journal-American,* September 27, 1947.

10. Ibid.

11. Ibid.

12. Letter from LaVern to Choc, September 29, 1947.

13. Ibid.

14. *Plainview Daily Herald*, November 23, 1947.

15. LaVern's letter to Choc, October 29, 1947.

16. Ibid.

17. LaMotta, *Raging Bull.*

18. *New York Herald*, November 27, 1947.

19. *Plainview Daily Herald*, November 30, 1947.

20. LaVern's letter to Choc, November 29, 1947.

21. Ibid.

22. Art Fleischer, *The Ring,* February 1948, 3.

23. Ibid., 12.

24. Ibid., 34.

25. LaVern's letter to Choc, December 31, 1947.

Chapter 10

1. Liebling, *Sweet Science.* Liebling used the phrase, "the sweet science," to describe boxing.

2. *New York Post*, January 17, 1948.

3. Ibid.

4. *Plainview Herald*, January 11, 1948.

5. Dundee, *My View from the Corner*, 24–25.

6. LaVern's letter to Choc, January 5, 1948.

7. Ibid.

8. LaVern's letter to Choc, January 15, 1948.

9. Angelo Dundee, interview by author.

10. *New York Enquirer*, January 12, 1948.

11. *New York Sun*, January 17, 1948.

12. *New York World Telegram*, January 17, 1948.

13. Ibid.

14. Ibid.

15. Ibid.

16. *New York Journal American*, January 25, 1948.

17. *New York Post*, January 17, 1948.

18. Ibid.

19. *On the Waterfront*, directed by Elia Kazan (1954).

20. *Abilene Reporter-News*, January 22, 1948.

21. *Gastonia Gazette*, February 9, 1948.

22. *New Yorker*, January 20, 1948.

23. Ibid.

24. From an article in possession of the Roach family (writer unknown; ca. February 1, 1948, likely in the Maplewood, NJ, area).

25. LaVern's letter to Choc, January 20, 1948.

26. *New York Herald Times*, January 18, 1948.

27. LaVern's letter to Choc, January 26, 1948.

Chapter 11

1. Ty Primm, *Observer Sports,* January 19, 1948.

2. Evelyn, interview with the author.

3. *Plainview Herald*, March 11, 1948.

4. "Cerdan-Roach Bout Is Closed for March 12: Ex-Marine and Frenchman Accept Garden Terms: Latter Here Next Week" (article appeared between January 26 and February 2, 1948; newspaper unknown. Article in possession of the Roach family).

5. LaVern's letter to Choc, February 2, 1948.

6. Ibid.

7. LaVern's letter to Choc, February 8, 1948.

8. *Miami Herald*, February 20, 1948.

9. Jimmy Burns, *Miami Herald*, February 14, 1948.

10. Ibid.

11. Ibid.

12. *Plainview Herald*, March 9, 1948.

13. Ibid.

14. Associated Press, interview with Mitchell Curtis, March 8, 1948.

15. Ibid.

16. *New York World-Telegram*, March 12, 1948.

17. *Plainview Herald*, March 12, 1948.

18. Lester Bromberg, *New York World-Telegram*, March 10, 1948.

19. Bill Corum, *New York Journal-American*, March 12, 1948.

20. Lewis Burton, *New York Journal-American*, March 12, 1948.

21. Hy Goldberg, "Sports in the News" *Newark* (NJ) *Evening News*.

22. *New York Daily News*, March 13, 1948; *Miroir*, March 16, 1948.

23. *New York World-Telegram*, March 11, 1948.

24. LaVern's letter to Choc, March 8, 1948.

25. *New York World-Telegram*, March 12, 1948.

26. Burke, *No Regrets*, 124.

27. *New York Herald Tribune*, March 11, 1948.

28. Burke, *No Regrets*, 112.
29. *Plainview Herald*, March 11, 1948.
30. *New York Journal-American*, March 12, 1948.
31. *Newsweek*, March 22, 1948.
32. *Boxing News*, July 8, 1966.
33. *New York Journal-American*, March 14, 1948.
34. *New York Times*, March 13, 1948.
35. *New York Herald-Tribune*, March 13, 1948.
36. The *Ring*, 1949–50, numerous issues.
37. *New York Herald-Tribune*, March 13, 1948.
38. *New York Daily News*, March 13, 1948.
39. Burke, *No Regrets*.
40. W. C. Heinz, *New York Sun*, March 14, 1948.
41. Ibid.
42. Ibid.
43. Ibid.
44. Ibid.
45. John Lardner, *Newsweek*, "The Professor's Stop Watch," March 29, 1948, 76.
46. Burke, *No Regrets*, 125.
47. Bill Corum, *New York Journal-American*.
48. While *Miroir* listed it as Cercan's 108th victory, the Box.Rec website lists it as Cerdan's 106th.
49. *L'Humanité*, March 13, 1948.

Chapter 12
1. Evelyn, interview by the author.
2. Ibid.
3. LaVern's letter to Choc, May 13, 1948.
4. Evelyn's letter to Vera, June 11, 1948.
5. Ibid.
6. LaVern's letter to Vera, July 11, 1948.
7. *Washington Times Herald*, July 10, 1948.
8. Ibid.
9. LaVern's letter to Choc, July 21, 1948.
10. Ibid.
11. LaVern's letter to Choc, August 4, 1948.
12. LaVern's letter to Vera, September 3, 1948.
13. Choc Hutcheson, interview by the author.
14. Evelyn's letter to Vera, September 16, 1948.

15. Evelyn's letter to Vera, September 20, 1948.
16. Burke, *No Regrets*, 132.
17. LaVern's letter to Vera, September 22, 1948.
18. LaMotta, *Raging Bull*, 123.
19. Choc's notebook, 8.

Chapter 13

1. Earl Chism interview by the author.
2. *New York Times*, June 17, 1949.
3. Burke, *No Regrets*, 137.
4. Max Baer boxing record.
5. *Plainview Daily Herald*, July 14, 1949.
6. Choc Hutcheson interview by the author.

Chapter 14

1. Madison Square Garden's *1948–1949 Boxing Magazine and Program*, 47.
2. Evelyn interview, by the author.
3. LaVern's letter to Vera and Herb, November 24, 1949.
4. LaVern's letter to Choc, November 27, 1949.
5. Evelyn's letter to Vera, December 10, 1949.
6. Ibid.
7. Burke, *No Regrets*, 138.
8. Ibid., 139.
9. Angelo Dundee interview by the author.
10. "Roach Spurns Graziano for $700 Bout Here," *Philadelphia Inquirer*, January 11, 1950.
11. LaVern's letters to Vera and Choc, December 16, 1949.
12. LaVern's letter to Choc, December 16, 1949.
13. LaVern's letter to Choc, December 8, 1949.
14. LaVern's letter to Vera, December 28, 1949.
15. LaVern's letter to Choc, January 6, 1950.
16. Evelyn's letter to Vera, January 8, 1950.
17. *Philadelphia Daily News*, January 12, 1950.
18. Evelyn's letter to Vera, January 12, 1950.
19. *Plainview Herald*, January 13, 1950.
20. LaVern's letter to Vera, January 13, 1950.
21. Evelyn's letter to Vera, January 13, 1950.
22. Evelyn's letter to Vera, January 16, 1950.
23. LaVern's letter to Vera, January 17, 1950.
24. LaVern's letter to Choc, January 19, 1950.
25. LaVern's letter to Vera, January 20, 1950.

26. *Plainview Herald*, December 25, 1947.
27. LaVern's letter to Choc, February 5, 1950.
28. LaVern's letter to Choc, February 10, 1950.
29. *New Bedford Standard-Times*, February 12, 1950.
30. *New Bedford Standard-Times*, February 15, 1950.

Chapter 15
1. Spielman, *Spiritual Journey of Joseph L. Greenstein*, 234.
2. Finlayson and Page, "Death at Arm's Length" (magazine article in author's possession, publication information unknown).
3. Dundee, *My View from the Corner*, and personal interview.
4. LaVern's unfinished letter to Choc, February 20, 1950.
5. Evelyn's letter to Vera, February 20, 1950.

Chapter 16
1. Evelyn, interview by the author.
2. Ibid.
3. *Oneonta Star*, February 24, 1950.
4. *Time*, "Sport: Ten & Out," March 6, 1950.
5. *New York Times*, February 23, 1950.
6. *New York Times*, February 25, 1950.
7. Jack Cuddy, United Press, February 23, 1950.
8. Evelyn interview, by the author.
9. Ibid.
10. *Oneonta Star*, February 24, 1950.
11. *New York Times*, February 23, 1950.
12. *San Antonio Light*, February 23, 1950.
13. Evelyn interview, by the author.
14. *New York Times*, February 23, 1950.
15. Evelyn interview, by the author.
16. *Houston Post*, February 23, 1950.

Chapter 17
1. *Plainview Daily Herald*, February 23, 1950.
2. Evelyn interview, by the author.
3. *Abilene Reporter-News*, January 10, 1951.
4. Cummiskey, "The Big News Tonight" (copy of original script in author's possession; used by permission).
5. Texas House of Representatives' bill honoring LaVern.
6. *Washington Times-Herald*, February 23, 1950.
7. *New York Times*, February 25, 1950.

8. *Berkshire County* (MA) *Eagle,* February 24, 1950.

9. *Dunkirk Evening Observer*, February 24, 1950.

10. Ibid.

11. *Times Herald* (New York City), February 25, 1950.

12. *Fort Worth Star-Telegram*, February 24, 1950.

13. Rev. Bateman to LaVern's parents, February 27, 1950.

14. Ibid.

15. *Plainview Daily Herald*, February 25, 1950.

16. *Times Record* (New York City), February 25, 1950.

17. Rev. Bateman's letter.

18. Dr. A. Hope Owen, February 28, 1950.

19. *Syracuse Post-Standard*, March 1, 1950.

20. *Syracuse Post-Standard*, March 4, 1950.

21. *Fitchburg* (MA) *Sentinel*, March 28, 1950.

Chapter 18

1. Oates, *On Boxing*, 126.

2. Ted Sares, "My First One: LaVern Roach v. George Small, 1950," badlefthook.com.

3. Oates, *On Boxing*, 85.

4. Louis O'Brien's letter to Lavern (in author's possession, courtesy of Evelyn Trice).

5. Collection of letters from the Roach family.

6. Evelyn Trice, reflections of LaVern Roach, April 7, 2015 (in author's possession).

7. *Oneonta* (NY) *Star*, March 2, 1950.

8. *New York Daily News,* March 2, 1950.

9. *Olean Times*, March 28, 1950.

10. Nat Fleischer, "In Defense of Boxing," *The Ring*, May 1950.

11. Dundee, *My View from the Corner*, 42.

12. *Troy* (NY) *Record*, December 22, 1950.

SOURCES

Books

Alvarez, Eugene. *Parris Island: Once a Recruit, Always a Marine*. Charleston, SC: History Press, 2007.

Barr, Michael. *Remembering Bulldog Turner*. Lubbock: Texas Tech University Press, 2013.

Bradley, James, with Ron Powers. *Flags of Our Fathers*. New York: Bantam Books, 2000.

Burke, Carolyn. *No Regrets: The Life of Edith Piaf*. New York: Alfred A. Knopf, 2011.

Dundee, Angelo, and Mike Winters. *I Only Talk Winning*. Chicago: Contemporary Books, 1985.

Dundee, Angelo, and Bert Sugar. *My View from the Corner: A Life in Boxing*. New York: McGraw Hill, 2008.

Fleischer, Nat. *The Ring Record Book. 1947 Edition*. Norwalk, CT: O'Brien Suburban Press, 1947.

———. *The Ring Record Book: 1948 Edition*. Norwalk, CT: O'Brien Suburban Press, 1948.

———. *The Ring Record Book: 1952 Edition*. Norwalk, CT: O'Brien Suburban Press, 1952.

Fried, Ronald K. *Corner Men: Great Boxing Trainers*. New York: Four Walls Eight Windows, 1991.

Grombach, John V. *The Saga of the Fist*. Cranbury, NJ: A. S. Barnes and Company, 1977.

The Handbook of Texas. Austin: The Texas State Historical Association, 2013.

Hauser, Thomas. *The Black Lights: Inside the World of Professional Boxing*. New York: McGraw Hill, 1986.

Hillenbrand, Laura. *Seabiscuit: An American Legend.* New York: Random House, 2001.

———. *Unbroken: A World War II Story of Survival, Resilience, and Redemption.* New York: Random House, 2010.

LaMotta, Jake, with Joseph Carter and Peter Savage. *Raging Bull.* New York: Prentice-Hall, 1970.

Liebling, A. J. *The Sweet Science.* New York: North Point Press, 1951.

Oates, Joyce Carol. *On Boxing.* New York: Harper Perennial, 1987.

Roberts, James B., and Alexander G. Skutt. *The Boxing Register: International Boxing Hall of Fame Official Record Book.* Ithaca, NY: McBooks Press, 1997.

Schaap, Jeremy. *Cinderella Man.* Boston: Houghton Mifflin, 2005.

Skehan, Everett M. *Rocky Marciano: Biography of a First Son.* New York: Pocket Books, 1977.

Spielman, Ed. *The Spiritual Journey of Joseph L. Greenstein.* Cobb, CA: First Glance Books, 1998.

Sugar, Bert Randolph. *Boxing's Greatest Fighters.* Guilford, CT: Lyons Press, 2006.

Uris, Leon. *Battle Cry.* New York: Harper Collins, 1953.

Van Natta, Don, Jr. *Wonder Girl: The Magnificent Sporting Life of Babe Didrikson Zaharias.* New York: Little, Brown and Company, 2011.

Walsh, Peter. *Men of Steel: The Lives and Time of Boxing's Middleweight Champions.* London: Robson Books, 1993.

Wofford, Vera Dean. *Hale County Facts and Folklore.* Vols. 1 and 2. Lubbock, TX: Pica Publishing Company, 1978.

Films

Edith et Marcel (1983)
The Harder They Fall (1956)
La Vie en Rose (2007)
On the Waterfront (1954)
Raging Bull (1980)
Rocky (1976)
Somebody Up There Likes Me (1956)

Periodicals

Boxing News
Boxing 1948–1949 Magazine and Program for Madison Square Garden
LIFE
Look
New Enquirer
News of the United States Marines

The *Ring*
Sir Magazine
Stars and Stripes
Time

Newspapers
Abilene Reporter-News
Amarillo Times
Atlanta Journal
Atlantic City Press
Baytown (TX) *Sun*
Cincinnati Post
Fort Worth Star-Telegram
Houston Post
Kansas City Times
Lubbock Avalanche Journal
Maplewood (NJ) *News*
Miami Herald
Newark (NJ) *News*
New Bedford (MA) *Standard Times*
New York Daily Mirror
New York Daily News
New York Enquirer
New York Herald-Tribune
New York Journal-American
New York Post
New York Sun
New York Times
New York Times Herald
New York World-Telegram
Philadelphia Enquirer
Plainview (TX) *Herald*
Star-Ledger (NJ)
Times Record (Troy, NY)
Washington Post
Washington Times Herald

Sportswriters and Journalists
Abramson, Jesse, *New York Herald-Tribune*
Boddington, Clem, *Sir Magazine*
Bonacci, Jack, *Herald Statesman*

Broadbent, Betty, *Maplewood News*
Bromberg, Lester, *New York World-Telegram*
Buck, Al, *New York Post*
Burns, Jimmy, *Miami Herald*
Burton, Lewis, *New York Journal-American*
Cohen, Leonard, *New York Post*
Corum, Bill, *New York Journal-American*
Cuddy, Jack, United Press
Curtis, Mitchell, Associated Press
Cummiskey, Joe, WPAT, N.J. Broadcasting Co.
Cunningham, Bill, *Boston Post*
Daley, Arthur, *New York Times*
Finlayson, Ann
Fraley, Oscar, *The Times Record*
Goldberg, Hy, *Sports in the News*
Grayson, Harry, Newspaper Enterprise Association
Grimsley, Will, Associated Press
Hand, Jack, Associated Press
Heinz, W. C., *New York Sun*
Hilburn, H. S., *Plainview Herald*
Hutcheson, Choc, *Lubbock Avalanche Journal*
Jennings, Jim
Kelly, Bill, *Lubbock Avalanche Journal*
Lardner, John, *Newsweek*
Magill, Dan, Jr., *Atlanta Journal*
Marenghi, Anthony, *Star-Ledger*
McMullen, Lorin, *Star Telegram*
Miller, Jane, Associated Press
Nichols, Joseph C., *New York Times*
O'Brien, Dick
Page, Marjorie
Parris, Collier, *Abilene Reporter-News*
Patzer, *New Bedford Standard Times*
Primm, J. T. (Ty), *Observer Sports*
Ratner, Bill, *Newark News*
Robinson, Pat, International News Service
Smith, Red, *New York Herald-Tribune*
Van Every, Edward, *New York Sun*, Associated Press
Ward, Gene, *New York Daily News*
Weissman, Harold, *Daily Mirror*

Wolfson, Norman L.

Interviews

(All interviews were conducted by the author. The numerous interviews for this book were conducted over a period of four years and are not dated.)
Birdsong, Ronnie Roach
Chism, Earl
Dundee, Angelo
Garrett, Raby
Hutcheson, Choc
Klingmeyer, Ray
Mason, Johnny
McClain, Mavis Churchwell
Terrell, Cloyce
Trice, Evelyn Roach

Letters

All letters from LaVern Roach to Choc Hutcheson are from the papers of Choc Hutcheson and are now the property of Evelyn Roach Trice. All letters from LaVern Roach and Evelyn Roach to family members are from the papers of Evelyn Roach Trice.

Websites

www.ancestry.com
www.badlefthook.com (see, esp., Ted Sares, "My First One: LaVern Roach v. Georgie Small, 1950," November 17, 2010)
www.boxingnews24.com (see, esp., Brian Zelly, "The Saddest Song of All," October 28, 2011)
www.boxrec.com
www.eastsideboxing.com
www.oldtimestrongman.com/strongmen/the_mighty_atom.html

INDEX

as prolific letter writer, 112

Roach, Molly Fitzsimmons (grandmother), 20

Roach, Richard James (son), 172, *180,*
  231

Roach, Ronnie (step-daughter), *157,*
  180
  life of, 85, 157, 231, 237
  Roach's death and, 204
  Roach's fondness for, 87, 156–57,
    157, 158, 160, 164

Roach, Rosa Inez (mother). *See also*
  parents of Roach
  background, 9
  birth of children, 9, 14–15
  courtship and marriage, 9
  later life of, 230
  and Roach's boxing career, 20, 24,
    56

Roach, Stanley James (father). *See also*
  parents of Roach
  background, 9–10
  courtship and marriage, 9
  health problems, 39, 56, 59–61, 71
  later life, 230
  and Roach's boxing career, 19,
    23–24, 56
  Roach's discharge and, 62–65
  as struggling laborer, 9–10, 14–15,
    17, 19, 21, 39, 75

Robinson, Sugar Ray
  Abood on, 95, 173
  career, xvii, 56, 70, 77, 96, 124, 140,
    173, 178, 182, 227, 229–30
  Roach's desire to fight, 8, 187, 222

Roosevelt, Franklin D., 42, 57

Rosa, Manuel, 88–89

Rosati, Danny, 93–94, 105

Rubio, Norman, 91, 96, 105

St. Nicholas Arena (New York), 3–6, *4,*
  72, 81, 88, 98, 100, 102–3, 190–91,

196, 196–98, 211, 226–27. *See also*
  Small fight

Small, Georgie, *188*
  background, 6, 189–90
  career, 111, 190–92, 228
  as friend of Roach, 6, 228
  life after boxing, 228–29
  marriage, 192, 228
  Roach on, 7, 193
  Roach's death and, *205,* 208,
    210–11, 213

Small fight (Feb. 1950), *2,* 3, 6–8, *196,*
  196–98
  importance of, 7–8, 185, 187
  investigations of, 207–11, 215
  near cancellation of, 215–17
  pre-fight preparations, 195–96
  Roach's health prior to, 7, 185, 193,
    207–9
  Roach's hospitalization and death,
    199–203
  as televised, 4–5, 195–99, 219–20
  venue for, 3–4

Stallone, Sylvester, xviii, 91, 230

Stark, O. R., 117, 129, 145, 156,
  160–61, 215

Stillman's Gym (New York City),
  76, 79, *80,* 97, 99, 135, *135,* 158,
  161–62, 164

Strauss, Sol, 127–28, 140–41

Taylor, Jimmy, 4, 164, 185–87, *186*

television
  boxing and, 4–6, 73, 193, 226
  postwar growth of, 4–5
  Small-Roach fight on, 4–5, 195–99,
    219–20

Texas Amateur Athletic Foundation
  (TAAF) tournament, 25–26

Thornton, Al, 129–31

Towne, Arte, 81–82, 94

Trice, Weldon, 230–31

ABOUT THE AUTHOR

Frank Sikes, a third-generation West Texan, grew up in Plainview, where LaVern Roach, along with Jimmy Dean, were hometown heroes. *West Texas Middleweight* is his first book.